Space, Oil and Capital

T0289781

The historical development of capital has produced a progressive increase in the demand for raw material and has consequently resulted in the concentration of capital in, and the geographical expansion of, the production of natural resources, globalizing and intensifying the competition for the control of production and markets.

This book is an attempt to explain, at the theoretical and empirical level, the relationship between the production of oil and the process of inter-capitalist competition in the global economy, and why it is necessary to appreciate the underlying process of the social production of space in determining the access to, and control of, global oil production and world markets. Labban argues that the competition for oil is part of a broader inter-capitalist competition, which expresses inter-capitalist competition at its most fundamental level, as competition for the production and realization of profit from the application of capital to material nature. He uses case studies of oil in the former Soviet Union and contemporary competition for investment in Russian and Iranian oil to illustrate the competition for the control of oil and emphasize its contradictory geographical basis. Unlike other studies of the contemporary geopolitical struggle for oil, Labban's book emphasizes the origin of the struggle for oil in inter-capitalist competition and the instrumental role that the production of global space, through the dialectical tensions between transnational oil corporations and resource-owning states, plays in determining the profitability of oil production and the availability of oil in the world market.

This highly interesting and topical book will appeal to those undertaking research in political economy, economic geography, resource geography and international relations.

Mazen Labban is Assistant Professor of Geography at the University of Miami, USA.

Routledge studies in international business and the world economy

Space, Oil and Capital

Mazen Labban

LONDON AND NEW YORK

Transferred to digital printing 2010

First published 2008
by Routledge
2 Park Square, Milton Park, Abingdon, Oxon OX14 4RN

Simultaneously published in the USA and Canada
by Routledge
270 Madison Ave, New York, NY 10016

Routledge is an imprint of the Taylor & Francis Group, an informa business

© 2008 Mazen Labban

Typeset in Times by Wearset Ltd, Boldon, Tyne and Wear

British Library Cataloguing in Publication Data
A catalogue record for this book is available from the British Library

Library of Congress Cataloging in Publication Data
Labban, Mazen.

Space, oil, and capital/Mazen Labban.
p. cm.
Includes bibliographical references and index.

1. Petroleum industry and trade–Economic aspects. 2. International
economic relations. 3. Geopolitics. 4. Petroleum industry and
trade–Russia–Case studies. 5. Petroleum industry and trade–Iran–Case
studies. I. Title.

HD9560.5.L17 2008
338.2′3–dc22

2007042979

ISBN10: 0-415-77391-1 (hbk)
ISBN10: 0-415-59478-2 (pbk)
ISBN10: 0-203-92825-3 (ebk)

ISBN13: 978-0-415-77391-1 (hbk)
ISBN13: 978-0-415-59478-3 (pbk)
ISBN13: 978-0-203-92825-7 (ebk)

For my parents,
Saaduddine al-Labban and Mona al-Masri

Contents

Acknowledgments

I would like to express my gratitude to the following individuals for their support and encouragement. First and foremost, I would like to express my deepest appreciation to Dick Peet for his boundless generosity, intellectual and otherwise. This book would not have been possible without Dick's unwavering camaraderie. I am fortunate to have had the chance to benefit from his vast and critical intellect, and I continue to do so. I thank Jody Emel for introducing me to the world of oil and much else of which I would have otherwise remained ignorant, and above all for her continued confidence in my scholarship. My intellectual debt to Neil Smith runs deeper than the occasional citation and I'm grateful for his consistent support. Andy Merrifield and Erik Swyngedouw are solid comrades with a lot of dialectical thinking to share. Richard Grant, Peter Muller, Jan Nijman and Rinku Roy Chowdhury are more than colleagues, and their genuine support and invaluable advice are deeply appreciated. I would also like to thank John Ziadie for his competent and patient assistance.

At Routledge, I would like to thank Terry Clague for taking on this project and, together with Thomas Sutton, Sarah Hastings, Karen Blenkinsop and Wearset's Kelly Alderson, for carrying it through in the smoothest way possible.

My family, especially my parents, will be the happiest to see this book materializing. I thank all of them for their endurance, and especially my brother Rami who provided me with more support than he may be aware of.

There are not enough songs in the world to express my total love and infinite gratitude to Laura Schneider. Much in the following pages owes to the many conversations that went well into the night and to Laura's endurance of hours of Shostakovich during the day. Without her love, patience, good humor, and her insistence that I should take time off from my desk to make dinner, neither this book nor its author would have been possible. Gracias, Laura.

1 The expansion of capital, oil scarcity and the contradiction of space

Inter-capitalist competition for the control of oil is at the center of the political geometry of global capitalism. Beyond assertions of its vital centrality to the emerging geopolitical economy, particularly the continued hegemony of the US, little attempt has been made to theorize the relations among the production of oil, the process of capital accumulation, and the production of geographical space. Geopolitical analyses reduce the competition for oil to rivalry among nation states caused by a combination of an increase in consumer demands and growing populations and a decline in the quantities and quality of available resources. Thus, the rise in world consumption and inevitable decrease in the amount and quality of available oil resources not only explain geopolitical competition, but are certain to lead to what Michael Klare has called "resource wars," and, on some catastrophic views, to nothing short of the extinction of the human species altogether. Wars are destined to erupt wherever shared resources are located until, in a matter of few years, no oil will be left to produce the energy necessary for the survival of the global human population and six of the seven billion people on this planet will become "redundant."[1] Political economic analysis has been careful to avoid the Malthusian, and erroneous, premises of this argument and point to the historical forces that made oil a "strategic commodity" upon which the integration of capitalist economies under US hegemony in the post-war period has depended, making the global competition for the control of oil a central aspect of the survival, or decline, of US hegemony in the global economy.[2] Despite glaring differences in their explanation of the sources of geopolitical competition for oil, both conventional geopolitics and political economy share a focus on the security of supply of oil, determined by its geological finiteness, in terms of its limited quantities or in terms of its location, thus making the competition for oil a competition for the control of the geographical spaces in which it is located or through which it is transported to consumers in order to ensure its uninterrupted flow into the global economy. I aim to reverse this relationship in the chapters that constitute this book and argue that it is not the geological finiteness of oil that leads to geopolitical competition and makes space important, but the production of geographical space in the process of competition that is crucial to producing the finiteness of oil. In other words, I shall show that the competition for oil is not to guarantee its supply but to guarantee that a part of it stays out of the market in order to make its production profitable. The problem of oil is not its scarcity but its abundance. It is, moreover, cheap to produce, making it necessary for competing oil producers, national (state) and transnational oil companies, to put in place mechanisms that prevent overproduction and oversupply in the market by regulating capital invested in the production of oil. In the process, geographical space becomes decisive in controlling the production of oil and negotiating the contradictions of the expansion of global capital into oil reserves, rather than simply the passive locus of competition.

The debate over the supply of oil pits geology against economy. It revolves around factors that are difficult to determine, mainly the size of recoverable reserves, how much oil is left in the ground, and the economic and physical viability of extracting it. On the "depletionist" side, geologists have argued that oil is geologically finite, in that there is a limited quantity of it generated millions of years ago and which can only be located in a so-called oil window at a specific depth of 7,000–15,000ft.[3] There is no oil outside this window. All major oilfields had been already discovered by the 1960s and recent discoveries have been either insignificant in size or uneconomical to mine. Most of the easily accessible oilfields have been mined and their productivity has begun its irreversible decline. Oil production is near its peak, i.e. almost half of all available reserves have been extracted, if it has not already passed it. Global oil production is therefore bound to decline and eventually cease some time in the near future, when the energy needed for lifting oil out of the ground will exceed the energy derived from burning it, or when more money is required to lift it than money is made from selling it.

This argument is based on an analysis of oil production in the US by Marion King Hubbert, a geologist who worked for Royal Dutch Shell and the United States Geological Survey. In 1956, Hubbert predicted that US production should peak some time between 1968 and 1972, around 40 years after the peak of discoveries in the US. Indeed, oil production in the US started declining around 1970, at about the same time that Hubbert had started applying his analysis of US oil production at the global scale. He predicted in 1969 that global oil production should peak some time between 1990 and 2000. It did not, which spurred geologists to re-examine and modify Hubbert's predictions, moving them eventually ten to 20 years ahead. "Detractors" from the peak oil thesis, largely energy economists, criticize the notion of geological shortage on the grounds that it is difficult, if not altogether impossible, to determine the ultimate size of recoverable reserves.[4] The size and recoverability of oil reserves are functions of capital investment and technological developments that often lead to the discovery of new reserves; the exploitation of nonconventional sources such as oil shale and tar sands; increased access to existing reserves and their upward revaluation through the application of techniques that enhance their productivity, such as horizontal drilling and gas reinjection. Moreover, removal of legal and political obstacles, such as economic sanctions, stringent laws of investment, or protected wildlife sanctuaries, expands oil production into hitherto inaccessible reserves. The size and productivity of oil reserves, therefore, are not fixed and are not determined by geological limits as much as by economic, political, and technological developments in production. Reserves grow; they do not only deplete. Also, consumption does not grow in one direction. More efficient use of oil as a raw material and source of energy, gradual substitution of more abundant and renewable resources for nonrenewable ones, slow down in demand from rising market prices – caused partly by more difficult and costly extraction – extend the life of dwindling reserves. Indeed, the size of proven reserves of crude oil across the world has only grown over the past 30 years, in absolute terms (see Figure 1.1), and in relation to world consumption and production (see Figure 1.2). While the world consumption of crude oil grew from 63 to 84.5 million barrels per day from 1980 to 2006 (around 34 percent), the size of world proven crude oil reserves more than doubled, from around 645 to around 1,317 billion barrels by the end of 2006.[5] Reserves-to-production ratio increased from 27.54 to 42.67 between 1980 and 2006 (see Figure 1.3).

The scarcity or abundance of oil is ultimately a social–spatial relationship, not merely a geological fact or technical appraisal. Certainly, oil is ultimately finite and nonrenewable, on one hand, and its availability is a function of technology and investment capital, on the other. The real scarcity of oil, however, derives primarily from the monopoly of landlord states and oil

Figure 1.1 World proven oil reserves in billion barrels, 1980–2006 (source: US Department of Energy, Energy Information Administration, Office of Energy Markets and End Use).

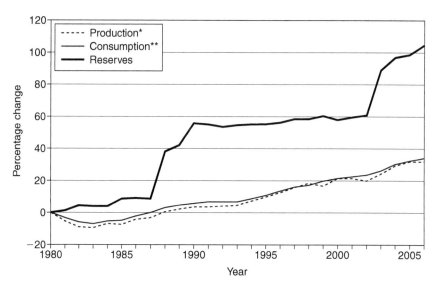

Figure 1.2 Cumulative change in world oil production,* consumption,** and reserves since 1980 (source: US Department of Energy, Energy Information Administration, Office of Energy Markets and End Use).

Notes
*   Includes crude oil, natural gas plant liquids, lease condensate and other liquids, and refinery processing gain (the difference in volume between refinery input and output).
** The sum of supplied petroleum products (production and net withdrawals from primary stocks, plus imports minus exports) and of crude oil burned directly.

companies, national and transnational, over extraction and access to reserves in order to avoid the build-up of inventories and to maintain inflated market prices. Oil lifting costs range between $4 per barrel in the Middle East and $7 per barrel in high-cost regions in the Western hemisphere, while its market price hovers around $70 per barrel. There would not be a problem were it not for the chronic tendency in the oil industry to overproduce and oversupply oil markets, driven not by consumer demand but by the profitability of the oil industry itself. The progressive growth of fixed capital in the oil industry, in absolute terms and in relation to labor, requires larger amounts of oil to valorize it. In other words, it is necessary to produce oil in large quantities to reap a return on investment in the enormous quantities of capital fixed in its production, from drilling pipes to refineries, linked through a vast web of pipelines, tankers, trucks and storage facilities – including the reserves themselves. The value of the current global oil infrastructure is estimated at $10 trillion, in addition to around $90 trillion worth of oil in the ground, assuming world proven reserves of 1.3 trillion barrels at $70 per barrel. There is, therefore, around $100 trillion to be made without further major investments. Thus, paradoxically, as reserves grow and oil becomes more abundant, it must be made scarce in order to produce and realize the surplus profits of the oil industry.

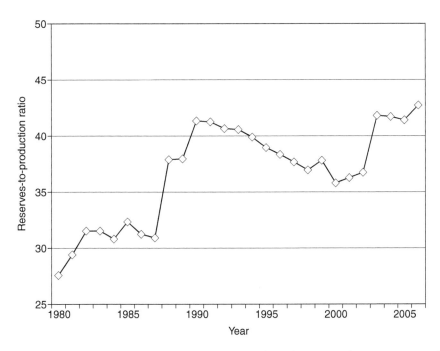

Figure 1.3 Reserves-to-production ratio, 1980–2006 (source: US Department of Energy, Energy Information Administration, Office of Energy Markets and End Use).

The problem of overproduction and oversupply is exacerbated by its opposite: underproduction and undersupply, which particularly hurts the profits of landlord states, but in the long run also major oil companies. A slow decrease in market supplies leads to a disproportionately higher increase in the market price, eventually slowing down demand and income. States and oil companies can adjust to such market fluctuations, but the major problem is the effect that undersupply has on the production of oil. High market prices make production in high-cost regions profitable, causing the migration of capital into new regions and the incorporation of more reserves into production, creating new competition in the market and leading, eventually, to decline in market prices and profitability. Hence the contradiction for oil producers: making oil artificially scarce results in making it abundant again and reproduces the problem of controlling its production.

Oil producers must, therefore, negotiate the contradictions between scarcity and abundance to regulate the flow of capital into the oil industry, such that not too much nor too little capital is invested in the production of oil. Competition for oil is fundamentally competition to control this flow of capital to prevent overproduction and the expansion of competition – ultimately to protect monopoly profits. At the heart of this process is a contradictory process of spatial integration and fragmentation that regulates the flow of capital into reserves and that emanates from the conflicting interests of the different factions of capital, namely extractive capital (oil companies) and landed capital (landlord states). The spatial contradiction becomes, therefore, an effective and necessary means in regulating the scarcity of oil and determining the profitability of the oil industry.

How does the contradiction of space mediate the (contradictory) extension of capital into the production of oil? The development of capital is expressed historically in the concentration of the means of production: the instruments and objects of labor necessary to carry out the labor process, leading to increase in demand for raw material, which ranges from the material that directly forms the substance of the product to the material consumed in its production as a source of energy. Raw material is not directly available in nature, however, and enters the labor process as an object that has already been "filtered through previous labor." In other words, raw material is itself the product of one form of labor, which enters another form of labor as its object. With the development of the division of labor, extractive industries became the principle providers of all other branches of industry with what Marx called their "most important element" – the necessary objects without which production cannot proceed (see Marx 1976: 288; 1981: 213). Resource extraction becomes the necessary link, within capital as a whole, between the different branches of industry and the objective conditions of production, lending it extreme importance for the accumulation of capital as a whole. Oil, in particular, has a very wide range of use in various industries and, most importantly, a very high energy content compared with other fuels in terms of weight and volume.

Increase in the demand for raw material leads first to an increase in their market price. This spurs capital into the production of raw material in search of high profits, leading to the concentration of capital and decline in profitability in extractive industry, exacerbated by the eventual fall in the market prices. As with other industries, to counter the decline in the profitability of capital invested in the production of raw material, producers increase either the mass of production or the productivity (exploitation) of labor, both of which lead necessarily to an increase in the mass of resources to be extracted. With the development of capital in extractive industry, the primary source of demand for resources becomes the contradictions of growth in extractive industry itself, between the concentration of capital and the decline in profitability. The concentration of extractive capital, the development of the social productivity of labor in this branch of industry, becomes both the consequence and cause of increase in demand for a larger mass of resources. In the case of non-reproducible resources such as oil, the tendency towards capital concentration and increase in demand for the resource needed to valorize it translates the dependence on larger amounts of resources into deeper territorial fixity, deepening the link of capital as a whole, through the extractive industry, to land and the resources in it. As capitalist production develops, a portion of capital has to be immobilized for (remaining) capital to move freely (see Harvey 1999). As capital expands and circulates in deeper layers of global space, it becomes more immobilized and pinned down to the accidental location of key natural resources, such as oil. The contradiction between circulation and accumulation materializes in geographical space as a tension between mobility and fixity, and, as we shall see, as a contradiction between geographical integration and fragmentation.

Decline in profitability and increase in the concentration of capital in extractive industry has two contradictory consequences, both of which lead to the centralization of capital: intensified competition for large reserves to valorize capital invested in the production of raw material and intensified competition for the control of reserves to prevent overproduction and decline in prices and profits, or, what amounts to the same, to make the resource in question scarce. Producers of raw material are, therefore, plagued with the contradiction of having to continuously expand the mass of available resources, making them more abundant, while controlling production and availability on the market by controlling access to resources, making them scarce. Thus, competition for oil is not to secure its continuous supply, but to secure that not so much of it is produced that may threaten the profitability of the industry. Scarcity of oil is not a product of geological limits or increased demand for it in the market leading to its depletion, but the condition upon which oil enters production and the market to reap surplus profits. Its source lies in the capitalist relations to property.

The expansion of extractive capital brings it up against the barrier of landed property, the owners of the resource to be extracted. Both factions of capital depend on the contradiction of space to negotiate the contradiction between overproduction and scarcity. Whence the contradiction? Resources existing in nature do not embody value because they are not the product of human labor, i.e. they are not commodities in the strict sense. They acquire the commodity-form, exchange-value, by being privately appropriated (and made artificially scarce). Only then can they enter the market, can they be bought and sold as private property. The private appropriation of naturally occurring resources is the source of the monopoly power of resource owners embodied in their ability to withhold them from the market. Legal entitlement of the owner to resources in the land allows him to restrict the access of capital to the resource, making it artificially scarce in order to reap higher rents from its exploitation. The power of landed property over capital, however, can only be exercised as a "power of negation," by withholding resources from production. Legal entitlement can only act as a barrier to the expansion of extractive capital, but it is only valorized economically (in the form of rent, share in profit, royalty tax, etc.) by the extension of capital into the resource. Thus, the condition of rent deriving from the power of landed property to act as a barrier to capital depends on its opposite, the extension of capital into the land, the employment of labor in the production of the use-values and surplus value: the source of rent. While the control over access to the resource entails an absolute division of space into mutually exclusive territories, according to which resource owners, ranging from private individuals to states administering the national wealth, can exercise their monopoly power over exclusive portions of space, the economic valorization of landed property depends on its integration in the fluid circuits of capital. The encounter of productive capital and landed capital produces a geographical contradiction between integration and fragmentation, which mediates the process of capital expansion into resources, and becomes the means by which the scarcity of the resource is produced. When the two factions of capital combine in the same entity, such as the national oil company, the contradiction is not resolved, but internalized.

Inter-capitalist competition for the control of oil reserves and production has, historically, led to the increasing centralization of control of the industry in the hands of large transnational corporations. The centralization of capital, the fusion of different enterprises into large corporations, brings production and markets under the control of fewer capitalists and allows them to maintain surplus profits by eliminating excessive capital from production, thus minimizing costs, reducing the threat of overproduction and market gluts. In extractive industry, centralization of capital places resources under the control of fewer producers, allowing them to control scarcity and negotiate the contradiction between extending and restricting the access of capital to the resource. The development of the oil industry throughout the twentieth century, as with the development of extractive industry in general, has been centered on the monopoly of production by a few large corporations. In the oil industry, outside of the Soviet Union, the so-called "seven sisters" dominated oil production for most of its development.[6] By the 1960s, transnational oil companies had direct access to 85 percent of global oil and gas reserves; the Soviet Union controlled the remaining 14 percent. The monopoly of transnational oil companies was largely based on semi-colonial and imperialist relations with Third World countries, which allowed them unrestricted access to large swaths of land and complete control over the production of oil, for a royalty paid to the state. This was challenged with the national liberation of Third World countries, and the development of economic nationalism restricted the access of foreign companies to oil reserves and placed part of the control over production in the hands of state-owned national oil companies. This process, still in development today, reversed the proportion of control over world oil reserves, placing more control under national oil companies, without, however, abolishing the monopoly of the oil industry. The largest 15 companies, in terms of reserves, controlled 68.5 percent of world oil reserves by the end of 2006. In terms of production, the largest 14 controlled 52 percent of world oil production (see Table 1.1). Thus, the nationalization of the oil industry shifted part of the control of oil reserves and production from transnational oil companies to national corporations and widened the competition in the oil industry to include the resource-owning or resource-administering state as another faction of capital. This did not slow down the competition nor the centralization of capital. By the late 1990s, in the middle of an oil slump, a wave of mergers and acquisitions swept the industry, consolidating control over reserves and production again in the hands of transnational oil companies. Six of the so-called seven sisters merged into ExxonMobil and ChevronTexaco (now Chevron), with Chevron and BP splitting Gulf oil between them, the bulk going to Chevron; BP also acquired Amoco; French Total went on to merge with Fina and Elf Aquitaine into TotalFinaElf. The consolidation of the Russian oil industry, discussed in detail in Chapter 5, represents another stage in this process taking place especially in developing countries, with the development of the hybrid national oil corporation that is partly state-owned, partly publicly traded, and sometimes partly foreign-owned, as in the case of Gazprom and Rosneft.[7]

Competition for oil, or raw material in general, must be understood in relation to the internal movement of capitalist accumulation in general and the concrete historical geographical development of global capitalism. Accumulation is

Table 1.1 Reserves and world share of oil and gas companies with reserves of more than 3,000 million barrels

Oil and gas companies with reserves of more than 3,000 million barrels (state and percentage of ownership)*	Liquids reserves in million barrels*	Percentage of world total based on EIA estimate of 1,317,447 million barrels at the end of 2006**	Percentage of world total crude oil and natural gas liquids production (2002)**
Saudi Aramco (Saudi Arabia 100)	264,200	20.1	10.6
NIOC (Iran 100)	137,500	10.4	4.9
INOC (Iraq 100)	115,000	8.7	3.5
KPC (Kuwait 100)	101,500	7.7	2.2
PDV (Venezuela 100)	79,700	6.0	4.4
Adnoc (Abu Dhabi 100)	56,920	4.3	2.6
Libya NOC (Libya 100)	33,235	2.5	
NNPC (Nigeria 100)	21,540	1.6	2.7
LUKoil	16,114	1.2	2.1
Qatar (Qatar 100)	15,200	1.2	
Rosneft (Russia 75)	14,345	1.1	
Pemex (Mexico 100)	13,671	1.0	4.6
PetroChina (China 90)	11,962	0.9	2.8
Sonatrach (Algeria 100)	11,712	0.9	
ExxonMobil	11,229	0.9	3.4
Gazprom (Russia 50.002)	9,829	0.7	
Petrobras (Brazil 32)	9,716	0.7	
BP	9,565	0.7	2.5
Chevron	8,146	0.6	2.6
Petronas (Malaysia 100)	7,559	0.6	
Surgutneftegas	7,339	0.6	
Total	6,592	0.5	
ConocoPhillips	6,189	0.5	
Royal Dutch Shell	5,382	0.4	3.1
TNK-BP	4,115	0.3	

Sources: **Petroleum Intelligence Weekly* 2006; **US Department of Energy, Energy Information Administration, Office of Energy Markets and End Use.

the ultimate end, and it is driven by the contradiction between progressive concentration of fixed capital and decline in the rate of profit, in industry in general but particularly in extractive industry, leading to growing demand for raw material in order to put larger concentrations of capital in motion and counter the decline in the rate of profit. The contradiction of space arises in the process from the contradiction between the conditions of accumulation for capital in general and the conditions of accumulation for individual factions of capital, forcing the contradictory extension yet restriction of capital into land and the resources in it. The expansion of capital expands the contradictions of capital accumulation and inter-capitalist competition at the same time that it embeds them deeper in material nature. At the most fundamental level, the contradictions of extractive industry are the contradictions of capital accumulation as a whole, not only expressed as, but becoming contradictions with, nature and contradictions of space. Oil, more than any other raw material, demonstrates the spatio-material contradictions of capital and the importance of the extension of capital into natural resources for the continued accumulation of capital as whole. Consequently, competition for oil is a condensed expression of inter-capitalist competition reduced to its essence: competition for the appropriation of the material conditions of production for the production of profit. The development of capital must, therefore, translate into more intense competition for oil and the centralization of oil reserves and production, both of which depend on and reproduce the contradiction of space. It is at this fundamental level, rather than in extra economic factors such as population growth or geological limits, that the competition for oil must be understood.

I examine the geographical contradictions of the oil industry in the three empirical case studies that constitute Chapters 4, 5, and 6. Chapters 2 and 3 expand the argument presented in this introduction on two levels. In Chapter 2, I present a detailed theoretical explanation of the contradictions in capital accumulation between the decline in the rate of profit and the concentration of fixed capital. The focus is on the causes of concentration and centralization of capital in the extractive industry and the development of the geographical contradiction from the expansion of extractive capital against the barriers of landed property. This chapter serves as a theoretical backdrop to the case studies presented in the last three chapters.

Chapter 3 presents an account of the development of the geographical contradiction through an examination of the development of inter-capitalist rivalry through three, interlocked historical moments: classical imperialism, the postwar period, and neoliberal globalization, each of which represents the development of the geographical contradiction in its historically specific form. The purpose of this chapter is to explain the centrality of geographical space to the historical development of capital by going beyond the abstract generalizations discussed in Chapter 2 and the particular question of oil, to embed the geographical contradictions of capital in the concrete historical development of global capitalism. Chapter 3, therefore, serves to locate the current inter-capitalist competition for oil in a broader historical and geoeconomic context.

Chapter 4 examines the development of the oil industry in the Soviet Union from the standpoint of the contradiction between dependence on expansion and integration into the world market and isolation from foreign capital. Despite its apparent independence from the world economy, the Soviet economy depended on the world market for exports of oil in exchange for capital and technology – a contradictory dependence exacerbated by the abundance of oil reserves and by the quantitative logic of the Gosplan, which led continuously to overproduction and the need to dispose of oil surpluses that could not be absorbed domestically, making the Soviet Union, with its isolation to foreign capital, a serious threat to the profitability of the global oil industry. Commercial integration, however, transformed into integration through direct investment as the Soviet economy withered throughout the 1970s and became more dependent for its survival on foreign capital, financial and technological. The opening of the Soviet economy renewed the scramble for Soviet oil among transnational oil companies before the final implosion of the Soviet Union, itself partly the product of a voluntary and deeper integration into the world economy, gave it full throttle.

Chapter 5 examines the development of this process by analyzing the development of the Russian oil industry throughout the privatization and liberalization spree of the 1990s followed by an apparent process of renationalization, or reverse privatization, at the turn of the century. I shall argue that far from nationalization, the recent development of the Russian oil industry has led to the creation of a state-managed oil industry comprising of private companies and partly state-owned companies. I focus, in this chapter, on the process of capital centralization in the Russian oil industry, which internalized the geographical contradiction between the attempt of the Russian state to bring foreign capital into the industry yet consolidate its control over it, leading ultimately to the creation of the hybrid national oil company as an expression and embodiment of this contradiction. The contradictions in the development of the Russian oil industry are a product of the movement against the privatization and liberalization of the 1990s. The case of Iran, examined in Chapter 6, represents the opposite. Isolated from the world economy by its own constitution and US sanctions since the Revolution of 1979, the Iranian government has, since the early 1990s, sought to open the economy to foreign capital for the development of its oil and gas production, ridden by damages from the war with Iraq and decline in the productivity of aging and depleting oilfields. The contradictory movement to opening the Iranian economy is not too dissimilar to that of the Soviet Union, and is driven by the dependence on foreign capital restricted by barriers from investment laws and US sanctions. I focus, in this study, on the embodiment of this contradiction in both the development of the Iran and Libya Sanctions Act since 1995 and the development of Iranian investment laws over the same period. Each of the case studies is written to stand on its own, with an introduction summarizing and expanding the aspects of the theoretical argument most relevant to the case study. For the last two chapters, I relied on extensive research in the *Wall Street Journal*, the *Financial Times*, the *New York Times*, *The Economist*, the *Oil and Gas Journal*, *Petroleum Economist*, and *Petroleum Intelligence Weekly*; and on the *New York Times* and the *Wall Street Journal* for some of the material in Chapter 3 (section III) and Chapter 4 (the period after 1970). To cite each and every article I used in my research would have resulted in a long bibliography without any apparent use for the reader. I want, therefore, to acknowledge my debt to the many reporters whose work I've mined, interpreted, and misinterpreted in the process.

2 Contradictions of capitalist accumulation

Inter-capitalist competition, the production of raw material and the contradiction of space

The contradiction of space is an expression of the contradiction between the interests of different factions of capital (financial, productive, landed, and commercial – but also "national" factions of global capital) and the interests of the capitalist class as a whole, or of capital as a "formal unity" of different factions, nationalities, states, and markets (Lefebvre 1991; see also Harvey 1999). This contradiction is explored historically in the following chapter. In this chapter, I draw on Marx's analyses in the third volume of *Capital* to explain the contradiction arising from inter-capitalist competition as a contradiction between the production of surplus value, the source of profit, and the distribution of profit among competing capitalists. The argument could be summarized as follows: under the compulsion of competition, capitalists seek ways to squeeze surplus value out of the working class as a whole, to produce the largest profits from capital they invest in production, leading to a progressive concentration in labor-saving means of production. The development of capital is, therefore, expressed as a contradictory tension between the concentration of the means of production and a decline in the general rate of profit of capital as a whole, as a result of growth in the objective means of production in relation to the labor necessary to employ them in the production process – the source of surplus value and profit. The development of labor productivity replaces living labor, the source of surplus value, with dead labor, machines, tools, buildings, etc. Capital counters the tendency of the rate of profit to fall by increasing the exploitation of labor to extract larger masses of surplus value, which leads, however, to further growth in the means of production (including, not in the least, the raw material necessary to put more productive labor to work), resulting in further decline in the general rate of profit and consequent development of labor productivity, and so on and so forth. This contradiction is at the heart of the development of capital – the growth of constant capital being the source both of the tendency for the rate of profit to decline and the means to counter this tendency temporarily, and is expressed as both growth in the value and magnitude of the means of production in relation to living labor: the organic composition of capital.

But if profit is produced in the production process, it has to be realized in the sale of commodities in the market. In its second moment, inter-capitalist competition becomes competition for the capture of larger shares of the total profit produced by workers in all spheres of production. It is here where the conflict between the interests of the capitalist class as a whole (the extraction of surplus value from the workers) and the interests of individual capitalists (capturing the largest possible share of total surplus value) becomes most acute. Surplus value produced in society as a whole is appropriated by the capitalist class as a whole, but, because of the unevenness of capital concentration, individual capitalists do not directly realize the surplus value produced by the workers they employ. Thus, the competition among capitalists finds expression not only as competition for the *production* of greater masses of social surplus value, but also its *realization* as profit in the market and redistribution among individual capitalists.

Total surplus value produced in society is determined by the aggregate organic composition of individual capitalists and their magnitudes, but the fraction of the total surplus value that individual capitalists appropriate is proportional to the fraction their capital represents of total capital. Capitalists do not realize the profit produced by workers in their respective spheres or enterprises, but a share of profit that may be less or more than the surplus value produced by their workers. As we shall see below, assuming all capital exploits all labor at the same rate and all capital has the same turnover time, although the individual rate of profit is lower in branches of production and enterprises characterized by a higher organic composition of capital (where the ratio of the means of production to living labor is larger in terms of magnitude and value), capital with an organic composition below the social average, i.e. with larger outlays on labor than on the means of production compared with other capitals, produces a bigger part of social surplus value than it captures, "losing" part of this surplus value to capital with an organic composition higher than the social average. That is, industries with organic compositions of capital lower than the social average extract more of the total social surplus value but receive less of it by transferring part of the surplus value produced by their workers to industries with a higher organic composition in the process of exchange. Conversely, capitals of relatively higher organic composition return a greater portion of surplus value produced in society than they extract. The profitability of capital as a whole depends on the exploitation of labor as a whole by capital as a whole. But the profitability of individual capitals depends on the possibility of realizing an "extra cut," to extract profit in excess of the surplus value produced by workers employed by that particular capital.

As the share of a particular capital in total profit is determined by two factors, i.e. its individual rate of profit, deriving from its internal composition, and its size proportional to total capital, the attempt by individual capitalists to capture a larger share of the total surplus value also leads to progressive growth in investment in labor-saving fixed capital, and consequently in the circulating part of constant capital (raw material), and to a tendential fall in the general rate of profit combined with its tendential equalization across different spheres of production (and across different geographical regions). In the long run, capital as a whole produces at a lower general rate of profit. It remains to the individual capitals in the competition to try to capture the largest share of it by revolutionizing the means and methods of production, creating monopolistic conditions of production, controlling markets, etc., to escape the equalization process and realize surplus profits: profits above the prevalent average. Larger and less profitable capital becomes dependent on larger (and cheaper) volumes of raw material to be valorized in the production process. The development of capital in extractive industry, the oil industry in our case, thus takes on the same tendencies as fixed capital concentrates in the extraction of resources to prevent decline in its profitability and to extract larger shares of social surplus value. Yet, since it is the sphere of industry directly tied to the accidental location of resources and objective natural conditions of production, the development of extractive industry is more directly determined by property in land and resources and, therefore, by the power of landed property as another faction of capital competing for a cut in total surplus value produced in society.

The power of landed property, however, goes further than its (parasitical) claim to rent, a share in surplus value extracted by productive capital from workers producing on the land. Landed property, by exercising power over extractive industry, determines the development not only of extractive industry, but the development of capital as a whole in as far as monopoly of land determines the mobility of capital and prevents the equalization of profit rates across space and branches of industry. Under normal conditions of capital mobility, capital moves from spheres of production with lower rates of profit to those with higher rates of profit, which results in equalizing the differences in the organic composition of capital across different spheres of production. Seen from a geographical standpoint, under normal conditions of capital mobility, capital moves from one place where the rate of profit is lower to another where it can achieve higher rates of profit, thus equalizing the conditions across geographical space. The migration of capital from one industry or region to another, therefore, erodes the monopolistic conditions under which particular capitals realize surplus profits. As it also alters the relative mass and value of commodities on the market, it leads to change in market prices and to altering the rate of profit from the standpoint of its realization in the market. Thus, capitals enjoying surplus profits have to erect barriers against the free movement of capital in order to prevent the equalization of the rate of profit and to continue the transfer of surplus value from other spheres and branches of industry. It is here where the power of landed property becomes decisive, for restricting the access of capital to the resource, or, which amounts to the same, removing land and resources from production, affects not only the availability and price of the resource as raw material entering the production process, but the uneven distribution of profit among capitals in different spheres of production and different geographical regions. Especially in the case of the oil industry, whose products enter almost all other spheres of production (and individual consumption) and, thus, have direct effect on the profitability of capital in almost all other branches of production, the competition between extractive capital and landed property over access to the land and control of raw material production has decisive effects on the general profitability of capital and on differentiation in the profit rates among competing capitals. However, the power of landed property can only be exercised in negation. No matter how decisive it can be in controlling the production of raw material by restricting the access of capital to natural resources, it depends on productive capital for the employment of resources in the exploitation of labor and the production of surplus value: the source of rent. Thus, the contradiction between the interests of capital as a whole and the interests of individual factions of capital finds expression at the most fundamental level, the level of acquiring the objective means of production, as a contradiction between productive capital and landed property. This, in turn, is materialized as a contradiction between geographical expansion and integration on the one hand (to put land in the production process, to produce surplus value), and fragmentation and isolation on the other (to withhold land from production, to reproduce surplus profit).

In the following, I first establish the significance of the extractive industry as the crucial segment of social production that ties capital in its totality to the natural conditions of production by providing other branches of industry with their necessary means of production. In this section, the discussion is focused on the production and exchange of use-values among capitalists in different branches of industry. In the section that follows, I discuss the contradiction in the accumulation of capital between the tendency of the rate of profit to fall and the concentration and centralization of capital. Here, the discussion is largely focused on the contradiction between the production and realization of value, the basis of profit, in competition among capitalists in different spheres of production and capitalists in the same branch of industry. The third section examines the contradictions that arise from the expansion of capital into land: the focus is primarily on the contradictory interdependence of productive capital and landed property in the reproduction of surplus profit.

The elements of labor and the mutual dependence of the branches of industry

Labor is a process that appears on the side of the worker in the "form of unrest" and on the side of the product in the "form of being, as a fixed, immobile characteristic." During the labor process, labor "constantly undergoes transformation … from the form of motion into that of objectivity" (Marx 1976: 296). The "simple elements" of the labor process in general are work itself, as a "purposeful activity," the object on which work is performed, and the instrument that mediates between the worker and the object. Labor as activity forms the subjective means of production, and the object and instrument of labor form the objective means of production – the form of objectivity that makes the labor process, as subjective activity, possible. At an advanced stage of the division of labor, the products of social labor become also its necessary conditions, i.e. the products of one segment of social labor enter another as its necessary means of production.

The primary object of human labor is earth, and the labor process proceeds first by separating the objects of labor from their immediate environment in the totality of nature. Thus, although the object of labor is originally present in nature, it only becomes the object of labor when labor abstracts it from the totality of nature. The separation of materials and things "spontaneously provided by nature" from their "immediate connection with their environment" provides labor with its necessary objects and, hence, with its objective necessity (Marx 1976: 284). At more advanced stages of the social division of labor, this process of separation becomes characteristic of one specialized sphere of production, extractive industry, which performs for social labor as a whole the primary task of separation and provides other spheres of production with the necessary objective means of production, objects and instruments. The object of labor in industry at an advanced stage of the division of labor is not spontaneously provided by nature, but it is an object of labor that has "undergone alteration by means of labor," i.e. it is the product of extractive industry: *raw material*. Raw material may "form the principle substance of a product, or it may enter its formation as an accessory;" it may be introduced to another raw material in order to modify it, as coal is added to iron; or it may help "to accomplish the work itself," as in "materials used for heating and lighting workshops" (Marx 1976: 288). Apart from living labor, raw material is the "most important element in all branches of production," without which production cannot take place (see Marx 1981: 213). The development of industrial production in general is, therefore, dependent on, and expressed as, development of production in industries that produce raw material.

The instrument of labor is a "conductor of activity" between the worker and the object of labor, i.e. the "thing, or a complex of things, which the worker interposes between himself and the object of his labour," comprising the objective conditions required in the labor process. The relationship between the worker and the objects of labor in the labor process is not immediate: the worker is in "direct possession" of the instrument of labor, not the object of labor, and this mediation thickens with the complexity of the instrument and the process of production. At a more developed stage of industrial production, the object of labor can only become an object of labor with the development of instruments capable of realizing it as such. In extractive industry this implies the development of instruments capable of transforming the earth, or nature, into an object of labor.[1] Indeed, the extraction of materials from nature, or the use of natural forces as means of production, became possible only with the development of industry proper and the knowledge and technologies capable of transforming nature into use-values, i.e. objects and instruments useful for industrial production. Thus, although the object of labor for extractive industry appears to be "provided directly by nature," not the product of past labor, its becoming an object of labor is determined by the existence of instruments of labor capable of transforming it into a useful means of production.

The industries that produce the instruments of labor, together with the industries that produce raw material, are industries that produce the means of production. As with the objects of labor, the instruments of labor in one branch of industry become the products of other branches of industry, and the development of extractive industry becomes itself dependent on, and expressed as, development in branches of industry that produce other means of production. The process of extraction takes place as a crucial part of industrial production seen in its totality and it is, therefore, a process within industrial production and integral to it, rather than a process outside of it or merely preceding it.[2]

Specialized industries that produce the means of production provide other branches of industry with the necessary objects and instruments consumed in the production process, which has at its end the final consumption by society as a whole. The mutual interdependence of the different branches of production derives from the social division of labor, which, at the same time, conceals it behind their apparent fragmentation. The fragmentation of the different branches of production appears in the simultaneous existence of various types of commodities on the market at one point in time, and obscures the spatiotemporal nature of the inner connections between the various branches of production in the production of the final commodity. What is hidden in the appearance of independent commodities that stand on their own in their abstraction is the structure of relationships among the various branches of production that constitutes the structure of social labor as a whole. Individual producers in different branches of industry, despite their mutual dependence on social labor, produce in isolation from each other such that production in one branch of industry may exceed, or fall short of, the need of the other, and, at a more general level, production may exceed or fall short of social need (backed up by purchasing power). As apparent fragmentation and isolation conceal, and rest on, actual mutual dependence, actions of single capitalists have (unforeseeable and largely uncontrollable) consequences for capitalist production as a whole.

Extractive industry appears to stand on its own as an independent branch of industry existing simultaneously with other branches of industry, only by looking at its products in the market standing in isolation from the branches of industry that consume them and the branches of industry that produce the means of production. The apparent detachment of extractive industry as a specialized branch of industry that stands on its own has, as its consequence, two contradictory effects: the apparent separation of the total production process from the natural conditions of production and the abstraction of extractive industry from the inner contradictions of the process of capital accumulation. Extractive industry, however, when seen as one branch of industrial production with necessary and inner connections to capital as a whole, forms the necessary mediation between production as a whole and the natural conditions of production within the process of capital accumulation. It points to where the contradiction between capital as a whole and individual factions of capital becomes mediated by the social relation with nature, i.e. where inter-capitalist competition for the production of profit appears as, or becomes, competition for access to and control of the natural conditions of production. It is therefore insufficient, or erroneous, to analyze competition for raw material in itself in isolation from the general process of capitalist accumulation and inter-capitalist competition. Only by seeing it as part of the contradictory development of capital can we fully appreciate the importance of extractive industry and the competition for raw material.

The contradictions of capitalist accumulation

Capital is a social relationship between, and within, social classes, but it is also a general social relationship with nature (Marx 1981). The social relationship with nature in capitalist society, as expressed in the labor process, is determined by the social relations among the different classes, or factions within social classes. As the analysis is primarily concerned with explaining inter-capitalist competition for oil as an instance of the mediation of the social relationship with nature by inter-capitalist contradictions, we assume Marx's theory of value and the exploitative relationship between capital and labor. The accumulation of capital rests on the expanded exploitation of social labor by the capitalist class as whole. The extraction of surplus value from the worker is, of necessity, dependent on the transformation of material nature in the labor process: the expansion of labor exploitation, thus, implies an expansion in the "exploitation" of nature. Exploitation of land and resources is merely their utilization, as use-values, in the process or as the basis of real exploitation: the extraction and appropriation of surplus value from living, human labor. Profit derives from the exploitation of labor rather than the exploitation of nature, which, in this case, serves as the medium through which the creation of value and surplus value takes place. The development of extractive industry, as any branch of industry under capitalism, rests on the creation of surplus value from the exploitation of labor in this industry and, as it is structurally embedded in relations among the different branches of industry, on the redistribution of social surplus value among different factions of capital and competing capitalists.

Growth of capital and the tendency of the rate of profit to fall

The value of a commodity is equivalent to the total labor time contained in its production: dead labor (past labor congealed in instruments and objects of production) and living labor, paid labor and unpaid labor. The total value of commodity C can be expressed as $C = c + v + s$, where c represents capital expended on the means of production, i.e. constant capital; v represents capital expended on the purchase of labor power, i.e. variable capital; and s is surplus value, unpaid labor, contained in the commodity. Only human labor *adds* value in the process of production, therefore the part spent on the purchase of labor is variable, whereas the value contained in the means of production is only *transferred* without any quantitative alteration. Hence, it remains constant. Constant capital and variable capital together constitute the *cost price* (k) of the commodity, the total capital that a capitalist spends on the production of a particular mass of commodities during a definite period of time. The value of a commodity ($C = k + s$) is, therefore, always greater than its cost price (k), the difference being surplus value.

For the capitalist to make a profit, the commodity must sell above its cost price even if it does not sell at its total value. The variation in profitability is, therefore, a function of how much of the surplus value contained in the commodity the capitalist can capture from the sale of the commodity. Capitalists go into production if they can realize an average profit, if their commodities can sell at a *production price* equivalent to its cost price plus a profit calculated according to a general rate of profit. Production price must, therefore, be greater than cost price, but it may be greater or smaller than the total value of the commodity, depending on if and how much individual capital realizes profit above or below the social average rate of profit (p'). Thus, if the *cost price* of a commodity is specific to individual capitals, *production price* is independent of particular capitals, i.e. it is an average determined by total capital advanced in production. In other words, production price is determined not by the cost price of any individual capital, but by the price that a commodity costs on average under (hypothetical) average conditions of production in a particular sphere of production.

Profit is realized only when the commodity is sold in the market, but it is created in the labor process. It is an excess of value over the cost price of a commodity, contained in the commodity as profit in potentiality, rather than an excess of sales price over its value. Profit is realized in the market but does not derive from it. If the commodity is sold at a price higher than its *production price*, then the capitalist makes profit above the social average – *excess* or *surplus profit* – even if the total value of the commodity is not realized. This implies that another capitalist realizes profit under the social average, and surplus value is transferred from one owner of commodities to another. (Transfer of value can occur either in the direct exchange between capitalists or through the alteration of workers' wages if the commodity realizing surplus value determines directly, or indirectly, the wages of labor – such as oil. This, of course, depends on the strength of labor unions and the intensity of the class struggle in preventing decline in the real value of wages.) One capitalist takes a larger share of the total surplus value produced by social labor, hence appropriating the surplus value produced by workers employed by other capitalists.

Profit is "the form of appearance of surplus value" and total profit appropriated by capital is equivalent to total surplus value produced in society. Yet, whereas the *rate of surplus value*, or the rate of exploitation, is surplus value measured against variable capital $(s' = s/v)$, the *rate of profit* is surplus value measured against total capital outlaid in the production of a commodity, or its cost price $(p' = s/c+v$, or $p' = s/k)$. The rate of profit is tied to, and always smaller, than the rate of surplus value. But it is possible that the same rate of surplus value finds expression in different rates of profit – the variation derives from the variation in the relationship between constant to variable capital. In other words, it is possible that different capitalists exploit their workers to an equal extent but still realize different rates of profit, and vice versa.

The particular rate of exploitation and rate of profit of one branch of industry or one capital are not directly affected by its absolute magnitude. The magnitude of a particular capital in relation to total capital, however, determines its share of total profit. More importantly, the relative magnitude of different capitals with different internal compositions determines the formation of the average rate of profit, and hence the distribution of total surplus value among competing capitals. The rate of profit of a particular capital is determined by its *organic composition*, that is the relationship between its constituent parts: constant capital and variable capital, or *c*/*v*. The organic composition of capital depends on its *technical composition* (the relationship between the mass of the means of production and the quantity of labor required to produce a certain volume of commodities over a definite period of time) and on its *value composition* (the relationship between the value of constant capital in relation to the value of its variable part). While the first varies with changes in labor productivity (the amount of labor necessary to employ a definite mass of means of production), the second varies with fluctuations in prices of the means of production and the wages of workers. The organic composition is its value composition in so far as "it is determined by its technical composition" … "the actual *basis* of its organic composition." Changes in the relative quantities of the components of capital, or the ratio between the magnitudes of constant and variable capital, does not necessarily, or directly, alter the *value* of its components. Nor does a change in the technical composition of capital necessarily follow from a change in the value composition of capital. Although they are directly related, both can vary independently in the same or opposite directions. The development of labor productivity allows fewer workers to put larger amounts of means of production to work, thus increasing its technical composition, while cheapening the means of production from increased productivity can lower its value composition if it is not accompanied by a proportionate increase in quantity, and so on.

The rate of profit of a particular capital is in direct relation to the rate of exploitation and to its organic composition. While the rate of profit is directly proportional to the rate of surplus value, it is inversely proportional to the organic composition of capital, such that if the rate of exploitation is held constant, the rate of profit falls with the increase in the organic composition of capital:

$$p' = \frac{s}{c+v}; \text{ but since } s' = \frac{s}{v}, \text{ then } p' = \frac{s'v}{c+v}, \text{ which is reducible to:}$$

$$p' = \frac{\dfrac{s}{v}}{\dfrac{c}{v}+1}$$

Conversely, the rate of profit rises with an increase in the rate of exploitation if the organic composition remains constant or increases at a smaller rate.

Under compulsion of competition, the drive of the capitalist to squeeze profit from labor tends to the perpetual development of labor-saving technologies that replace living labor, the source of surplus value and profit, with dead labor. The development of labor productivity results in the expansion of the mass of the means of production in relation to the quantity of requisite human labor, bringing about a disproportionate increase in the part of capital expended on the means of production (constant capital) in relation to the part expended on the purchase of labor power (variable capital), unless the means of production are cheapened at an unlikely rate equivalent to the growth in their mass. (Growth in productivity also has the effect of cheapening labor power and reducing variable capital as constant capital grows.) But, since only human labor creates new value in the process of production, whereas the value of constant capital is only transferred without any quantitative alteration, the expansion of constant capital in relation to variable capital brings about a decrease in the surplus value produced in relation to the total cost of production, hence a decline in the relationship of profit to cost of production, the rate of profit (see Marx 1976: 312 ff). The development of capital finds expression, therefore, as a contradiction between the growing composition of capital and the tendency of the rate of profit to fall. Capital in general becomes less profitable because labor becomes more productive.

The profitability of particular capitals, however, is not directly determined by their respective organic composition and rates of profit, but by a general average according to which they enter into production. The *average rate of profit* is determined by the exploitation of social labor as a whole by capital as a whole – by an average rate of exploitation and an average composition of capital. Let us follow Marx in assuming that all capitalists across different industries (and geographical regions) exploit their workers to the same extent, such that the rate of exploitation is the same.[3] The rate of profit is then determined by the product of two factors: the variation in the organic composition of particular capitals or branches of industry and their relative magnitudes in relation to total capital. The average rate of profit varies with the amounts of capital invested in spheres of production with an organic composition of capital lower or higher than the social average. An increase in the magnitude of capital does not alter the rate of profit for that particular capital if the ratio between variable and constant capital remains the same, but it alters the average rate of profit for social capital as a whole by altering the relative weight of that capital as part of the social whole and thus its relative share of the total surplus. The size of capital invested in spheres of production with a particular organic composition of capital (and rate of profit) alters the social average rate of profit, such that the average rate of profit approximates to the rate of profit of the sphere of production or capital which forms the greatest relative size of all capital invested across social production as a whole. More capital invested in spheres of production with lower rates of profit will bring down the social average rate of profit. If the larger magnitude of social capital is transferred to spheres of production with higher rates of profit, then the social average rises with it.

The average rate of profit is, therefore, determined by the distribution of the total social capital across spheres of production with varying rates of profit. The movement of capital from one sphere of production to another, or from one region to another, drives the tendency of the equalization of the rate of profit across all spheres of production or geographical space. In their attempt to realize profits higher than average, capitalists, under the compulsion of competition, lower the profitability of all capital while inching closer to a general rate of profit. The social average itself is never constant, however, and is an outcome of long periods of "oscillation" deriving from technical changes in labor productivity and the actual values of commodities that enter the production process. As competing capitalists operate independently of each other in their pursuit of surplus profits, the equalization process is, therefore, simultaneously a differentiation process. A simple increase in the magnitude of capital does not alter its rate of profit if the constant and variable components of capital increase in the same proportion. But, the increase in the magnitude of capital increases the relative *mass* of profit accruing to this capital while simultaneously altering the average rate of profit for all. The size of capital alters the mass of profit, such that bigger capital appears to produce more profit. Indeed, this is how capital appears to "produce" profit.

Let us illustrate the above with a simple hypothetical example of four producers (I–IV) producing, say, apparel, pharmaceuticals, oil, and cars, with the same rates of exploitation (100 percent), turnover times, and normal market demand for their commodities, but with varying compositions of capital and individual rates of profit. They all invest the same amount of capital, $10 million, with different proportions laid out on constant and variable capital:

	k	s	C	p'	Prices of production $= k + kp'$
I	$8_c + 2_v$	2	12	20%	$11.25
II	$8.5_c + 1.5_v$	1.5	11.5	15%	$11.25
III	$9_c + 1_v$	1	11	10%	$11.25
IV	$9.5_c + 0.5_v$	0.5	10.5	5%	$11.25
Total	$40 million	$5 million	$45 million		$45 million
Average				12.5%	

The four producers together invest $40 million and their workers produce a total surplus value of $5 million. Their commodities together contain $45 million in value and, since all capitalists invested an equal amount of capital ($10 million), each returns an equal share of the total product ($11.25 million) according to an average rate of profit of 12.5 percent. In other words, each capitalist invested his capital with an aim of realizing the general rate of profit, and they all did. Yet, the commodities of producers I and II contained more value than they returned, whereas the commodities of producers II and IV returned more value than they originally contained. Although all four producers made profit, a transfer of value took place among them, with I and II "losing" $750,000 and $250,000 to IV and III, respectively. Thus, the most profitable investment is the one that laid out the least on variable capital, and we should expect further investment to gravitate towards the most profitable spheres. Let us, therefore, assume that there is enough market demand to absorb four times larger investments by capitalist III, or, which amounts to the same thing, for three more producers to enter production in this branch of production as III:

	k	s	C	p'	Prices of production $= k + kp'$
I	$8_c + 2_v$	2	12	20%	$11.14
II	$8.5_c + 1.5_v$	1.5	11.5	15%	$11.14
III	$36_c + 4_v$	4	44	10%	$44.56
IV	$9.5_c + 0.5_v$	0.5	10.5	5%	$11.14
Total	$70 million	$8 million	$78 million		$78 million
Average				11.4%	

Assuming that all producers manage to dispose of their commodities according to the new average rate, the total surplus value grew and all producers managed to make profits, but they all made less profits than before, including producer III, who now captures a greater share of the total profit because of his larger investment. The greater share came from decreased profits for all other capitalists: producers I and II now "lose" $860,000 and $360,000 respectively, while producer IV gains only $640,000 instead of the $750,000 he gained previously. Producer III gained $560,000, more in absolute terms than before, but less in terms relative to his investment. Let us finally imagine that producer II managed to cut his costs down by investing in labor-saving technologies, approximating the same composition of capital as producer III, while at the same time expanding production and investing $20 million:

	k	s	C	p'	Prices of production $= k + kp'$
I	$8_c + 2_v$	2	12	20%	$11.0625
II	$18_c + 2_v$	2	22	10%	$22.125
III	$36_c + 4_v$	4	44	10%	$44.25
IV	$9.5_c + 0.5_v$	0.5	10.5	5%	$11.0625
Total	$80 million	$8.5 million	$88.5 million		$88.5 million
Average				10.625%	

The four producers together now invest twice as much as they started with. Although they all still make profit – a larger mass of profit taken altogether, from $5 to $8.5 million – they all now realize a smaller rate of profit with another uneven pattern of distribution of total profit. Producers II and III now possess commodities with values above their total value and potential profit. Surplus value is still transferred among the four producers but in lesser quantities and different proportions: producer I now "loses" $937,500 to all other producers; producer IV, producing under the most favorable condition, gains the most: $562,500 above the value contained in his commodity; while producers II and III gain $125,000 and $250,000 above their commodity values, respectively.

Capitals with different organic compositions produce different rates of profit, but they all realize the same rate of profit, i.e. the average rate of profit. The profit that capital realizes is independent of the profitability of the particular capital in question. It is a social average arrived at accidentally from their competition with each other for a larger share of the total surplus value. An equal rate of profit inherent to all capitals is an accident, if it ever occurs: capitals always make profit above or below the surplus value they appropriate from their workers. Although all capitalists share an interest in exploiting total labor, squeezing as much profit as possible out of all workers regardless of whom they work for, they compete among each other to realize larger shares of total surplus value, leading in the long run to an equalization of the rate of profit across spheres of production (or geographical regions). Or, more precisely, to the "constant equalization of ever-renewed inequalities" as individual capitalists, despite their structural interdependence, operate independently of each other. The tendency towards equalization is accompanied by a progressive increase in the total mass of profit produced but a decline in its ratio to total capital employed in production. The distribution of profit among competing capitals is determined by their magnitude relative to total capital and their organic composition, such that larger capitals appear to make more profit and industries with an organic composition below the social average lose part of the surplus value to capitals with an organic composition higher than the social average. All capitals realize the same average profit, but they appropriate different parts of the total surplus value according to their organic composition and size of their investments.

So far, the analysis has proceeded on the assumption that there is enough market demand to absorb all commodities produced in society, with competition across spheres of production but without much competition within each sphere of production, and that commodities are sold at their production price. But this is hardly the case, since producers have to sell their commodities to realize the potential profit contained in them, and the competition across different spheres for larger shares of the total surplus is intertwined with competition within the same spheres of production. In the same sphere or branch of production, producers operating independently of each other bring the same commodity to the market and, thus, face the prospect of exceeding market demand and the inability to realize all, or any, of the surplus value contained in their commodities. The declining rate of profit is, therefore, only exacerbated by potential market gluts arising from the growth in the magnitude and productivity of capital, unless the movement of capital is restrained.

Realization of surplus value: the mediation of the market

The process of production under capitalism is the dual production of use-values, the transformation of material nature into useful objects, and surplus value, the difference by which capital grows and which is nothing but unpaid labor. Immediate production, however, is only the "first act" in the general process of production, completed, from the standpoint of the capitalist, when surplus value objectified in the commodity is realized as profit in the "second act" of exchange, bringing to an end the process of extracting surplus value (which is then plowed again into another, expanded round of production). Surplus value, created in the production process, is appropriated as profit only after it is *realized* in the market. The conditions for the production of surplus value and the conditions for its realization are different: whereas the production of surplus value is restricted by social productivity (forces of production), its realization is restricted by "society's power of consumption" of the total product produced by society. The conditions for the realization of surplus value are restricted further by the development of social productivity. In other words, the expansion of production in pursuit of expanding the extraction of surplus value in the labor process, which constantly replaces living labor with dead labor, comes into direct conflict with the narrowing of the sphere of realizing surplus value by diminishing society's power of consumption. The production and realization of surplus value come into contradiction with each other at every stage of the development of capital, such that the expansion of the market becomes a necessary condition for the expansion of production, and not only its result (cf. Marx 1981: 353, 134–135).

The production price of commodities emerges from inter-capitalist competition across different spheres of production, given normal conditions of capital mobility and similar levels of exploitation and labor productivity within the different branches of industry. The problem for particular capitals is to realize the value contained in the mass of commodities at their prices of production in order to realize the average rate of profit and not to transfer value to capitalists in other spheres of production in the process of exchange. Capitalists in the same branch of industry, however, bring to the market the same commodity and must, therefore, compete with each other for the sale of their commodities. From this competition among capitals in the same sphere of production emerges an average *market value* corresponding to the total value of commodities produced under average conditions of production and constituting the bulk of commodities produced in a particular branch of industry. Commodities are sold at their market value only if their supply meets social need, "with money to back it up." That is to say, the market value of commodities coincides with their production price if, first, there is enough social demand perfectly equivalent to the total bulk of commodities and, second, if the quantity of social labor spent in their production is equivalent to the quantity of social labor available for their purchase. Two problems arise from the nature of capitalist production that prevent commodities from selling at their market value: seen as a single commodity, the mass of commodities forming the total product of society contains more value than is compensated for in wages, making the amount of labor time dispensable for the purchase of commodities insufficient for the purchase of the total product – some commodities will not be sold;[4] second, capitalists do not go into production to satisfy social need but to realize profit, investing independently in industries with high rates of profit regardless of the social need for their products, bringing about fluctuations in the supply of commodities that constantly alters their market price above or below market value. The supply of commodities is the result of constant migration of capital into spheres of production with higher than average rate of profit, with the constant threat of oversupply that brings market prices down and with it the rate of profit of those particular spheres.

Commodities rarely sell at their market value. When the supply of commodities exceeds the social need, e.g. when competition is strong, commodities will sell below their market values. The total mass of commodities on the market will represent, in terms of purchasing power, a smaller value than they contain: part of the labor contained in them will be "wasted" as their market price falls below their market value. When the mass of commodities does not meet the social need and competition is weak, then commodities will sell at a market price above their market value, or above their value in the case of commodities under inelastic demand or structural scarcity (commodities that cannot be substituted, such as oil), capturing surplus value produced in other branches of industry. Supply, however, not only determines the deviation of market price from market value, but also influences the determination of market value itself. As mentioned above, under hypothetical (normal) market conditions, *market value* corresponds to the value of commodities produced under average conditions as long as they constitute the bulk of commodities on the market. When competition is strong and supply is in excess of effective social demand, then market value is determined by commodities produced under the most favorable conditions, and these commodities may then sell at, or close to, their value, regardless of their constituting the bulk of commodities. Under such conditions, commodities produced under less favorable conditions may fail to realize any profit and may indeed have to be sold at below their cost price, with negative profits. Under opposite conditions, when demand is strong or supply falls short of meeting social need, then market value is determined by commodities produced under the worst conditions, even if they do not constitute the bulk of commodities. Commodities may then sell at above their value.[5] Market value (rate of profit) is determined not only by the relationship of the total product to effective social demand, but also by the internal distribution of commodities produced under varying conditions of production within the total mass of commodities brought to market. If commodities produced under either more favorable or worse conditions dominate, or form a "relatively significant quantity," it is either mass that comes to govern market value.

Let us illustrate with three oil producers, I–III, producing at the same rate of

	k	s	C	Production price	Market price
I	$4.5_c + 0.5_v$	0.5	5.5	$5.5/bbl	$16.5
II	$9_c + 1_v$	1	11	$11/bbl	$16.5
III	$13.5_c + 1.5_v$	1.5	16.5	$16.5/bbl	$16.5
Total	$30 million	$3 million	$33 million; 3 million barrels		$49.5 million
Average				*Market value* $11/bbl	$16.5/bbl

labor exploitation, $s' = 1/1$, and same rate of profit (with the same turnover time), $p' = 1/10$. Thus, $C = 90_c + 10_v + 10_s$. The first produces at a cost of $5/barrel (bbl), the second at $10/bbl, and the third at $15/bbl – roughly the same as three oil producers in the Middle East, the North Sea, and the Gulf of Mexico, respectively. They each produce 1 million barrels per day and sell in the same market. There is enough effective demand to absorb the total product, so market price is determined by producer III producing under the worst conditions.

All producers together realize a total profit above the average rate. The production price of the total product is $33 million, but it is sold at a market price of $49.5 million, 50 percent too much, with producers I and II capturing $11/bbl and $5.5/bbl in excess profits. Considering the amount of profit that producer I made, we should expect capital to migrate to where producer I is producing. Let us assume that producer I now produces three million barrels per day, while producers II and III still produce one million barrels each, and that there is still social need for the total product. Thus, our producers assume a market price still determined by producer III:

	k	s	C	Production price	Market price
I	$13.5_c + 1.5_v$	1.5	16.5	$5.5/bbl	$49.5
II	$9_c + 1_v$	1	11	$11/bbl	$16.5
III	$13.5_c + 1.5_v$	1.5	16.5	$16.5/bbl	$16.5
Total	$40 million	$4 million	$44 million; 5 million barrels		$82.5 million
Average				Market value $8.8/bbl	$16.5/bbl

If all producers manage to sell their product, then they all together realize a profit of $38.5 million above market value; or a $7.7/bbl above the average market value, reduced now from $11/bbl to $8.8/bbl. Both producers I and II still make surplus profits. It is possible that our producers miscalculated the effect of supply on market demand, however, and that the latter did not grow. In this case, with additional investment, the market became oversupplied by two million barrels. Five million barrels will have to be sold at the price of three million barrels, if society could afford to still pay the $49.5 million it paid for the first three million barrels at a market price of $9.9/bbl. In this case, producers II and III will have to dispose of their oil at below its cost price, while producer I would still capture profits in excess of the average market value ($8.8/bbl) and his production price ($5.5/bbl). In other words, producer I forces producers II and III to withdraw their oil from the market and go out of production, unless producers II and III can prevent producer I from putting part or all of his oil on the market, or deny producer I access to capital to invest in further production. Alternately, producer, II or III will shift part of their investment to enhance the productivity of their fields or to regions where I produces, either through direct investment in the same region or by merging with I to form one large capital producing at the average cost price. As we shall see in the three case studies, oil producers have employed a combination of these strategies, depending on the particular circumstances.

Let us finally imagine that effective social demand actually grew by the anticipated 2 million bbl/d and that producer III managed to supply the additional quantity:

	k	s	C	Production price	Market price
I	$4.5_c + 0.5_v$	0.5	5.5	$5.5/bbl	$16.5
II	$9_c + 1_v$	1	11	$11/bbl	$16.5
III	$40.5_c + 4.5_v$	4.5	49.5	$16.5/bbl	$49.5
Total	$60 million	$6 million	$66 million; 5 million barrels		$82.5 million
Average				Market value $13.2/bbl	$16.5/bbl

All producers together now realize a total profit above the average rate. But since the increase in supply came from producer III, the average market value is now higher and the difference between market price, still determined by producer III, and market value is now smaller (market price is $3.3/bbl above market value, compared to $7.7 difference in the previous case). Producer III benefits by increasing the share of his capital in total capital and increasing the mass of his profit. All producers together benefit less, as they now only realize $16.5 million over and above the value of the total product, as opposed to the $38.5 million difference realized when additional investment came from producer I.

The contradiction between the individual and collective interests of the three hypothetical capitals is evident. It is not enough that they all together realize profit, for the unevenness of their production costs and relative magnitudes translates into the mass and rate of profitability of the total product and unevenness in the distribution of profit amongst them. This, however, does not preclude producers selling commodities at surplus profits from searching for ways to equalize the rate of profit amongst themselves. (In the oil industry, as we shall see below, because of its territorial fixity, the natural productivity of oilfields and landed property in the form of the state play a crucial part in preventing such equalization and reproducing the uneven distribution of profit among producers.) If capitals in a branch of industry all sell their commodities at above their values, then there is a transfer of surplus value across spheres of production. That allows all producers within the given branch of industry to realize surplus profits even if they realize different rates of profit in comparison with each other, as long as they realize profit above their average market value. It is, therefore, reasonable to suppose a hierarchy of coexisting general rates of profit, ranging from industries (and places) with strong monopoly privileges that allow them to realize surplus profits, such as the oil industry, to spheres of production where competition is strong and monopolies are not yet established, or are not easy to form (see Sweezy 1942: 274). This also means that not all capitals are selling their product in its entirety and realizing the total value contained in it, as producers with surplus profits absorb larger shares of total social value available for the purchase of commodities.

The tendency of the rate of profit to fall and the development of labor productivity: the limits to the exploitation of labor

The development of the capitalist mode of production is expressed as growth in the productivity of labor, and therefore a decline in variable capital in relation to constant capital, i.e. growth in the organic composition of capital (Marx 1976: 772 ff). Growth in the organic composition of capital, however, leads to a declining rate of profit. But, since growth in the organic composition of capital characterizes all spheres of production in a society and not particular spheres or individual capital, the growth in the average organic composition of capital "must necessarily result in a *gradual fall in the general rate of profit*" (Marx 1981: 318). Individual capitals or branches of industry may still enjoy a rise in their individual rates of profit as the general rate falls.

The decline in the rate of profit is a progressive tendency and it does not appear in an "absolute form," since all capitalists, operating independently from each other, attempt to reverse the decline by extracting more surplus value from labor. Thus, the profit rate might increase, e.g. with the introduction of technological innovations, but it does so at a decreasing rate. Or, expressed in terms of surplus value, the rate of exploitation may increase at a declining rate, due to the physical limits of exploitation (workers can perform a certain amount of work in a given, limited, period of time), limits to how low wages can drop (workers have to reproduce themselves and thus have to retain some purchasing power), and political limits, depending on the intensity of the class struggle. Finally, at a higher stage of capital accumulation, the rate of profit becomes less sensitive to changes in the rate of exploitation the greater the organic composition of capital (see Harvey 1999).

The progressive decline in the rate of profit does not preclude an increase in the total mass of social labor exploited by capital, neither an increase in the mass of surplus value appropriated by social capital as a whole (regardless of increase in the number of workers). Marx (1981: 347) summarized the contradiction thus: "The profit rate does not fall because labour becomes less productive but rather because it becomes more productive." As the productivity of labor grows, the same number of workers or the same mass of labor (working day) can put to work an increasing mass of the means of production, fixed (machinery, instruments, buildings, etc.) and circulating (raw material, energy, etc.). The absolute mass of profit that labor produces can, therefore, grow progressively despite the progressive fall in its rate. Indeed, on the basis of capitalist accumulation, this becomes a necessity, as the concentration of capital becomes a necessary condition for further accumulation, as much as the result of the process of accumulation itself.

The concentration of capital, and the growth in the organic composition of capital, is the cause for both the decline in the rate of profit and growth in the absolute mass of profit (not yet realized). The decline of the rate of profit is a decline in surplus value in relation to total capital. The contradiction is that the concentration of capital (growth in constant capital) appears both as the reason for the decline in relative surplus value (the rate of profit) and also as the cause for growth in the absolute mass of surplus value appropriated by total capital. If the *mass* of profit is to remain the same with the decline in the *rate* of profit, then total capital must increase by a ratio proportional to the decline in the rate of profit. If the mass of profit is to *grow*, however, with a declining rate of profit, then total capital (employed in production) must grow at an even higher ratio than that of the falling rate of profit, unless the fall in the rate of profit can be reversed.

The tendency of the rate of profit to fall is checked, and at times reversed, by "counteracting influences" which give the decline in the rate of profit the character of a tendency. These influences, or factors, do not annul the general law of the falling rate of profit, but only slow it down or weaken it, because, as we shall shortly see, the factors that are brought about to counter the tendency of the rate of profit to fall are actually the same that caused the falling rate of profit in the first place. Marx (1981, chap. 14) discusses five "counteracting factors": the increase in the rate of exploitation of labor; the reduction of wages below their value; the cheapening of the elements of constant capital; the relative surplus population; and foreign trade.[6] We only deal with the first two factors in this section as we are concerned with the extraction of surplus value in the labor process. The third factor is discussed in the following section, and "monopolization" in the two sections that follow, under the centralization of capital and landed property.

The increase in the rate of exploitation counters the falling rate of profit, or even reverses it, if it rises at a higher rate than the organic composition of capital. The rate of labor exploitation can increase either by lengthening the working day or by increasing the intensity of work and reducing the amount of necessary labor time by labor-saving technologies. As is often the case, capital resorts to both. Marx (1976) calls the first the extraction of absolute surplus value; the second, the extraction of relative surplus value. The prolongation of the working day is already its prolongation beyond labor time necessary to reproduce labor power and forms "the starting point for the production of relative surplus value." Relative surplus value, from this standpoint, is absolute, and absolute surplus value is relative since it rests on the possibility of labor producing more than is necessary for its existence or subsistence. The difference within the identity of absolute and relative surplus value appears in the attempt to raise the rate of surplus value.

The intensification of labor, the extraction of greater surplus value relative to necessary labor time, is the result of developments in labor productivity. More productive labor, however, implies a necessary quantitative expansion in the magnitude of constant capital, especially its circulating part (raw material and energy), if the mass of surplus value is to increase with it. Intensifying the labor process, therefore, leads to growth in the constant component of capital in relation to the variable component, and thus involves an increase in the organic composition of capital. Increasing the rate of exploitation may slow down the decline in the rate of profit, but it does not cancel it altogether and renders it a tendency whose "absolute realization" is forever delayed. The prolongation of the working day, the extraction of absolute surplus value, also has its limits and cannot alleviate the falling rate of profit indefinitely, for it also presupposes an expansion in the constant part of capital: more workers, or workers laboring for longer hours, consume more material and instruments in the production process. If this is not accompanied by a proportional decline in the cost of the means of production, then the prolongation of the working day presupposes a growth in the organic composition of capital. The result of increasing labor productivity and/or prolonging the working day is an increase in the organic composition of capital that counters the increase in the mass of surplus value produced. Furthermore, the development of labor productivity results in an ever increasing mass of commodities containing, as a totality, an increasing mass of value yet, as individual products, a declining mass of value, making the problem of realization more acute in two ways: overaccumulation of (cheaper) commodities and decline in the purchasing power of workers as a result of decline in the amount and value of necessary labor time, i.e. wages.

Recall from the illustration above oil producer II producing at $10/barrel. Producer II sinks in the ground $10 million every day in exchange for one million barrels, laying out 90 percent of his capital on constant capital and 10 percent of it on variable capital. Say he employs 1,000 workers for eight hours a day, of which four constitute necessary labor time (the time the workers are compensated for in wages) and four constitute (unpaid) surplus labor. Let us assume that a similar producer producing in the same region (producer II′), procured technologies that allow a twofold increase in the productivity of labor. Assuming no change in the natural productivity of the exploited oilfield, now the same quantity of labor, i.e. the same number of workers working the same number of hours for the same wages, can produce two million barrels of oil per day by employing twice the mass of constant

	k	s	C	p'	Product	Production price
II	$9_c + 1_v$	1	11	10%	1 million barrels	$11/bbl
II′(a)	$18_c + 1_v$	1	20	~5.3%	2 million barrels	$10/bbl
II′(b)	$9_c + 0.5_v$	0.5	10	~5.3%	1 million barrels	$10/bbl

capital as before (a); or half the amount of labor is now necessary for the production of the same commodity (b) (and if producer II′ cannot find effective demand for the extra one million barrels, then he will have to employ his workers for four hours per day and withdraw half of his capital from production, or lay off half his workers to produce one million barrels at the new rate of productivity):[7]

Increase in productivity produced a larger mass of commodities containing a larger mass of value in absolute terms, but smaller when divided by the individual product. The same amount of work, value created by the workers (paid and unpaid), is now spread over a larger amount of the product. Or, the same product now contains half the amount of work: one million barrels at first contained 8,000 working hours (half of which paid for in wages); now the same commodity contains 4,000 hours of work (2,000 of which are necessary). This is the necessary labor time required for the production of the commodity and everything above it constitutes surplus value. To guarantee a market share for the additional barrels, producer II can now sell his product at below its prevalent social value ($11/bbl) yet above its individual value ($10/bbl) and pocket surplus profit, until his technological advantage is eroded with the generalization of the technologies used by competitors seeking the extra profit. The result is a cheaper product (and lower profitability) across the whole economy, in industries whose product directly or indirectly forms the working wage.

The cheapening of commodities by increasing the productivity of labor is a motive for all producers, resulting in the decline of not only the amount of necessary labor time required for the production of commodities, but also decline in the value of necessary labor power required for their production. Hence a decline in wages. In other words, the development of labor productivity leads to increase in surplus value in relation to the mass and value of necessary labor (paid labor).

In the current illustration, under conditions of improved productivity, 4,000 instead of the 8,000 hours are now required to produce one million barrels of oil; but while before, according to our assumption, 4,000 of the 8,000 hours were necessary for the purchase of labor power, under the new conditions, with the twofold increase in productivity and the cheapening of commodities by around 10 percent, less and cheaper labor power (say by 10 percent less), 1,800 hours instead of 2,000 hours, now constitute necessary labor time (the amount of work that the labor performs to produce the commodities necessary for his or her existence). This raises surplus value from 2,000 hours to 2,200 hours of the same 4,000 hours workday, increasing the rate of surplus value (s/v) from 1/1 to 22/18, although the same amount of labor time ($s + v$) going into the production of the commodity remains the same:

II′	k	s	C	s'	p'	Product
Before	$9_c + 0.5_v$	0.5	10	100%	~5.3%	1 million barrels
Now	$9_c + 0.45_v$	0.55	10	122%	~5.8%	1 million barrels

With the cheapening of labor power, less variable capital is now required to put the same amount of labor (and means of production) to produce the same mass of commodity, one million barrels, which, however, now contains a larger mass of surplus value in absolute terms and in relation to a smaller mass of total capital employed in production. Although the organic composition of capital increased, the rate of profit increased with it as the rate of surplus value grew. But because the organic composition of capital is already high, the rate of profit grew at a rate much smaller than the rate of surplus value: 0.5 percent against 22 percent.

Now let us imagine that, due to bargaining pressure, instead of reducing wages, producer II' contrived to procure longer working days from his (500) workers and that instead of eight hours/day, they now work for ten hours/day totaling 5,000 hours, for the same wages. They now employ 25 percent more constant capital and produce 25 percent more oil per day, and since their wages remain unaltered and 2,000 hours of labor time remain necessary for their repro-duction, the workers relinquish 3,000 hours of their working day to their employer for free, raising the rate of exploitation from 1/1 to 3/2:

II'	k	s	C	s'	p'	Product
Before	$9_c + 0.5_v$	0.5	10	100%	~5.3%	1 million barrels
Now	$11.25_c + 0.5_v$	0.75	12.5	150%	~6.4%	1.25 million barrels

As the rate of surplus increased here at a higher rate than before, the rate of surplus value also increased despite an increase in the organic composition of capital. But in this case also, the rate of profit increased at a much slower rate than the rate of exploitation: a little more than 1 percent against 50 percent. Also, producer II' is again required to advance a larger sum of (constant) capital to put his productive workers to work. Depending on the intensity of the class struggle, it is likely that producer II' might manage to increase the rate of surplus by both increasing the working day and lowering wages to offset the increase in the cost of production (if the cost of constant capital remains unal-tered). He will then squeeze an even higher rate of profit without altering the total value of the commodity, bringing, however, an increase in the rate of profit smaller than the increase in the rate of exploitation and the organic composition of capital:

II'	k	s	C	s'	p'	Product
Before	$9_c + 0.5_v$	0.5	10	100%	~5.3%	1 million barrels
Now	$11.25_c + 0.45_v$	0.8	12.5	178%	~6.8%	1.25 million barrels

Producers cannot lower wages indefinitely, nor can they prolong the workday beyond the limits of physical labor. The rate of exploitation cannot, therefore, grow at a commensurate rate to counter the growth in the organic composition of capital. Both, moreover, would provoke workers' resistance and a threat to the profitability of capital. Furthermore, the increase in the rate of exploitation and the adoption of more labor-intensive methods, etc., may counter the falling rate of profit created in the production process, but it does not solve the problem of its realization in the "second act" – in the market. The problem is exacerbated by two factors pushing in the same direction: the increase in the mass of commodities on the market and the cheapening of labor power – both results of the increase in labor productivity that put on the market a total commodity containing more value as an aggregate product but less as an individual one. More commodities have to be sold for capital to realize profit. The expansion of production heightens both the contradiction between the production and realization of surplus value as a whole and the competition among capitals to realize it. As the expansion of the market – social need backed up by money, or effective demand – cannot absorb the total mass of commodities produced by society, competing capitalists must seek alternative means to lower costs of production and eliminate the threat of overproduction. Overaccumulation and the intensification of inter-capitalist competition ultimately lead to the elimination of rival capitals by their integration into larger concentrations of capital, i.e. the centralization of capital. Before we examine this tendency, the final expression of capital accumulation, we must examine the economy in the cost and use of constant capital, especially raw material, as a counteracting factor to the falling rate of profit.

Concentration of capital in extractive industry and economy in the use of capital

The drive by capitalists to reduce the cost of constant capital, the means of production, is not as compelling as the drive to reduce the cost of living labor, the basis of extracting surplus value. Yet, the development of productivity leads inevitably to an increase in the mass of the means of production necessary to put labor to work, which raises the value composition of capital if it is not accompanied by a simultaneous decrease in the value of constant capital. The cheapening of the elements of constant capital, both fixed and circulating, can thus counter the tendency of the rate of profit to fall by preventing the value composition of capital from increasing to the same extent as its technical composition. We can assume, as with the case of the value of labor power (wages), that the development of productivity in branches of industry that produce the means of production consumed in other branches leads to an increase in the mass of those commodities accompanied by a decrease in their prices. The result of the development of labor productivity is, therefore, the increase in the technical composition of capital at a higher rate than its value composition, i.e. an increase in the volume of constant capital in relation to variable capital at a higher rate than the increase in its value relation. This is expressed as the development of productivity and growth in the concentration of capital in branches of industry that produce the means of production – raw material, in the specific case of this study. The development of productivity in this sphere of production, as long as it employs advanced, large-scale capitalist methods of production and organization, takes on the same tendency for overproduction and the rate of profit to fall, leading to the further development of productivity and an increase in the mass of the product accompanied by a decline of its value (hence price). Larger volumes of raw material have to be sold to realize the value contained in them, regardless of effective demand in other branches of industry or individual consumption. This means that more resources have to be tapped to valorize the larger mass of capital sunk in their extraction as raw material.

When seen as a whole, all production is dependent, in various ways and degrees, on the objective natural conditions of social labor. Through extractive industry, the development of all capital is tied to the natural productivity of labor producing the objective means of production. The development of productivity in industry increases the demand for raw materials, raising their market prices at the same time that it effects the migration of capital into their production. Prices decline as productivity develops and production expands in extractive industry, transferring the competition for raw material from the branches of industry that consume it as use-value to those that produce it as an embodiment of surplus value to be realized. Cheaper raw materials result from the development of productivity in extractive industry which translates into savings on the cost of constant capital in branches of industry consuming the raw material. But cheaper raw material also implies decline in profitability in extractive industry, leading to the contradictory tendencies to develop labor productivity further to squeeze more surplus value in the production of even larger masses of raw material and the necessity to restrain its supply on the market and induce artificial scarcity in order to restore (declining) profitability.

Capitalists save on the cost of constant capital not only by consuming cheaper means of production, but also by employing less wasteful methods and instruments of production – by economizing on the use-value, not only value, of the objective conditions of labor to counter the falling rate of profit. Less wasteful production from improved instruments of production, higher quality raw material, more efficient production and use of energy, seems, on the surface, to preserve better the labor employed in the production of the total product (including the dead labor congealed in constant capital). Economy in the use of constant capital, however, is nothing but an expression of the development of labor productivity seen from the standpoint of the objects and instruments of production, which leads to preserving labor in so far as it can dispose of it and replace it with (more efficient) constant capital. Reduction of waste, recycling, efficiency in the use of materials and energy, etc., are not so much expressions of the prudence of capitalist production as much as expressions of the continuous attempt to capture more surplus labor in the final product, even when this rests on wasting the "human material" itself (see Marx 1981: 180–181). Improvement and economy in the use-value of the means of production implies an improvement in the method of extracting surplus value from living labor, leading not to a reduction in the mass and value of constant capital in relation to variable capital, but its opposite. The development of labor productivity through more prudent use of capital leads to growth in the organic composition of capital and further decline in profitability expressed in a larger product containing relatively less value.

The attempt to counter the declining rate of profit by economizing on the value and use-value of the constant elements of capital can, at best, delay the decline in the rate of profit by shifting it from one branch to another until it becomes generalized across the whole mode of production. The result is a total increase in the organic composition of capital rather than its decline. One distinguishing characteristic between manufacturing and extractive industry regarding raw material, is that in the former, raw material forms the object of labor to be transformed in the process, and its increase in terms of volume is the product of developed labor productivity in the branches of industry that produce it. In extractive industry, raw material is the product of the labor process applied directly to nature, whose object is provided spontaneously by nature. Hence, the development of extractive industry finds expression particularly in ever-growing magnitudes of the fixed component of constant capital, in addition to growth in constant capital in relation to variable capital (see Marx 1981: 893–894). Growth in the circulating part of constant capital required to put fixed capital and living labor to work becomes relatively determined by the "natural productivity" of labor, not only its social productivity. The growth of fixed capital in extractive industry, and the extraction of surplus labor from living labor, becomes dependent on making nature more "productive." In extractive industry, "we not only have the social productivity of labour to consider but also its natural productivity, which depends on the natural conditions within which labour is carried on" (Marx 1981: 901). The same capital, constant and variable, sunk in oilfields of varying productivity would yield a different product, as would the productivity of the same capital plowed into the land during different seasons. This, however, does not imply that one product would contain more value than the other. On the contrary, different volumes of the same product will, under varying natural conditions, contain the same amount of labor.[8] The same labor produces a cheaper (and larger) commodity when applied to more productive fields (which will realize surplus profit). The growth in the production of raw material becomes progressively the result of the growth of fixed capital in extractive industry itself and the need to valorize it by increasing the volume of circulating capital to capture labor involved in the production of the total product. The tendency to chronic overproduction of raw material is the result of the development of capitalist production, i.e. the concentration of capital, development of productivity, and decline of profitability in extractive industry as expression of the development of capital as a whole.

The centralization of capital

The movement of the capitalist economy results from the myriad individual decisions that capitalists make in competing with each other; but the results of these decisions do not always coincide with the strategies of individual capitals. Thus, the tendencies in the capitalist economy are irreducible to the decisions of individual capitals, although they emanate from them. This is the case with the centralization of capital, which takes increasing importance with the development of capital and the intensification of inter-capitalist competition for the production and realization of surplus value. The centralization of capital completes the accumulation process and allows a more rapid expansion of production at a larger scale and higher rate than simple concentration because it does not depend on actual growth in the size of total capital, but on its redistribution on fewer capitalists. The centralization of capital creates capital of a greater magnitude without further investment in the means of production. It is the final expression of "primitive accumulation," by which one capitalist dispossesses another and by which larger combinations are created from the amalgamation and/or elimination of smaller individual capitals.

The more intense the competition, the more the centralization of capital becomes necessary for its survival, especially in periods of slow economic growth and crises of overaccumulation. Hence the waves of centralization at the end of the nineteenth century, during the 1930s, and the latter half of the post-war period, beginning in the middle 1960s and extending into the present (see Duménil and Lévy 1993; Mandel 1975, 1995). The centralization of capital is an effective means in the competition for the production and distribution of surplus value amongst competing capitalists. As we saw above, the size of capital and its share of total capital determine the general rate of profit and the portion of the total profit accruing to individual capital. But it is also an effective means of controlling production and eliminating overaccumulation by allowing capitalists to remove excessive production capacity at the same time that they equalize the conditions of production and the rates of profit across space. It thus allows the restoration of profitability without investment in new productive capital and the further development of labor productivity by eliminating redundant means of production and labor. In extractive industry – non-reproducible resources in particular – the centralization of capital has the additional advantage of increasing the mass of available resources under the control of fewer producers while, at the same time, denying access to resources to competitors without actual expansion of available resources or the discovery of new ones. The centralization of capital also expands market shares under the control of fewer capitalists without producing new commodity gluts, with the additional advantage of reducing the risk of lower cost producers flooding the market with cheaper commodities. Even if this were to take place, the control of larger shares of the total commodity allows fewer capitalists to control its availability, and hence its price, on the market. Thus, the amalgamation of enterprises into fewer and larger ones allows capitalists greater control over the production of surplus value at both ends of the process. Or to use Marx's terminology, in the two "acts" of production: the first act of its creation and the second, equally crucial, act of its realization.

The centralization of capital is only a tendency and, as such, it is a contradictory process. Rather than resolve or transcend the contradictions of capital accumulation, the centralization of capital internalizes the contradictions and takes them to a higher level. In so far as the accumulation of capital involves its concentration at a larger scale, it involves the growth of constant capital in relation to variable capital. The centralization of capital, while it initially allows capitalists to protect profits from further decline by controlling production and prices, leads, in the last instance, in the opposite direction by accelerating the accumulation of constant capital and increasing the organic composition of capital. Capitalists may open small-scale and labor-intensive branches of production or subcontract part of their operations to prevent the further accumulation of constant capital. Yet inter-capitalist competition re-emerges, only now it is more intense, due to the high level of concentration achieved by the centralization of capital. The centralization of capital resolves the problem of distribution by allowing capitalists to divide markets and profits among themselves and to raise the minimum requirements for the entry of competitors into production in order to prevent overproduction and decline in prices and profitability. However, it does not entirely resolve the contradiction in the creation of surplus value in the labor process. Under the compulsion of more intense competition, capitalists are still compelled to cut down costs by replacing living labor with constant capital. Capital is a process of self-expansion, and the increase in the profits of fewer centralized enterprises means the increase in the availability of profits that need to be capitalized for the process to renew itself. Capitalists are caught in the same contradiction of having to limit production (to maintain high prices) yet transform accumulating profits into more productive, labor-saving capital, plowing back their growing profits into the expanded production of surplus value. The result is renewed overproduction, except now it is at a much higher scale. The contradiction between the interests of one capital and the interest of capital as a whole becomes more acute as each capitalist scrambles to maximize the share of the total surplus value that he can extract. As all surplus value is produced from the transformation of material nature in the labor process, the renewal of inter-capitalist competition at a higher scale with the centralization of capital must translate into an intensive competition for the control of the material basis of production. The development and expansion of capital drives its contradictions ever deeper into the material basis of existence.

Land and landed property: the conditions and barriers to capital accumulation

Increase in the dependence of capitalist production on larger volumes of (cheaper) raw material, as the circulating part of larger concentrations of constant capital, makes its quantitative and geographical expansion simultaneous along with its deeper extension into material nature, both as use-value (exploitation of material nature) and exchange value (appropriation and formal valorization of material nature).[9] The transformation of nature in the labor process under capitalism proceeds with, and rests upon, its transformation into private property. The privatization of the means of production, the basis of capitalist accumulation, begins by the separation of the objective means of subsistence and production from the real producer. The transformation of the real producer into wage-worker proceeds with the simultaneous transformation of land into a commodity that could be owned and exchanged before both are combined again in the production process (Marx 1976; see also Marx 1964, 1975).[10] The unity of human labor with the objective conditions of production, including land and the resources in it, becomes, on one level, mediated by capitalist relations of private ownership. Yet, as the access of capital to land and resources, on another level, becomes mediated by private property in land or landed property, the exploitative relationship between capital and waged labor – the extraction of surplus value – becomes, in turn, mediated by the contradictory relationship between productive capital and landed capital.

Land is an (external) objective necessity, a universal condition for, and means of, production, which gives landed property power over the accumulation process. Even when conquered and internalized by capital, land retains its externality to capital, for land, no matter how commodified, is not like any other commodity – it is not the product of human labor, and hence it is not reproducible. The basis of power deriving from landownership is, therefore, fundamentally different from that based on the ownership of other means of production, and it is the ownership or control of this peculiar commodity that entitles its owner to a share in the total surplus value produced by society. Rent collected by landowners is part of total surplus value produced by social labor transferred from other factions of capital to landed capital. The redistribution of surplus value, however, is not simply an end to the process of production and realization of surplus value in the labor process, but, as expression of a class relation among different factions of capital, it is a determining moment in the process of reproduction of capital and its continued accumulation at an expanded scale. Political power attached to landed property grows as land-based resources increase in significance with the development of capital, and the contradiction between capital and landed property becomes more acute as continued accumulation becomes dependent on larger volumes of raw material and expanded "exploitation" of natural resources. "Nationalization" of land or underground resources does not abolish landed property, rent, or the landowning class. Rather than negate private landed property, land and resource "nationalization," state ownership or state management of resources, gives landed property its highest expression by transforming the property of all resources, their management or regulation within a given territory to the state, giving the state the character of total capitalist landlord. Hence, the contradiction between capital and landed property is not abolished, but is taken to a higher level as capital now faces the territory of the nation-state as the external obstacle of landed property, to be conquered and internalized. Both as owner or regulator of property in land and resources, the state, in the case of resource extraction, stands in opposition to capital as land property. Thus, the state enters intercapitalist competition as another faction of capital that stands in conflict with other factions of capital, regardless of their "nationality" (see Chapter 3). As landlord, however, the state remains dependent on productive capital for the extraction and appropriation of surplus value in the production process as mere ownership or control of resources does not in itself produce rent. The amalgamation of capital and state, in national or state-owned oil companies for example, does not abolish or transcend the contradictory interdependence of productive capital and landed capital, but internalizes and reproduces it, as we shall see in the cases of Russia and Iran (Chapters 5 and 6) and in the peculiar form it assumed in the Soviet Union (Chapter 4). In what follows, we shall try to elaborate the contradiction between landed property and capital in order to understand further the contradiction among different factions of capital in the production, realization, and distribution of surplus value.

The contradiction between capital expansion and landed property

Our concern with land is confined to the problem of the accumulation of capital based in its extension into land and resources, and hence to the relationship between productive capital and landed property in extractive industry. We begin with a general, economic definition of land, which includes the underground and aboveground resources, in so far as these elements could be monopolized by an exclusive owner: "Landed property presupposes that certain persons enjoy the monopoly of disposing of particular portions of the globe as exclusive spheres of their private will to the exclusion of all others" (Marx 1981: 752). Exclusive ownership of certain segments of the earth, or elements of nature, is a legal relationship that gives the landowner social power, in as far as it determines the availability of land and the access of productive capital to the land's productive capacities – this forms the basis of ground rent, the landlord's entitlement to a share of total surplus value. But it is the *economic value* of landownership, its valorization in the production process rather than its legal definition, that transforms mere legal entitlement into political economic power and forms the source of rent. The legal entitlement to land does not by itself endow it with any value nor grant its owner any entitlement to an imaginary value inherent in the land. Yet, the legal entitlement to land gives the landowner the power to withdraw land from productive use and to determine its availability as a space for capital investment, as a means of production available to capital. In this respect, landed property exercises its power over capital as "power of negation" and, as such, landed property determines the production of surplus value by exercising power over the mobility of capital and the equalization of the rate of profit across different branches of production or among competing capitals in the same branch of industry. But landed property remains dependent on the extension of capital into the land for its valorization and the resources in it. Thus, the basis of rent is in direct contradiction with its source.

Unleased land is "economically worthless" from the standpoint of rent accruing to the owner, and land withheld from productive use does not yield rent because it is not incorporated in the production of value and surplus value. Nevertheless, portions of land (and resources) are always deliberately withheld from productive use and withdrawn from the circuits of capital until their use can yield higher rent, i.e. when production and market conditions allow the production and realization of higher quantities of surplus value from which higher rents could be extracted by the landowner (Marx 1981: 891). But productive capital also gains from withholding land from productive use in order to control production and prevent overproduction that could lead to market gluts and decline in profits. In capitalist society, there is a permanent scarcity in land and resources, socially induced and bearing no relation to actual shortage. Land and the resources in it may be available in abundance, yet may still be scarce. Indeed, the more abundant, the more they should be made scarce if they are to yield profit under given market conditions. This scarcity is the result of the "private will" of the landowners not to lease land under unfavorable economic conditions, or the "private will" of capital to control or prevent investment in the land (by competing capitals) under unfavorable conditions. But these economic conditions are independent of the "private will" of either, for, as we argued above, the development of capital results from myriad individual decisions that capitalists make in competing with each other, despite their shared interests (in opposition to the working class). The results of these decisions do not always coincide with their intended consequences (which lends the centralization of capital at higher scales significance in minimizing the scope, yet not intensity, of such contradictions). Nevertheless, the power of the landowner to withhold land from production and erect barriers to the mobility of capital is also one way by which the landowner can directly affect general economic conditions, by preventing the equalization of the rate of profit.

Thus, the "artificial" monopoly of land, which bears directly on the sectoral and geographical mobility of capital, is valorized only in so far as the land is put to use by productive capital, and is hence determined by economic conditions external to landownership. By preventing entry of additional capital into particular branches of production or particular territories, monopoly of land protects the *surplus profits* produced by capital with access to the land (which forms the source of rent collected by the landowner). Both extractive capital and landed property have to negotiate a contradictory "balance" between opening land and resources for valorization by capital (for the production of profit) yet withholding land from production and denying access of capital to it (to maintain surplus profits). This contradiction must find expression as, but is also negotiated with, a geographical contradiction between spatial integration and spatial fragmentation. In the case of non-reproducible land-based resources, such as oil and gas, "artificial" monopoly is reinforced by "natural" monopoly arising from the fact that access to the resource is limited by conditions that capital cannot reproduce elsewhere under given socio-technological conditions of profitability. This by no means replaces the social determination of the availability of the naturally occurring resource with its "natural determination," or the determination of some "natural" limits. Natural monopoly may enhance the artificial monopoly of exclusive ownership, but it is nevertheless determined by the level of capital accumulation and technological development necessary to make possible the *profitable* production of the resource, i.e. the production of surplus value from the resource and not only its production as use-value.

Rent, monopoly, and surplus profit

Appropriation of rent, regardless of its specific form, is the "economic form in which landed property is realized" (Marx 1981: 772). Rent is a "contractually fixed sum of money" that can assume various forms, paid to the landowner by the capitalist in exchange for the use of the productive capacity of a definite extent of land (or the resources in it) over a particular period of time during which capital is "fixed in the earth," either in a transient manner – improvement of the land itself – or in a more permanent manner, as in the building of structures required for the production process to proceed. This addition to the land, without necessarily transforming the land itself, transforms land into means of production. Land (or the resources in it) becomes fixed capital when productive capital is fixed in it (ibid. p. 756).[11] All land pays rent as long as it is employed in production, regardless of its qualities. The question is: how can production on the worst kind of land pay "genuine rent," i.e. rent over and above average profit, without deduction from profit and wages?[12]

Unlike other elements of constant capital, fixed or circulating, unimproved land in itself (or undeveloped resources) does not embody value since it is not the product of labor and therefore land does not transfer any value to the final product. Land becomes a commodity, however, by acquiring the commodity-form or "price-form," i.e. by acquiring exchange value (even when it does not embody value), when it is offered for sale or rent by its owner: as a condition, it has to be monopolized (see Marx 1976: 197; 1981: 772). Yet this imaginary "price-form", conceals a real value-relation, not one, however, which derives directly from the value produced from the land in particular. As with the distribution of social surplus value among productive capitals, in which case each capital receives a share proportional to its size rather than the surplus value it individually produces (see above), rent is redistribution of surplus value determined by the total size of capital invested on lands of different qualities and of different areas. Rent is surplus value transferred to the landowner not only from capital producing on the land. In so far as it forms part of surplus value "over and above profit," it is, therefore, always *surplus profit* transferred not only from capital producing on the land to the landlord but also across different spheres of production, among capitals producing at different rates of profit. It makes no difference if the landowner and the capitalist coincide in the same entity, as in the case of national oil companies. For capital producing on the land to pay rent and still make profit, it must realize profit over and above average, regardless of the surplus value extracted from labor producing on or from the land. Surplus value pocketed by the landowner is part of surplus value transferred from capitals producing at below the average rate of profit to the landlord through capital producing on the land at above the social average rate of profit (which keeps part of the surplus profit to itself).

Rent, as with other forms of profit, is a share of total surplus value distributed among different capitals according to the distribution of different magnitudes of capital across lands of various qualities and quantitative extent. The "natural productivity" of land, however, as with the productivity of labor in specific branches of production, affects the production of total surplus value by lowering the average cost price and cost of production (for everyone) and altering the share in the volume of the total product produced under specific conditions of productivity. As we argued above, surplus profit, the origin of rent, is determined by the possibility of producing commodities at below their average price of production (cost price plus an average profit) and realizing the surplus value embodied in them by selling them in the market at a price above average and, in some cases, above the total value embodied in the commodity. Surplus profit as such is transferred from producers whose commodities embody more surplus value than average. Landed property does not intervene in the process of creating and realizing surplus value, but determines the realization of surplus profit by controlling the availability of land and maintaining monopoly conditions for certain capitals, i.e. by controlling the mobility of capital across different types of land.

(This is the basis of maintaining monopoly profits in general, which in this context takes the form of controlling access of capital to land. But the realization of surplus profit takes the form of a built-in barrier to large concentrations of capital. Surplus profits hardly find their way back into production, lest they result in an increase in production and fall in prices, thus eroding the very basis upon which surplus profit rests. Large concentrations of capital must find other outlets for their accumulated surpluses, even in less profitable production in order to maintain their monopoly privileges. Recent surges in profits of oil companies, deriving from increases in prices and lower taxes rather than any revolution in the methods of production, were accompanied by a decline in rates of investment. Profits found their way to dividends rather than back to the production process, against a general call upon oil companies to invest more to bring prices down. There is no reason to expect such voluntary measures from big capital.)

As the demand for greater volumes of natural resources to be transformed into raw materials and valorized in the production process grows with the development of social productivity, so does the competition for the control of land itself. The increase in demand for raw material makes the extension of capital into land for the direct control of the production of raw material necessary for its uninterrupted accumulation: to secure the continuous flow of the elements of constant capital and the reduction in their production costs. Competition for the control of land, however, is not only confined to the attempt to increase and cheapen the production of raw material required in manufacture but also, from the standpoint of extractive industry, to ensure that its supply does not grow enough to erode surplus profits and decrease rent. In other words, competition for resources is irreducible to competition for increasing access to resources as use-values (or denying access to competitors) but is also, at a more fundamental level, competition to regulate the flow of capital into the production of resources in order to maintain surplus profit, i.e. to pay rent above the average rate of profit.

Landed property represents the external barrier that prevents the free movement of capital and the equalization of the rate of profit across all spheres of production, thus maintaining the monopoly conditions that protect surplus profits: the transfer of surplus value across competing capitals. It is here again where the interests of individual factions of capital, or individual competing capitals, come into contradiction with the interests of capital as a whole. For the desire to destroy all barriers and open all space for the free mobility of capital, as a basis for the equalization of the rate of profit across space, comes into direct conflict with the desire to reproduce the very same (geographical) barriers that ensure monopoly conditions and surplus profits for particular factions of capital. Landed property forms one such barrier. The progressive concentration and centralization of capital forms another, by determining the "minimum capital" required for profitable production, i.e. production that realizes *surplus profits*. As large concentrations of capital become necessary for profitable production, however, landed property becomes more dependent on larger amounts of capital to valorize land and resources in it. The ultimate expression of this interdependence is the amalgamation of extractive capital and landed capital, which only manages to internalize the contradiction rather than transcend it, and make it more acute. If "resource wars" are to make any sense at all, they are to be understood as an expression of the contradiction in the accumulation of capital between the interests of the capitalist class as a whole – capital as a "formal unity" – and the interests of individual, rival factions of capital for the extraction and distribution of profit from the labor process applied directly to material nature.

Raw material and the accumulation of capital

The production of raw material is the fundamental mediation between production in general and the natural conditions of production. The products of the extractive industry form the objective material elements of capital and the development of capital is, therefore, dependent on the development of the extractive industry. The development of capital depends on, and finds expression in, the growth and development of extractive industry, and, as Marx (1976: 752) observed, increase in the products of extractive industry finds expression in the growth of constant capital of other industries. Extractive industry has its own peculiar characteristics deriving from the nature of its object and conditions of production: in the social division of labor, it is the sphere of industrial production that is in direct confrontation with the natural conditions of production. Nevertheless, despite its special character, extractive industry shares with general capitalist production the same developmental tendencies since the extraction of raw material became dependent on large concentrations of (fixed) capital.

Hence, we must stress this dual character of the extractive industry and examine it as an industry in itself and as a branch of industry within the general division of labor, in order to appreciate its real significance in relation to the accumulation of capital. On one level, therefore, the importance of the extractive industry and the dependence on its products grows with the development of capital in terms of use-value and value (to counter the tendency of the organic composition of capital to grow by employing cheaper raw material). Growing competition for (cheaper) raw material grows with the development of capital, effecting the migration of capital into the production of raw material. The more capital advances into the production of raw material, however, the more the development of the extractive industry becomes dependent on the growth in the organic composition of capital, i.e. on the concentration of capital. Extractive industry becomes dependent on larger concentrations of fixed capital, and the rate of profit in this branch of industry falls with its development, making it dependent on larger volumes of resources to valorize capital employed in extraction, regardless of demand in other branches of industry.

The development of capital is expressed as growth of the means of production: the result and consequence of the development of labor productivity. The development of labor productivity, however, leads to growth in the magnitude and value of the constant component of capital (objective means of production) in relation to its variable component (living human labor) leading to a decline in profits in relation to total capital, despite growth in the mass of surplus value extracted from labor and growth in the mass of profit realized by capital as a whole. Capitalists extract surplus value from social labor as a collective unity, but they realize parts of this value as competing individual capitalists acting independently of each other. Under compulsion of competition, capitalists seek ways to maximize their share of total surplus value. As larger capital with relatively high organic composition returns a larger share of total surplus value, competition among capitalists for the extraction of larger masses of surplus value from labor and competition over the distribution of surplus value lead to a further increase in the composition of capital and decline in the rate of profit for capital as a whole. The problem is exacerbated by the consequent overaccumulation of capital, its accumulation in production beyond social need, which leads to overproduction. As the production of surplus value falls in relation to capital, its realization in the market becomes more difficult as the mass of the total commodity grows beyond society's effective demand, forcing capitalists to seek ways to eliminate overproduction and restore profitability.

As inter-capitalist competition for larger shares of social surplus value is both competition across different branches of industry and among capitalists within the same branches of industry, decline in the profitability of capital (in both production and realization), resulting from its concentration across all branches of industry, leads to its vertical and horizontal centralization. The former combines enterprises in different branches of industry, the latter combines enterprises within the same branch of industry, into fewer and larger enterprises that can control production and equalize the rates of profit across different capitals. The centralization of capital proceeds also across space, combining capitals in different geographical regions into capitals of larger geographical extent. In the capitalist interstate system, international centralization of capital across geographical space combines capitals of different nationalities, either by their merger into one international enterprise (e.g. Royal Dutch Shell; TNK-BP) or by bringing enterprises of different nationalities under the control of one enterprise (e.g. Schlumberger's acquisition of PetroAlliance). In extractive industry, the centralization of capital combines productive and landed capital and, where resources are owned, controlled, or managed by the national state, the centralization of capital amalgamates international capital and the national state, without necessarily eliminating their contradictory duality. Increasing international centralization of capital comes into direct contradiction with the interstate division of global geographical space, internalizing the geographical contradiction between spatial integration and fragmentation as capital becomes dependent on both: the expansion of its sphere of production and realization of profit, yet its fragmentation to protect surplus profit.

The expansion of extractive capital and its international centralization is not simply an expansion in search of raw material, but an essential part of inter-capitalist competition for the production and realization of higher profits. The expansion of the need for, and production of, raw material is itself a result of this competition. Competition for oil is inter-capitalist competition reduced to its fundamental expression: competition for the extraction of profit from the application of labor to nature. The contradiction of space plays an essential part in this process and it is examined in the competition for oil in the three cases presented in Chapters 4, 5, and 6. In the next chapter, we examine the historical development of the geographical contradiction with the development of twentieth-century capitalism.

3 Imperialism and the geographical contradictions of monopoly capital

The geographical contradiction of capitalist globalization – contradiction between spatial integration and fragmentation – has developed in three forms expressing the concrete historical-geographical development of the internal contradictions of capitalist accumulation throughout the twentieth century. The geographical contradiction has its origin in the contradiction between the interests of capital as a whole and the conflicting interests of competing factions of capital. The interlocked forms that the geographical contradiction assumed at different moments throughout the twentieth century resulted from the concrete circumstances determining the contradictions of inter-capitalist competition. Thus, each of the three forms became dominant at one time, but they all overlap such that they cannot be separated ontologically or chronologically. We can summarize the three forms of geographical contradiction according to three forms of inter-capitalist competition in the global economy. 1) At the most general level, the fragmentation of global space into "national" (economic) territories, including formal colonies and "spheres of influence," prevailed in the period of classical imperialism, roughly between 1870 and 1945, and it was determined by the global expansion of, and competition between, national monopolies. Despite the development of multinational corporations and the integration of capital at the international level in the post-war period, the fragmentation of the global economy into national territories and the reliance of competing factions of capital on the power of the state persist. 2) The territorial division underlying global expansion was not confined to the spaces of the rival nation-states and as early as the late nineteenth century, fragmentation could be seen taking place at the supranational, or continental, scale, organized around three regions centered on what would later be referred to as the "global triad" of Western Europe, the US, and Japan (more recently, China has increasingly contested Japan's dominance in East Asia). The triadic dominance of global capital and the restriction of inter-imperialist rivalry to the three global economic powers, accompanied the development of capital in the post-war period. It remained confined to the territories outside the Communist bloc and, despite competition in the former colonies, inter-capitalist competition was largely confined to dominance in the territories of the competitors. It remains largely so today, despite the entry of new rivals and the further globalization of the world capitalist economy after the collapse of the Soviet Union and the socialist economies of Eastern Europe. 3) The emergence of the Soviet Union in 1917 removed large territories from the space of capital and, despite several attempts by capital to penetrate the Soviet sphere, capitalist expansion remained confined to the territories of the advanced capitalist countries and the Third World. Until the collapse of the Soviet Union towards the end of the 1980s, but especially during the first Cold War between 1947 and the early 1970s, the apparent dominant form of the geographical contradiction was determined by a binary division of the world into a "contained" Communist bloc and a self-contained (Western) capitalist zone. Inter-capitalist contradictions persisted within the capitalist camp at the same time that the capitalist classes of the US and Western Europe formed alliances against the working classes in the capitalist countries, national liberation and decolonization movements, and the potential spread of socialism in the Third World. The latter, although justified by Cold War imperatives, was relatively independent of it: it was largely a strategy to prevent the development of economies in Third World countries independent of Western capital – a strategy that has its origin in the old colonial division of labor. With the Third Worldization of countries of the former Communist bloc and despite the uneven economic development of Third World countries, the binary division of the world between capitalist and Communist zones transformed increasingly into the old binary division between an advanced global North and a lagging or developing global South. Thus inter-imperialist rivalry among and within the triad in the so-called period of neoliberal globalization intersects with what Amin (2004) has called "the collective imperialism of the triad" or, the neoliberal war on the South.

Beginning in the middle 1970s, with the relative decline of US economic hegemony and renewal of inter-imperialist rivalry, the three layers of geographical contradiction became ever more complex and intertwined. The generalization of inter-capitalist competition throughout much of the Third World and the former Communist areas and the emergence of capitalist rivals in China, Russia, and India, renewed inter-imperialist rivalry in its nationalistic form without completely eroding the binary division between North and South and the triadic structure of regional economic blocs. Conversely, the uneven development of the global economy along the North–South divide and the further consolidation of the global economy around the global triad did not transcend the division of the world into national states. The development of global capital, indeed, seems to have made it more dependent on the political power and material power of the national state, i.e. its command of the collective means of violence and destruction. The more capital becomes global, the sharper the competition among rival factions of capital that still attach themselves to specific national states. The more intense the competition, the sharper the geographical fragmentation of the globe and the geographical contradictions of capital.

Contradiction of space, inter-capitalist competition and the centralization of capital

The geographical contradiction between the globalization of capital accumulation and fragmentation of global space is the concrete historical–geographical result and basis of the specific form that the international centralization of capital assumed in the twentieth century, i.e. "finance capital," or, for reasons that we shall discuss shortly, more accurately, "monopoly capital" – which is itself the result of inter-capitalist competition for the production and realization of surplus profits (see Chapter 2). Bukharin (1929; 1972) was the first to discern and elaborate the geographical contradiction between two necessary tendencies of capital accumulation specific to twentieth-century imperialism in the expansionist and protectionist policies of monopoly capital. Geographical contradiction between integration and fragmentation, globalization and territorialization, is the result of the development of inter-capitalist competition in the world economy between large concentrations of national capitals that fused financial and industrial capital in "state capital trusts," engulfing the political military power of the state necessary to carry out the imperialist policies of expansionism and protectionism. As inter-capitalist competition subsided and, to a great extent, disappeared in the national economy, it intensified in the world economy, making the further centralization of capital ever more necessary, ultimately leading to its centralization at the international scale. The stronger the centralization of capital, however, the sharper the contradiction between the production and realization of profit, the sharper the contradiction between the interests of capital as a whole and the interests of competing factions of capital, and the sharper the contradiction between the necessities of expansion of capital in all its forms and the protection of profits. The smaller the extent of competition, the more intense the imperialist struggle and the stronger the need for (military) states. Geographical contradiction, the outcome of capitalist development in its monopoly form, becomes its necessary condition in the process of inter-capitalist competition and which capital must reproduce at various scales and in different configurations.

The centralization of capital is the result of competition among different factions of capital for greater shares of surplus value produced in society, which allows fewer capitalists to control production (to prevent overproduction) and the availability of commodities in the market and their price. As it creates large concentrations of capital, it also limits the entry into production of competing capitals by raising the minimum capital requirements for profitable production. Centralization is accomplished either by the expropriation of smaller capitals by larger ones, or the amalgamation of existing capitals into larger corporations. This process is dependent on the "credit system," or on the availability of financial capital. In the process, financial capital develops from mere "enabler" of the process to a position of greater control over it, as the dependence on larger credit grows – a position that allows financial capital to reap great shares of total profit in the form of commissions and fees on mergers and acquisitions. The dominance of financial capital, however, is transitional and it coincides largely with transitional periods of consolidation, of transition from competitive to monopoly capital (Sweezy 1942). Those who control the supply of money wield control over the process of centralization and determine the results of intercapitalist competition. The social power of financial capital, however, is inherently limited because it is realized only when appropriated by productive capital and employed *as capital* in the production of surplus value. It is exercised as "power of negation" rather than creation. The control of financial capital can become a barrier to the expansion of productive capital, but, as Harvey (1999: 250) aptly puts it: "there is no monetary power on earth that can by itself magically generate an expansion in commodity production." Only through the actual and concrete transformation of nature can surplus value be produced, and this can be subjected to the disciplining of financial capital "only to the degree that financier and industrialist become one" (ibid. p. 285).[1] Fusion of industrial with financial capital diminishes the dependence of industrial capital on external financial capital, as the concentration of surplus profits provides large monopoly enterprises with their own "internal financing." Although large industrial corporations may still borrow from financial institutions or raise funding through financial institutions, they are not forced to do so in order to carry out large-scale operations. Hence, they are not completely subject to the disciplining power of financial institutions (Baran and Sweezy 1966). (This, however, does not make all industrial corporations invulnerable to the predation of speculation, as the recent return of "robber barons" reveals.) Nonetheless, the generation of monopoly profits puts large sums of money capital in the hands of large industrial corporations which are not always capitalized, i.e. invested in the expansion of production, precisely not to erode the very advantages that caused monopoly profits in the first place. Indeed, the overaccumulation of money capital in the hands of productive (and commercial) enterprises has turned them partially into financial institutions.

The result of capital centralization and the formation of monopolies, is expansion of fewer and larger concentrations of capitals which increases their share in total profit produced in society without any necessary increase in the absolute volume of value produced in society and additional investment of capital in production. It redistributes a larger share of total surplus value in the direction of enterprises producing under conditions of monopoly at the same time as it eliminates, or at least lessens, the threat of overproduction. The centralization of capital has therefore accelerated, especially in periods of stagnation and recession (see Duménil and Lévy 1993; Mandel 1995). Centralization, moreover, centralizes commanding power in the hands of fewer capitalists by expanding their power beyond the confines of their private property, transferring power from the owners of the means of production to the administrators of social (financial and productive) capital. Capitalists increase their control over production and their share of the profit by increasing their commanding power, through a mixture of ownership and administration, over total social capital. One enterprise, or one individual capitalist, owning a "majority share" in another enterprise wields control over the whole capital invested in it. With the (international) centralization of capital, the control over capital expands over a greater extent of geographical space as it concentrates in the hands of few individuals and enterprises.[2]

The centralization of capital can take several forms, ranging from voluntary and non-binding "gentlemen's agreements," through cartels and trusts, to full mergers or acquisitions (as Chapters 4, 5, and 6 demonstrate, the oil industry exhibits moments of each of the three forms). Even beyond the formation of behemoth corporations through merger and acquisition, and despite intense competition, large corporations often operate within a "co-respective" universe in which they recognize each other's power and avoid provocation of retaliation. When they are not direct competitors in the same branch of industry, they are each other's customers and suppliers (see Chapter 2). Big corporations form a small community tied together by an ethic of reciprocity and solidarity, and whose members recognize the common power from their association (see Baran and Sweezy 1966: 50). Richard Evans, chairman of BAE Systems, currently the fourth largest defense aerospace corporation, described the industry, one of the most centralized and dominated by few very large monopolies (see below), as a "cottage industry" made up of a small number of connected players. "If Vance (Coffman of Lockheed Martin) or Phil (Condit, chairman of Boeing) is in London, I'd be upset if they didn't call round for a cup of tea," *The Economist* (2002) quoted Mr. Evans saying. There is no reason to doubt Mr. Evans's sincerity of sentiment. The association of competing capitals, however, survives for as long as each benefits from working for the common interests of the whole capitalist class rather than against it. But, as Marx (1981: 295) put it, this "unity of action ceases as soon as one entire side or another weakens" in the competition. It is then when capitalists operate independently and against each other, and engage in processes of "primitive accumulation" in which one capital dispossesses another if both do not mutually agree to form a yet larger unity, when already large corporations merge into yet larger corporations.

It is centralization by full merger or acquisition that has become increasingly dominant with the development of capital, especially in the post-war era, but increasingly so since the 1980s, and it is the centralization of capital at the international level that has accelerated both the integration of the global economy and the sharpening of contradictions in inter-capitalist competition. In its earliest phase, the centralization of capital proceeded largely at the national scale, although its concentration had already assumed an international scope. Larger shares of profits were collected from investments by European and US companies abroad, especially in the colonies and semi-colonies; Japanese capital was already making way in Southeast Asia. These profits became essential to the accumulation process under intensifying competition in the world economy. Although centralization at the international scale had proceeded modestly, it remained largely confined to the national economies, thus pitting "state capital trusts" against each other in competition in the world economy for investment opportunities and commodity markets. Trusts, cartels, and "gentlemen's agreements" at both the national and international levels were not uncommon (for specific cases in the oil industry, see Yergin 1991), but fusion of capitals of different nationalities remained rare (Royal Dutch Shell is one example). In the post-war period, however, international concentration developed into international centralization, and the national "state capitalist trust" gave way to multinational corporations as the main form of capitalist organization and major agents in the global economy. The primary agent for international centralization of capital was the intensification of inter-capitalist competition in an increasingly integrated world economy. This was, however, still structured by the divisions and protective barriers of the colonial period, some lingering from competition in the period of European colonialism, others hardening in the new competition, especially with ascendant US capital. Overaccumulation (concentration of money capital from surplus profits of monopolies) and overproduction (resulting from technological developments in preparation for the war in the US but later from the development of German and Japanese industries and, later still, with the entry of lower cost producers from Third World countries) created the need to expand both commodity markets and the sphere for capital investment – productive and unproductive (e.g. military expenditure) – and at the same time reproduce protectionist barriers. As inter-capitalist rivalry gained momentum by the end of the 1960s, protectionist measures proliferated. But as inter-capitalist rivalry was no longer confined to the competitive struggles among the capitalists of Western Europe and the US *in* and *over* the control of what had become the Third World, but had come to comprise rivalries *with* (and *among*) the capitalists of the Third World, the "new protectionism" that accompanied the expansion of capital since the early 1970s reflected the dual nature of emerging inter-capitalist competition as it targeted its two sources: competition among the advanced capitalist economies and competition from the developing capitalist economies of the Third World. We can see both developing in tandem since the early 1970s (see Mandel 1975, 1978; Halliday 1983; Gilpin 2000).[3] Protectionist barriers gave the international centralization of capital greater significance in its global expansion. The dominance of the world economy by large monopolies made the large volumes of capital necessary to enter into competitive and profitable production more crucial to competing capitals. This accelerated the international fusion of capital at the same time that it made capital dependent on the state's possession and control of large magnitudes of "national" capital and, in some instances, on cooperation among several states (see Mandel 1970, 1975).

Thus, the international centralization of capital reduced the extent of the competition only to make it more intense. It became a necessity for the expansion of capital under intensifying competition, sharpening further, however, the competitive struggle and the contradiction between the expansion of capital as a whole and the expansion of individual factions of capital. It also intensified the reliance of capital on the state, not only to provide large concentrations of national capital, but to protect the interests of rival factions of capital and to manage and stabilize the global economy as a whole (on the latter, see E. M. Wood 2003). The power of the (imperialist) state and the scope of its economic functions expanded with renewed inter-capitalist rivalry, expressing capital's need for strong states under circumstances of intensifying competition and increasing centralization. But the international centralization of capital changed the relationship with the (imperialist) state. I shall argue below, that the same process that freed capital from the confines of the nation-state also made the state relatively independent of specific factions of capital, without completely severing its ties with dominant "national" factions of capital. This set the conditions for its formation as a relatively independent faction of capital that enters inter-capitalist competition in this contradictory guise, i.e. as a faction of capital representative of all capital ("executive committee of the bourgeoisie"), yet in direct confrontation with other factions of capital. This is a process far from complete and one can discern it at various levels of development across the globe. In order to arrive at this formulation, we must look at the development of the relationship of capital to the imperialist state.

The contradictory fusion of monopoly capital and the imperialist state

Geopolitical competition is irreducible to interstate rivalry and cannot be properly conceived outside the process of (global) capital accumulation.[4] Over the course of the twentieth century, the capitalist–imperialist state became increasingly involved in the reproduction of both the capitalist forces of production (by providing the necessary social and physical infrastructure that no individual capital could, or would, provide) and relations of production (by exercising and legitimizing social relations of exploitation and domination), to the extent that to speak of state "intervention" in the economy, or the "role" of the state in capitalist development, becomes rather redundant, if not altogether erroneous, in so far as state and economy are treated as external to each other. The separation is maintained in both the reassertion of the importance of the state to transnational capital or assertions to the contrary about the erosion of state power against the expansion of capital at the global scale. It is equally unsatisfactory to argue that interstate rivalry is an "expression" of inter-capitalist competition and to vulgarize the orthodox Marxian view of the state as mere instrument in the hands of particular factions of the bourgeoisie. Only by separating capital and state can geopolitical competition, understood as interstate rivalry, be treated independently of inter-capitalist competition or a mere expression of it. It is, therefore, necessary to re-examine the relationship between state and capital to make sense of contemporary inter-capitalist competition, conceived as competition among different factions of capital, including the state as another faction of capital that stands in a contradictory relation of representation and opposition to other factions of capital.

The nature and degree of interdependence between state and capital varies across time and space, with variations in the relative power of different factions of capital and the variation in the autonomy of state from society, and the degree to which other social groups participate in it. Notwithstanding, the capitalist state *in general* cannot but operate from within the framework set by the requirements of capital accumulation. Different states, of varying economic, political, and military power, enjoy varying domains for exercising their power, but all capitalist states have a limited range of action set and imposed by the contradiction between competing factions of the bourgeoisie and the demands of capital accumulation as a whole. It is only when the state is the dominant faction of capital, with centralized control over large portions of (financial and productive) capital, such as in the case of most oil-producing countries outside the US and Western Europe, that the relation is reversed and the limits to other factions of capital are set and imposed by the state, which, nevertheless, must still operate within the limits of its position vis-à-vis global capital. In both cases, it is an assertion of the relative power of one faction of capital over capital in general.

The contradiction arises from the representative role of the state. Despite being one faction of capital with its own set of interests (and internal contradictions), the capitalist state must also defend, on behalf of all factions of the capitalist class, the interests of capital in its struggle against the working class; the imperialist and colonial relations between North and South; and the interest of "national" factions of capital against other "national" factions of capital (at the same time that the state must regulate the conflicts among different factions of national capital and individual capitalists). It is the latter that has so far reproduced the (imperialist) state despite the international globalization of capital, as capital expanded beyond the territory of one national state into the territories of other, rival national states. In the process, the form and power of the imperialist state underwent two contradictory changes in response to the transformation in the global capitalist economy (see Mandel 1975). The international centralization of capital, on the one hand, internationalized the imperial state, extending its political and military power as well as its economic functions while condensing them into one dominant state, as in the case of the US in the post-war period (see Panitch and Gindin 2005a). On the other hand, the internationalization of the state transformed all states into actors in an interstate system woven around the interests of global capital, or dominant factions of global capital, whose function became the actual erosion of the separation of "national" from "international" economy, by embedding the former into the latter (see McMichael 2004; Glassman 2004).

The international centralization of capital has also led to the formation of supranational governing bodies and regulatory institutions. This process remains incomplete precisely because it comes into contradiction with the (over-)extended power of the most internationalized of imperialist states (the US) and the persistence of contradictions among national factions of capital (as in the case of the EU especially, but also at the global scale), although, it has proceeded more successfully in ensuring the dominance of an increasingly transnational capitalist class (especially of the global North) over the globe. Seen from this standpoint, the creation of supranational state-like institutions depended on the (voluntary) dismantling or weakening of various state functions (social welfare, etc.), yet the strengthening of others (military, police). As we shall see below, this process becomes most explicit in the formation of the neoliberal state.

In summary, the international centralization of capital produced the peculiar strong-weak state, a contradiction that finds its exemplar representation in the neoliberal state (see more below), but which is at the heart of the bourgeois state. The development of a strong industrial bourgeoisie depended historically on dismantling the interventionist (absolutist) state. A "weak state" emerged from the process – weak, that is, in its relative position vis-à-vis the ascendant industrial bourgeoisie (see Mandel 1975). As much as the bourgeoisie depended on a weak state to expand its power over material production, it also depended on a strong state to repress and integrate the exploited classes in the process of reproducing the relations of production and to resolve conflicts among rival factions of capital to ensure the expansion of the capitalist mode of production as a whole. With the encroachment of labor on the legislative institutions of state (parliament), the bourgeoisie centralized its power more in the upper levels of state institutions, particularly the executive. The development of monopoly capital since the beginning of the twentieth century consolidated the power of the bourgeoisie in a state increasingly separated and alienated from the rest of society. What was at first an exceptional measure, called upon by the necessities of World War I, became the norm (see Agamben 2005).

The development of "state capital" in the post-war period moved the state directly into the process of production and placed a larger share of social capital under the control of the state, expanding and accelerating the process of capital centralization.[5] The "statist mode of production" (*mode de production étatique*), as Lefebvre (1976–1978) called it, is an expression of the formation of "state capital" in the narrow sense of the state becoming actual employer of productive capital (see Marx 1978: 177) and in the broader sense of the state providing the necessary, collective conditions of production, social and technical (including the military) without, or with the least, private expenditure (see Mandel 1975; Harvey 1999). In addition to subsidizing large industrial projects, the state provided occasions for profitable investments as the realization of profit became more difficult with the increasing centralization of capital. State expenditure (not least for military purposes) grew to account for a larger share of the total capital and national income (especially where the state directly controls large shares of productive capital in crucial sectors of the economy, as with oil-producing states). Thus, the growing integration of monopoly capital with the bourgeois state proceeded with the development of a quasi-autonomous state and its formation as a faction of capital relatively independent of other factions of capital, though, as with other factions of capital, equally dependent on the power of the capitalist class as a whole. With the development of monopoly capital, the state became an expression of "total capital," working on behalf, yet above, the interests of all factions of capital and mediating the contradictions among them.

The relative autonomy of the state from other factions of capital furnishes the basis on which it becomes a faction of capital. The contradiction of the capitalist state lies in its dual nature as representative of the political power of the capitalist class as a whole (primarily national but increasingly transnational) yet as a faction of capital that stands in opposition to, and competition with, rival factions of capital, domestic and foreign. (Hence, the proliferation of lobbies, think tanks, and other entities that mediate between different factions of the bourgeoisie and the state, the more the "personal union" and interpenetration between state and capital grows.) As such, the neoliberal attack on the welfare state in the 1970s is both an attack by capital on the privileges accrued to the working class by the welfare state and ascendance of certain factions of capital over others. Neoliberal privatization is a process of "accumulation by dispossession," as Harvey (2003) recently argued, which expanded capital's domain for "primitive accumulation." But as such, it is also a process of primitive accumulation within the capitalist class, i.e. expropriation of capitalists by one another. In the absence of a world government that acts on behalf of capital as a whole, and as with the imperialist state developing at the turn of the twentieth century, the bourgeois state – the neoliberal state – is both agent of global integration (as geographical basis of global capital expansion) and territorial fragmentation (as geographical basis of protecting individual factions of capital). The state, as such, internalizes the geographical contradictions of monopoly capital and emerges as a relatively autonomous faction of capital while it fuses deeper with global capital as a whole.

Thus, the contradiction between state and capital is irreducible to the contradiction between national states and global capital standing above and beyond individual states. The contradiction between capital and state is internal to capital and is determined by the contradictions between its different factions, not only in terms of financial, industrial, commercial capital, but also in terms of its national and regional factions of capital that need the state at the same time that they need to negate it in their expansion. As Harvey (2005; see also Mandel 1970) argues, rival factions of the bourgeoisie never confined their loyalties to particular states, although they attached themselves to particular state apparatuses for the protection of their interests. Transnational capital has less of a national origin, especially with the international concentration of surplus value extracted from over the globe, than an ever temporary "nationality." For example, nothing prevents Halliburton from shedding its "American" nationality if the government of the United Arab Emirates, where the company's headquarters are now located, can provide it with the same protection and advantages of the government of the USA. Competition among states to attract foreign investment is part of inter-capitalist competition, which relies on the fragmentation of the global political surface into exclusive nation-states. In the process of geographical expansion and global integration (monopoly), capital must strengthen the discontinuities in the political surface of the globe and erect the very (protective) barriers and entities that it must conquer in its expansion. Paradoxically, the same agents that appear to be responsible for undermining the economic power of the nation-state emerge as the defenders of the nation-state (see Picciotto 1991).

Imperialism

Imperialism is irreducible to the exploitation of the periphery by the advanced capitalist countries, the global South by companies in the global North. Imperialism, though replete with colonial conquests, is irreducible to colonial conquest alone.[6] As Hannah Arendt (1951: 126) concisely put it: "Imperialism is not empire-building and expansion is not conquest." Modern imperialism has developed not so much by territorial expansion and colonial administration, but by the economic dominance of large concentrations of capital over production and markets across the globe in underdeveloped and developed regions alike. Imperialism is also, therefore, inter-imperialist rivalry: an intense, competitive struggle among large capitalist enterprises for the control of the global economy through dominance and influence in the economies of the advanced capitalist countries as much as the underdeveloped regions. Indeed, seen historically, the (territorial) expansion of capital into the periphery of the world system is the result of the development of competition among capitalist empires, which returned to the core capitalist regions (North America, Western Europe, Southeast Asia) after World War II and expanded further with the globalization of capital throughout the post-war period to engulf competitive struggles with capital from developing countries in the Third World (China, India, Brazil, and Russia – in all of which, incidentally, the state wields considerable control over industrial production, especially in the arms industry and energy sector). The expansion of inter-capitalist rivalry, however, did not erode the "new international division of labor" between North and South, although, as we shall see in the final section of this chapter, it expanded and changed its nature with the generalization of the neoliberal state.

Luxemburg summarized the two interrelated aspects of imperialism in the following:

> Imperialism is the political expression of the accumulation of capital in its competitive struggle for what remains still open of the non-capitalist environment.... With the high development of the capitalist countries and their increasingly severe competition in acquiring non-capitalist areas, imperialism grows in lawlessness and violence, both in aggression against the non-capitalist world and in ever more serious conflicts among the competing capitalist countries.
>
> (Luxemburg 1951: 446)

The virtual disappearance of the "non-capitalist environment" does not alter the structure of imperialism that Luxemburg analyzed, elements of which are already present in Luxemburg's relational, geographical reasoning. Luxemburg (1951, 1972) placed central emphasis on the necessity of "external" markets, i.e. markets in the "non-capitalist environment," for the expansion and survival of the capitalist mode of production – a source of much (misplaced) criticism of Luxemburg's thesis on imperialism. Geographical expansion of capital, for

Luxemburg, was driven by the contradictions between the conditions of production and realization of surplus value in a closed capitalist economy and the impossibility of realizing total surplus value from growing production in the home markets of the advanced capitalist economies (see Chapter 2). Markets for all forms of capital (money, productive, and commodity capital) had to be created so that the surplus product of the capitalist economies could be disposed of, commodities transformed into "pure value" (money) and surplus value realized as profit that could then be capitalized for the reproduction of capital to proceed at an expanded scale. The reproduction of growing concentrations of capital depended on the expansion of the capitalist market and the creation of the world market, i.e. on the conquest of the "non-capitalist environment" by capital and the establishment of the capitalist relations of production (by force, hence the militarization of the imperial state).[7]

Luxemburg, however, did not restrict capitalist expansion into the "remaining" parts of the "non-capitalist environment" to the regions outside the most developed capitalist countries. Luxemburg may have problematically inferred a relation of structural necessity from contingent historical circumstances by assuming the necessary dependence of capital on the non-capitalist world. However, the non-capitalist world, as Luxemburg conceived it, was not simply the regions or countries that fell geographically "outside" the capitalist countries, but economic regions outside the process of (technical and social) reproduction of capital, i.e. the production and realization of surplus value. Luxemburg's geographical reasoning is deeply relational and she conceived the world economy beyond the models of the "interstate system" or the "core periphery system." Luxemburg conceived the relationship between the capitalist and non-capitalist worlds "in terms of social economy rather than political geography," irreducible to a one-sided relationship between capitalist and non-capitalist "countries." Geographical expansion of capital derived from (internal) relations between different parts of the total economy at various levels of development, as they are expressed in geographical space as a whole, rather than an external relationship between abstract spatial units that remained in the background of the movement of capital.[8]

Bukharin (1929; 1972) developed the analysis of capitalist imperialism further by examining the formation of the world economy as an integrated whole, primarily through the internationalization of capital, and the development of inter-capitalist rivalry in the territories of rival capitalists. Contra Luxemburg, Bukharin argued, first, that the expansion of capital does not result from the impossibility of realizing profit at home but from the possibility of realizing surplus profit abroad, making the export of capital, rather than the export of commodities, the primary means for the expansion of capital (see Bukharin 1972: 247). Second, exchange and geographical movement of capital did not necessarily occur between two different modes of production, capitalism and the "non-capitalist environment," but could take place within a purely capitalist economy. The absence of an "additional market" did not threaten the existence of the capitalist mode of production, for capital could expand into other capitalist territories along the lines of "least resistance." Competing firms benefited from the same protectionist barriers that their rivals erected against their commodity exports, forcing them to resort to the export of capital in the form of means of production and, especially, money (stocks and bonds).[9] Firms competed against each other by their "participation" in each other's markets and by establishing branches in foreign countries under the guise of independent corporations, accelerating the international concentration of capital and providing the basis for its centralization at the international scale.[10] "Primitive" accumulation is not, therefore, restricted to the practices of capital in the non-capitalist colonies, but can be accomplished by the conquest of weaker capital by stronger capital, i.e. by the centralization of capital, the final expression of primitive accumulation (see Chapter 2).

Thus, reference to pre-capitalist empires as models to explain contemporary imperialism is seriously flawed, in the same way that Schumpeter's (1991) description of imperialism as an atavism of a pre-capitalist past is. (Schumpeter did indeed speculate on the disappearance of the imperialist impulse in the most advanced capitalist society, the US: needless to say, history proved his speculation gratuitous.) Modern imperialism of the twentieth century, structured by the contradictions of monopoly capital, is a phenomenon specific to the concrete historical–geographical development of capitalism and is incomparable to the Empires of the past: pre-capitalist empires or non-capitalist empires. Pre-capitalist imperial conquest concentrated wealth in the empire through the plunder of already produced surpluses, a practice that found limits in the productive capacities of the pillaged societies. Capitalist imperial expansion, however, concentrated wealth in the metropolitan centers by expanding the sphere of production and realization of surplus value, hence by expanding the social relations of production and transforming the imperialized societies in ways that contributed to the accumulation of capital at home (cf. Magdoff 1978). Not that the expansion of capitalism transcended direct robbery – a process still going on under the rubric of privatization and in the predation of speculative capital on industrial enterprises. But, it is the expansion of capitalist production and its simultaneous centralization under the control of large monopolies that characterizes the development of imperialism throughout the twentieth century. Comparisons between the current imperial moment and pre-capitalist empires – the Roman Empire being the most frequently conjured model in the current debate on US imperialism – cannot explain the resurgence of inter-imperialist rivalry or its continuity with twentieth-century imperialism.

Mandel (1975) distinguished between three analytical models of imperialism to explain the development of inter-capitalist rivalry in the post-war period which are useful in shedding light on the current development of inter-capitalist competition. (a) *Super-imperialism* refers to a situation where a single hegemonic imperialist power (e.g. the US) transforms the other imperialist powers into dependent, 'semi-colonial' small powers. This model is dominant in both liberal and Marxian accounts of the post-war period, or the so-called Cold War.[11] The hegemony of this super-imperialist power however cannot only rest on its military supremacy, but implies the direct ownership and control of global capital as a whole and the elimination of rival competitors that might threaten its absolute hegemony. (b) *Ultra-imperialism*, on the other hand, refers to the fusion of international capitals of all nationalities into transnational capital spread evenly over the globe. Accordingly, inter-imperialist competition among states or national factions of capital disappears, and what remains in its stead is competition among, or more precisely among and within, transnational corporations. The state does not disappear, but transforms into a "supranational" world state. This was essentially Kautsky's position on the eve of World War I, which elicited an early critique by Bukharin (1929) and later Lenin (1975). It is also, to a great extent, reiterated in Hardt and Negri's conception of postmodern empire.[12] (c) Finally, *inter-imperialist competition*. The argument, in this instance, is that classical inter-imperialist rivalry continues into the post-war period but in a new form deriving from the international fusion of capital at the continental scale, intensifying and transforming inter-capitalist rivalry into "intercontinental imperialist competition."

The development of relatively independent capitalist rivals in Western Europe and Japan that were subsequently joined by rival capitalists from the later developing countries to challenge the global economic hegemony of US capital prevented the realization of a super-imperialist model in which the US capitalist class dominates global capital, or an ultra-imperialist organization of global capital in which inter-capitalist conflict is abolished. Inter-imperialist rivalry persisted, but began to assume a supranational form in the post-war period.[13] The formation of supranational blocs competing with each other in the world economy was already discerned by Bukharin, writing on the eve of World War I:

> Were "Central Europe" to unite according to the plans of the German imperialists, the situation would remain comparatively the same; but even were *all* of Europe to unite, it would not yet signify "disarmament". It would signify an unheard of rise in militarism because the problem to be solved would be a colossal struggle between Europe on the one hand, America and Asia on the other. The struggle among small (small!) state capitalist trusts would be replaced by a struggle between still more colossal trusts.
>
> (Bukharin 1929: 139–140)

This triadic continental form of inter-imperialist rivalry would also find expression in the "just" division of the world according to German geopolitics, with US dominance in the Western hemisphere, German dominance over Europe and Africa, and either Russian or Japanese control of Asia.

The division of the world into three pan-regions was a result of opposition to British-led free trade imperialism, or an attempt to counter British dominance of world economy. The contemporary consolidation of competition along similar triadic lines is reminiscent of classical imperialism in more than a formal way. Taylor notes that:

> The rise to dominance in the world-economy by the United States after the Second World War ended the general drift towards economic blocs and so

made the concept of pan-regions temporarily irrelevant. But with the current demise of US dominance of the world-economy, economic blocs, and even pan-regions are returning to the world political agenda.

(Taylor 1993: 58)

We might extend the argument further and argue that the formation of pan-regions, or economic blocs, is indeed the effect of the attempt by rivals to counter the rise of the US to world dominance in inter-imperialist struggles developing since the post-war period. The European Union is one contradictory result of the development of inter-imperialist competition – contradictory because it was partly promoted by the US. Much less successfully, Russia and China have, since the late 1990s, sought a strategic alliance in Asia to counter US global hegemony, eventually extending the offer to India as all three continue to compete with the US for dominance in Central Asia (see below). Inter-capitalist rivalry at the level of the national state has, so far, prevented the full formation of supranational blocs as fully integrated political entities, despite the advance of international centralization of capital and economic integration at the supranational regional scale.

The three models of imperialism outlined above are not mutually exclusive and they have developed together, unevenly, as layers that intersect and contradict with inter-imperialist rivalry at the national scale. Competition among different factions of capital has strengthened one model or another, and the geographical contradiction that associates most closely with it: transnational corporations, especially financial corporations, have pushed towards an ultra-imperialism that consolidates the power of transnational moneyed classes without completely transcending the competition amongst them in the world market. As Dicken (2003) shows, moreover, integrative tendencies in trade and foreign direct investment in production have been stronger at the regional level within each of the global triads, than at the global scale.[14] In the military and political spheres, factions of the US bourgeoisie have adhered to the post-war project of US super-imperialism. This is apparent in the projection of US military power and the increasing militarization of US foreign policy, in addition to the continued attempt to dominate global governance institutions such as the IMF and World Bank (and, to a certain degree, the UN Security Council), despite the relative decline of US global economic hegemony and to the increasing objections of other major capitalist rivals (especially in Europe).

Inter-capitalist rivalry at the level of the national state persists, and the fragmentation of world space into national territories persists, not only because the national state is an agent of integration (and management) of global capital and not only because it remains an instrument in the employ and control of competing factions of the bourgeoisie, in their wars against each other and the collective enemy, i.e. the working class, but also because of the degree of fusion of state with monopoly capital. This is especially the case where "state capital" has been necessary for the development of competitive capital in the global economy, such as the case with Russia, India, and China in the post-Cold War period and has emerged as a relatively independent faction of capital in global inter-capitalist competition. Capital preserved the state by swallowing it and fusing with it in the course of the development of inter-capitalist competition in world economy.

Inter-imperialist rivalry did not end with the decolonization of the Third World and the expansion of capitalism into the periphery of the world system. The apparent relative stability in the capitalist camp during the first half of the Cold War concealed latent contradictions of inter-capitalist rivalry, which surfaced and intensified as the world capitalist economy entered the crises of the 1960s. The neoliberal shift in the globalization of capital was born out of deepening crises in the world economy, still relatively constrained by the geographical contradictions of the Cold War. The opening of the former Soviet Union and the former Communist countries of Eastern Europe to the expansion of capital expansion and the emergence of new capitalist rivals in Asia, expanded inter-capitalist rivalry further as it generalized the contradictions of capital across global space. In the remainder of this chapter, I examine the development of inter-imperialist rivalry at three historical geographical moments in the globalization of capital since the end of the nineteenth century, keeping in mind the interpenetration and interaction of the three forms of geographical contradiction outlined at the beginning of this chapter. We shall see that at each of these three moments, the relationship between global capital and the capitalist state seems to have only deepened as the two aspects of imperialism – conflicts among the most advanced capitalist powers and the collective domination of the less developed capitalist countries – fused with each other. The first moment comprised the development of monopoly capital at the same time that the world achieved its final division among the more advanced capitalist economies. This moment was punctuated by World War I but continued until the end of World War II, when another period of capital accumulation began, this time faced with the closure of the capitalist world by the solidification of the Communist bloc. This second moment peaked in the late 1960s, when the industrialization of Germany and Japan and, later on, subsequent waves of industrialization in the economies of Southeast Asia, saturated the world market and intensified a crisis of overproduction and overaccumulation. By the 1980s, the capitalist world entered another phase of inter-capitalist contradictions, which was eventually punctuated by the collapse of the Soviet Union and the opening up of the former Communist bloc for the expansion of Western capital, yet also the emergence of new rivals such as Russia, China, and India, etc., to compete in the expansion of global capital. This third moment, the moment of neoliberal globalization, developed further the competition among large monopolies and accelerated the formation of larger monopolies, at the national and international level, and expanded the militaristic aspect of capitalist development, thus developing modern imperialism at a full scale.

Imperialist globalization and the production of contradictory space

"A new era of history, political as well as economic, opens with the depression of the 1870s," wrote Eric Hobsbawm (1975: 46). In the period between the 1840s and the middle of the 1870s, industrial capitalism transformed the globe "from a geographical expression into a constant operational reality … History from now on became world history" (ibid. p. 47). We must add that as industrial capitalism developed into a "world economy," geography also became "world geography." Imperialism of the later nineteenth century was a phenomenon specific to the development of monopoly capital, and contemporary inter-capitalist competition is a development, albeit in other forms, of the inter-imperialist rivalry of the last quarter of the nineteenth century as a result of the simultaneous expansion of industrial capital and the contraction of geographical space.

The formal conquest, partitioning and annexation of parts of the entire globe that were not under the immediate imperial rule of surviving empires (the Ethiopian, Chinese, and Ottoman empires in particular) proceeded at an enormous pace between 1880 and 1914. Between 1870 and 1900, European imperialist powers and the emerging US and Japanese empires partitioned the entire globe among them, closing the space for future expansion into new territory. Western European states increased their colonial possessions from around 35 percent at the beginning of the nineteenth century to 67 percent of the earth's surface by 1878. On the eve of World War I in 1914, their hold increased to around 85 percent (Magdoff 1978; Peet 1991). In Asia, when European powers did not formally annex territory, they carved out spheres of influence as in the sharing of power between Britain and Russia over Persia. Alternatively, they maintained "independent" states such as Afghanistan to serve as "buffer zones," which in this case also separated Russia and Britain in what is commonly referred to as the "Great Game." Britain expanded its Indian empire into Burma, and strengthened further its influence in Tibet and the Persian Gulf, while Russia expanded further into Central Asia and Eastern Siberia and Manchuria. Among European powers, Russia's expansion was the only expansion of an imperialist power into contiguous territory – a continuation of the tsarist expansion of several centuries. Imperialist expansion otherwise was carried out in distant territories. The parts of Asia that were not under Russian, Ottoman, Chinese, and British rule were divided between the Dutch in Indonesia and the French in Indochina. Japan, however, had also started wresting territory at the expense of China, in Korea and Taiwan, and at the expense of Russia in Manchuria. The US, which won the Spanish possessions in the Caribbean (in addition to the Philippines), did not formally annex any further territory in the Western hemisphere, but enforced the Monroe Doctrine and transformed the Americas into a US sphere of influence while maintaining an "open-door" policy in China. US hegemony in the Western hemisphere did not face any serious competition from other imperialist powers, even Britain – no European power was willing to challenge the Monroe Doctrine seriously.

Imperialism, however, did not only divide the world among the competing industrial powers, but also created, or completed, the more general division between the industrial capitalist economies in the "core" of the world economy and the predominantly agricultural, non-capitalist economies in the "periphery" – a globalization of the division of labor separating industry from agriculture as a result of the industrial revolution. Imperialism was the main means by which capital created a global economy functioning as a single unit, divided between a "developed" core and an "undeveloped" periphery, specializing in the production of raw material and foodstuffs under increasing demand from economic growth and technological development in the "developed economies" (Wolf 1982). This was achieved by the development of a massive network of land and sea transportation – especially steam-powered river transportation which enabled the colonization of the continental interiors of Asia and Africa – and by a host of machine guns and other advanced weapons technologies.[15] Hence, imperialism created two internally related geographical layers of division, one among imperialist powers, and a more general division between the "civilized" core and the "primitive" or "backward" periphery, thus establishing what Marx (1976) called a "new and international division of labor," i.e. one suited to the requirements of the main industrial centers.[16]

Throughout the nineteenth century, Britain held the largest part of Western European colonial possessions, extracting tribute from all over the globe, and "recycling" its imperial tribute in expanding further its territorial empire. Britain opened its domestic market to the products of the whole world, and British unilateral "free trade imperialism" established the authority of the world market in governing the interstate system. Britain's free trade imperialism "cross-fertilized" what had hitherto been two alternative strategies of capitalist state formation and "modes of rule," what Arrighi (1994) referred to as the territorialist and capitalist logics of power.[17] In the territorialist logic of power, the acquisition of territory was the objective achieved by the means of accumulated economic command. In the capitalist logic of power the relationship between means and objective is reversed: in this case, the accumulation of capital became the objective, while the control over territory the means. British imperialism initiated a fusion of the two logics of power such that the world economy established by British hegemony in free trade during the nineteenth century became equally a "world empire," with London at its center, both as center of colonial government of a territorial empire and as a global financial and services center. By 1914, Britain retained 44 percent of world foreign investment, while the new industrializing economies of the US, Germany, France, Belgium, the Netherlands, and Switzerland held 56 percent among them (Hobsbawm 1987). (London remains the center of the global financial economy, despite the rise of competing global financial centers, especially New York.)

By 1870, however, Britain began to lose its global hegemonic dominance with the rise of two economic powers: Germany and the US, whose national economy enjoyed a bigger domestic market and greater wealth of natural resources, and which soon became a great magnet for international migration of both labor and capital. A new inter-imperialist struggle for world supremacy thus begins in the last quarter of the nineteenth century, which, by the end of World War I (essentially a war between Britain and Germany), established the US as a potential global hegemony to rival the old European rivals – a potentiality the US will attempt to realize globally only after World War II. The two new contenders for global hegemony not only "cross-fertilized" the two logics of power, but fused them together such that they became indistinguishable. Germany and the US built their power on the basis of both capitalist accumulation and territorial expansion. US colonialism is often deliberately effaced from accounts of US history, but it is precisely the "internal" imperial expansion of the US that made its development into a global capitalist power less dependent on "external" colonial conquest.[18] Indeed, with US imperialism, territorial expansion became internal to the process of capital accumulation. German expansionism adopted this model by expanding into Europe, after its attempt to emulate the British overseas extension failed.

The era of imperialism marked an important transformation in the relationship between the bourgeoisie (capital) and the state, embodied in the emergence of Germany and the US as new imperial powers, and characterized by a growing convergence between interstate politics and the free market, as well as the merger of geopolitical and economic competition. Massive economic growth of the late nineteenth century led to political rivalry among states of competing industrial economies, to the growth of imperialist expansion, the growth of the arms industry and, ultimately, World War I. In contradistinction with the British "liberal" capitalists who sought to exclude the state from the functioning of the free market (but only relatively so), the new bourgeoisie sought the power of the state to eliminate the competition of its rivals, not only Britain, and to assert their dominant position in the emerging global economy. This took place in the context of growing production combined with declining rates of profit, which made the new industrial classes force their governments (Germany, Italy, France, the US) to keep rivals out of their domestic markets by erecting protective barriers, thus ending the era of nineteenth century economic liberalism.

Free trade at the international level, including colonial territories, never represented the norm in the relationships among the different factions of the bourgeoisie, but rather the exception. The reversion to protectionism in the 1870s was not an accident, but, as Engels put it, a "historical necessity" which did not merely express a "defensive reaction against English Free Trade" (see Luxemburg 1951: 449). Britain's adherence to free trade in the late nineteenth century did not originate in its strong commitment to the economic principle itself as much as from the fact that Britain had already secured a vast colonial empire by the time that the developing capitalists began their territorial expansion. Protective tariffs in France and Germany were not only directed against British "free trade imperialism" but also against each other's commodity capitals and the competition from US industries. Moreover, as Bukharin (1929) would later observe, protective tariffs were intended not so much to protect infant industries, but to protect high rates of profit in the home market that could subsidize competition abroad. Only Britain, the largest world exporter of capital and largest importer of world primary exports, kept its domestic market open for foreign products, allowing its protectionist rivals to control their domestic markets at the same time that they advanced their exports. While Britain held tariffs at 0 percent until 1914, the level of tariffs in Germany was 13 percent in 1914, and 30 percent in the US, a drop from 49.5 percent in 1890 and 57 percent in 1897 (Hobsbawm 1987).[19]

Protectionism, however, was not the only response to the "great depression" of the last quarter of the nineteenth century (1870–1890). The equally significant reaction to increasing competition and falling rates of profit was the concentration and centralization of capital. The concentration of national capital reduced competition among different capitals at home and intensified the competition among exported capitals abroad, which tried to secure by means of direct military control new, external domains for capital investment. Paradoxically, therefore, the end of economic liberalism and the revival of protectionism brought with it the end of an epoch in capitalism when the "national economies" of the capitalist countries constituted the "building blocks" of the world economy. A global economy was emerging, in which protectionist policies (hence a strong state) were necessary for the economic growth of nascent industrial powers at the same time that the territorial division of the world was becoming an impediment to the expansion of capital by restricting the expansion of the world market.

The emerging protectionism of the end of the nineteenth century was an expression of the growing rivalry among states, but only because those became deeply involved in the international competition among capitals. Economic competition at the end of the nineteenth century merged (again) with political rivalry, except now the rivalry had acquired a truly global scale. The merging of state and capital was perhaps most pronounced in the growing relationship between governments and industry, particularly the arms industry but also the oil industry – both strategic industries critical for warfare. Friedrich Engels observed in 1892: "as warfare became a branch of the *grande industrie* ... *la grande industrie* ... became a political necessity" (quoted in Hobsbawm 1987: 308). The state, with its strong military, became equally essential for industry – not only for exercising force in the colonies, but also as the main client for certain branches of industry, especially, but not exclusively, the arms industry, circulating value into the reproduction of capital through taxes levied on the working classes (see Luxemburg 1951).[20] The competition among rival states generated great demand for the products of industry, and required that the arms industry maintain a large productive capacity even in times of peace. War, or the perpetual preparation for war, coincided with the expansion of industry and, as the twentieth century will demonstrate, capitalist crises will be repeatedly alleviated by preparations for war, real wars such as World War II and the Korean War, and imaginary wars, such as the Cold War and the wars against Communism in the Third World throughout the second half of the twentieth century. As with all other capitalist industries, the arms industry was bound to produce surpluses that found no "markets." Obsolescent military technologies were, therefore, subsequently traded with allies (and enemies) in the colonies and later in the Third World, creating a ready market and steady income for the arms industries that had to remain profitable at the same time that they maintained a capacity to produce at a large scale when the need arose.

National rivalry and protectionist politics were well under way by the middle of the nineteenth century, but inter-imperialist rivalry developing since the 1870s was the consequence of specific developments in the capitalist economy. The capitalist economy at the end of the nineteenth century was on its way to becoming structurally global – the imperative to expand rendered even the division of the world into spheres of influence among the competitors only relatively and temporarily stable. The economic growth of capitalist industry reached its planetary limits – exacerbated by the October Revolution of 1917, which removed a vast area of the space open for capital expansion. Any future growth in capitalist production had, therefore, to transform the "objective spatial structure" of the globe (Wittfogel 1985: 50–51; see also Smith 2003) rather than expand into it. Geographical space now had to be actively created at the global scale according to the dictates of monopoly capital. By the first decade of the twentieth century, the old geography was "shattered" and a new geographical space was emerging. Capital could no longer expand into the "given," absolute space of the planet and the imperialist rivals could no longer simply divide the rest of the world into colonies and spheres of influence. Absolute global space had itself to be recreated as a consequence and basis of further capitalist expansion.

The geographical expansion of capital into "the pores of world economy," as Bukharin put it, was not simply a quantitative expansion of the domain of capital accumulation, but also a fundamental transformation of the geographical basis of capital accumulation, embedding its contradictions deeper in the material space it created and came to depend upon. Contradictory space emerged from inter-capitalist rivalry: space that is structured by a contradiction between globalization and fragmentation, deriving from the contradiction between the accumulation of capital as a whole and the accumulation of rival factions of capital – space that would be reproduced, in different forms and at various scales, in the renewal of inter-capitalist rivalry after World War II behind the appearance of a common alliance against Communism.

Cold globalization: inter-imperialist rivalry in the post-war period

The post-war period can be characterized by a contradiction between the attempt by the US bourgeoisie to establish US super-imperialism, by consolidating its hegemony over its capitalist rivals, and the attempt by the international bourgeoisie, the capitalist class as a whole, to establish ultra-imperialism by restoring the conditions for capital accumulation as a whole and eliminating the internal contradictions that had led to two destructive world wars spanned by a long depression that threatened the very existence of the capitalist mode of production. The threat of Communist expansion in Europe and anti-colonial national liberation movements in the European colonies made the task more daunting by exacerbating inter-capitalist conflict with external limits to the expansion of capital, already constrained by the geographical limits placed by the Soviet Union and its sphere of influence in Eastern Europe. Notwithstanding, the projects for an "American century" and for a conflict-free capitalist brotherhood were both frustrated by lingering inter-imperialist rivalry among the major European powers, primarily between Britain and France on one side and Germany on the other, and a developing rivalry between the US and European capital. Inter-capitalist contradictions at both the national and continental scale would become more pronounced and intense by the late 1960s as the geographical patterns of uneven development shifted in favor of the developing export-oriented economies of Germany and Japan. This first led to a slowdown in the profitability and accumulation of capital in the US but expanded soon after throughout the whole capitalist economy, thus ending the process of seemingly peaceful and conflict-free economic growth.[21]

Contradictions of inter-imperialist rivalry developing with the economic slowdown of the 1970s, however, have their origins in the contradictory attempt of the bourgeoisie after World War II to restore European capitalism but to keep it within the control of US capital, i.e. to create *European* capital in order to prevent inter-European rivalry yet without creating an independent European competitor to compete with the US in the world market. The economic asymmetries that resulted from the uneven destructive effects of the war on the opposite sides of the Atlantic made the rapid development of European capital dependent on the financial and technological expansion of US capital into Europe, kept under control in order not to relinquish ownership and control of European strategic industries to US capital. The expansion of US capital was necessary to alleviate the problem of productive overcapacity resulting from rapid development during the war, and to prevent a crisis of overproduction in the US economy. More than to generate foreign income, the expansion of US capital was necessary to keep high employment and high spending by workers in the US (see Armstrong *et al.* 1991). The project for a conflict-free, post-war capitalism thus depended on the controlled integration of the advanced capitalist countries and the liberalization of the capitalist economy, yet also on the protection of European capital from takeover by US capital and on the protection of the profitability of US capital in the face of potential crises. (The latter made the European bourgeoisie more wary of integration with, and dependence on, an unpredictable US capital and a US bourgeoisie that was certain to look after its interests to the detriment of the global economy in case of crisis.) The problem to the expansion of US capital resided in the dependence of European capital on strong Keynesian (quasi-protectionist) policies (including control over capital, commitments to high employment, etc.) and imperialist preferences (trade with the former colonies, non-convertibility of currencies, sterling especially, etc.) for its redevelopment, in the face of persisting protectionism in the US, which prevented the full liberalization of international capital. The persistence of high protectionism guarding the US market against foreign imports strengthened the dependence of European capital on trade with the former colonies – the same colonies that the US was trying to open to US capital without relinquishing the monopolistic position of US capital in its spheres of influence in Central and South America and Southeast Asia.

Thus, the attempt to create an (geographically) integrated capitalist economy in the post-war period was, from the beginning, frustrated by the persistence of protectionism in the uneven geographical development of interdependent capitals. The failure to establish an ultra-imperialism that accorded central space to US super-imperialism managed only to reproduce inter-imperialist rivalry, which remained concealed beneath the veneer of a common alliance against Communism.

Contradictions of US super-imperialism

Technological and organizational developments that accompanied preparations for World War II in the advanced capitalist countries did not directly contribute to global economic growth. Certainly, the war allowed governments to carry the costs of economic developments that would have only been taken slowly and hesitantly in peacetime, if taken at all. Huge masses of fixed capital and vast areas of agricultural land, however, lay in ruin after the war. The most extreme consequences were borne by the Soviets: 25 percent of prewar industrial assets were destroyed; 13 percent in Germany, 8 percent in Italy, 7 percent in France, and 3 percent in Britain (Hobsbawm 1994: 48). Only in the US was war good for the economy, which grew at a rate of 10 percent throughout the war years. World War II practically resolved the contradictions of US capital accumulation developing since the interwar period – the contradiction between a growing manufacturing and agricultural capacity against contracting domestic and foreign markets – by providing effective, high demand, subsidized by the federal government, which would make use of under-utilized or unused productive capacity and eventually lead to the further expansion of US industrial capacity. Productive capacity of US capital throughout the 1930s remained at an average of around 63 percent, reaching its lowest (42 percent) in 1932 and its highest (83 percent) in 1937, compared to an average of 85 percent during the previous decade. Labor productivity increased by 20 percent during the war and capital assets in June 1945 were 65 percent over their 1939 level, largely from government spending.[22] Yet, the expansion was good for the US economy for as long as the war lasted. Even before the war was over, the prospect of overcapacity, unemployment, market gluts, i.e. the specter of another depression, loomed large over the near future unless the actions necessary to prevent it were taken.

More than the reconstruction of European capitalism or the defeat of Communism, US plans for the post-war economy centered on dismantling European imperialism and on consolidating the economic hegemony of US capital resulting from the opposite effects of the war on the economies of the US and its allies and enemies in Europe and Japan. The Occupation authorities initially had no plans to stimulate economic recovery in Germany and Japan, presumably to discourage the resurrection of militaristic regimes but, in more immediate terms, to prevent renewed economic competition in the world market. Initial rehabilitation efforts consisted of emergency relief to bring the German and Japanese economies up to the same standards of living of the countries affected by their aggression. US policy towards the vanquished included reparations (which in the case of Germany were additionally intended to prevent the Soviet Union from seizing German industries, and had substantially got under way before the process was reversed), the deconcentration of industrial and financial capital (on the justification that it gave rise to militarism), the weakening of labor in Germany (to prevent a move towards socialism) and the strengthening of labor in Japan (in order to keep Japanese capital less competitive than US capital on the world market) (see Armstrong *et al.* 1991).

To offset the effects of cuts in wartime government spending, and to relieve industrial overcapacity, capitalists in the US needed foreign markets large enough to absorb surplus productive capacity and maintain employment and domestic spending. This depended on the reindustrialization of Germany and Japan on the one hand, and the return of Europe to liberal free market capitalism on the other. The removal of capital controls on Western European economies, a policy advanced by the US Department of State, found contradiction in policies advanced by the Department of the Treasury, which, under the influence of Harry Dexter White, pushed for strengthening Keynesian "national capitalism" in Europe and encouraging the persistence of capital controls on European economies on the grounds that this was the only way to guarantee full employment and maintain inflationary expansion (see Block 1977). The disagreement within the Roosevelt administration compromised the plans for a managed global capitalism presented at the Bretton Woods conference in 1944. The World Bank and the IMF, as envisaged by the US Treasury, were designed to enhance rather than weaken the power of national governments over their national economies, paradoxically by gaining power over national governments with regard to their economic and monetary policies. US bankers regarded the idea of supranational lending agencies with large capitalization and "credit creating power" detrimental to their interests, and, although wary of lobbying for free market liberalism at a time when the memory of the recession was not yet lost, pushed to limit the power of supranational institutions and to remove controls over the movement of capital.[23] If such controls on US capital flowing into Europe were tolerated by the US, it was in the expectation that their removal would eventually follow from the development of European economies (see Panitch and Gindin 2005a).

On the other side, the European bourgeoisie was not yet willing to concede its political independence for economic assistance, despite its dependence on US capital for the restoration of its power in relation to domestic working classes and its position in the world economy. It still had bargaining power that it could use to resist plans by the US and to advance its own interests, deriving from its control over vast territories that had hitherto remained closed to the expansion of US capital.[24] The mutual dependence of the European bourgeoisie on US capital for reconstruction and repayment of war debts – partly hindered by the high protectionist barriers that the US maintained against European exports – and the dependence of US capital on opening the European colonies would find expression in the contradictory attempt to preserve European imperialism (the basis for European capital expansion in the face of US protectionism), yet undo its geographical basis, which had hitherto placed limits on the geographical expansion of US capital. The post-war planning that officially began in Bretton Woods in July 1944, expressed and embodied the conflicts between the US and its European allies and the conflicts within the US bourgeoisie, which rendered the institutions that resulted from the meeting ineffective in the immediate reconstruction of post-war capitalism under US hegemony. Bilateral agreements, such as the British Loan and the Marshall Plan would evolve out of the failure of the post-war allies to arrive at a satisfactory multilateral arrangement, only to be complicated by the contradictions of ultra-imperialism under US hegemony.

The Marshall Plan was to eliminate the barriers to US capital expansion without compromising US imperialism by forging a pattern of "triangular trade" between the US, Europe, and the former European colonies. The US would purchase raw material from the former colonies with US dollars deposited in accounts in European banks that European capitalists could use to finance imports from the US and that the former colonies could use to finance imports from European countries, thus providing stimulus to European manufacturing industry (see R. E. Wood 1986). In this way, the former European colonies were enlisted to participate in the recovery of the metropolitan economies by substituting their markets for the lost markets of Eastern Europe and for the highly protected markets of the US. The success of the Marshall Plan in advancing an integrated global economy rested on the success of the triangular trade and the reproduction of the colonial division of labor at an enlarged scale as much as on the integration of the European economies. Paradoxically, however, this pattern of trade relations risked strengthening the geographical patterns of European imperialism that the US was trying to dissolve and which threatened to increase the barriers between dollar and non-dollar blocs, exacerbated this time by the prospect of increasing integration within Europe. Triangular trade failed, in part, because European exports failed to displace US competition in the former colonies.

The formation of NATO in 1949 and the outbreak of the Korean War one year later, provided an alternative to accelerate the integration of capitalist economies by locking the European countries into an alliance that prevented the formation of a continental rival closed to US capital.[25] The outbreak of the Korean War justified the costs of, and lent Congressional support to, National Security Council Directive 68 (NSC-68), which tripled the "defense budget" of the US from $13.5 billion to $50 billion. The approval of a high defense budget and the support of expanding rearmament into Western Europe propelled the US into the military Keynesianism that would alleviate the problem of recession in the domestic economy for some time, and would do the same to the economies of Western Europe once it expanded there. The Korean War, and subsequent wars, had an added advantage: it stimulated economic growth in the advanced capitalist countries without the physical destructive effects on their economies that the previous war left behind by moving war and destruction elsewhere, and by expanding the market for arms while expanding the geography of inter-capitalist rivalry, with and within the developing world.

The real or imaginary threat from the Soviet Union and the expansion of Communism in the Third World justified the large-scale arms race that fueled post-war economic growth. It was soon replicated on the other side of the Iron Curtain. Economic growth in both "camps" in the post-war period was, in part, motivated by the arms race: the constant preparation for a war that never happened but which centered the economies of both the US and the Soviet Union on, and concentrated political economic power in, their respective military–industrial complexes. As in any other capitalist industry, however, large-scale manufacture of arms produced an excess capacity larger than either of the Cold War rivals could "consume." The commitment to the arms race generated a lucrative export-oriented sector that required foreign outlets if it were to remain profitable and which found these outlets in an expanding network of strategic alliances maintained through arms sales and donations. As wars moved to the Third World, either as imperialist wars of aggression against the former colonies or (proxy) wars fought among countries of the Third World (see Mandel 1975; Halliday 1983), so did part of the arms market. Cold War rivalry thus strengthened military–economic integration within each camp.

The seeming threat of advancing Communism, manufactured so eloquently in the speeches of subsequent US Presidents from Truman to Reagan, served the US in gaining political ascendancy over its allies. Beneath the apparent formation of US super-imperialism there was a process going in reverse. The development of Western Europe and Japan shifted the center of the world capitalist economy away from the US, eroding the uncontested economic hegemony of US capital, although the US remained the largest producer and exporter of manufactured goods. *Absolute* US hegemony was, therefore, short-lived: as Mandel (1970; see also Mandel 1986) succinctly put it, the American century lasted scarcely more than one decade. Relative decline of US hegemony began at the moment of its formation and its hegemony over its allies within the capitalist world economy remained only relative. The ideological reproduction of the Communist threat and the maintenance of US rivalry with the Soviet Union played an important role in upholding US political and military hegemony over its old and new capitalist rivals by locking the European rivals into an alliance that prescribed limits to their political autonomy. The reproduction of a struggle against a common enemy served to displace irresolvable contradictions within a precarious inter-capitalist alliance onto the global plane of a general contradiction between capitalism and socialism. As Harvey put it:

> the Soviet threat and anti-Communism became the central ideological tool
> to ensure solidarity of potentially competitive regional class alliances. To

the degree that this ideology needed a material base, the geopolitical confrontation of the Soviet Union and the Communist bloc became central to
the survival of capitalism irrespective of Soviet policies or action.

(Harvey 2001: 343)

Indeed, the increasing militarization of the US economy and US foreign policy
after the war indicated its induction into the ranks of imperialist powers, not
unlike its older European rivals despite the concrete historical and geographical
differences, and, as such, was dictated by the necessities of inter-imperialist
rivalry more than any struggle against Communism. The preparation for war in
times of peace remained preparation for *inter-imperialist* war.[26] The Soviet
"threat" was not the real cause of uninterrupted arms production as much as the
convenient basis for manufactured crises that justified increasing military
budgets and "defense" spending, as well as maintaining an alliance intended to
save capitalism from its own internal contradictions.[27]

Geographical contradictions of the Cold War

The binary geopolitics of the Cold War was itself not exempt from the geographical contradictions of capital; two interrelated contradictions deserve brief
scrutiny. On the one hand, the dynamic expansion of the capitalist economies
proceeded as part of the effort to "contain" the Soviet Union. Indeed, the containment of the Soviet Union meant, of necessity, the expansion of capital and,
as such, capitalist expansion proceeded against a self-imposed containment of
capital itself within a delimited geographical territory. Certainly, the US and
Britain tried to wrest from Stalin as much territory outside the Soviet Union as
it was possible, by keeping East Europe open to (US) capital (despite
Churchill's urging to occupy it with US troops), but there was no comparable
attempt to kill the Bolshevik child in its cradle, as in 1918.[28] The European bel-
ligerents could not afford it and the US was not interested in a war with the
Soviet Union or in conducting territorial expansion on behalf of European
imperialism – something, in fact, the US was intent on dismantling. This
accepted "balance of power" was reflected on the other side in the Soviet self-
imposed containment of "socialism in one country" and satellite states in
Eastern Europe. Soviet territorial expansion, contrary to US fears (revived
repeatedly well into the 1980s), was completed as soon as a buffer zone separating Russia from Europe was erected under the control of the Soviet Union.
"Peaceful co-existence," reinforced by subsequent Soviet governments, was
already implicit in Stalin's "election speech" of 1946, in which he predicted an
eventual Anglo-American conflict, and a more general conflict *within* the
capitalist world that would necessarily arise from the development of monopoly
capital.[29] But Stalin had already dissolved the Third Communist International in
1943 as a gesture of goodwill towards his wartime allies. World socialist
revolution was forever congealed in the Soviet Union becoming a state engaged
in the game of global geopolitics, and in order to survive geopolitical competi-

tion, the Soviet Union, as a state, had to play by capitalist rules (cf. Taylor 1993: 84).

The contradictory coexistence of two antagonistic and seemingly isolated political worlds, accepted by both sides as mutually exclusive of each other and representing external threats to each other – nothing less than the threat of mutual nuclear annihilation – contradicted with the scores of commercial interconnections that tied both spheres together in one world economy. As we saw above, the US (and Britain) had plans to include the Soviet Union in their postwar economic plans that led to the Bretton Woods conference. Indeed, Marshall Aid was offered to the Soviet Union and Eastern European socialist countries almost simultaneously with Kennan's formulation of the policy of containment and Truman's famous speech of 1947 instituting the Cold War. Stalin's refusal to join the capitalist league, however, or to allow the expansion of capital into Eastern Europe, found its negation in the voluntary insertion of the Soviet economy in the world market, which was to deepen irreversibly by the beginning of the 1970s (see Chapter 4). This dual contradiction eventually led to the crises of the 1970s on both sides of the Iron Curtain, to the renewal of inter-imperialist rivalry and to the demise of the Soviet Union altogether. The gradual integration of the Soviet economy in the circuits of global capital was, indeed, an effect of the general economic decline and the resurgence of inter-capitalist rivalry in the West, for it resulted not only from the increased dependence of the Soviet economy on the world market but also from developing crises of overproduction in the advanced capitalist economies that needed outlets for capital to ease the intensifying rivalry among the competitors.

The contradiction between expansion and containment, or isolation, indicates continuity with the contradictions of monopoly capital between expansion and protectionism, albeit in negative form, what I shall call "negative territoriality" in relation to the isolation of Iran (see Chapter 6). In other words, containment was one kind of protectionism practiced in reverse and aimed not to prevent the expansion of the Soviet Union or of Soviet power into the Third World as much as the expansion of (European) capital into the Soviet Union. The coming of détente in the 1970s and the willingness of Western European countries, especially Germany, to increase economic and commercial relations with the East contrasted with the renewal of Cold War rivalry in the US, which threatened to keep US capital out of the lucrative Soviet sphere as European (and Japanese) capital advanced into it. Incidentally, the Cold Warriors of the 1970s, who saw détente as a Soviet ploy to gain advantage in the arms race by tricking the US into reducing its defense spending, had strong connections with the military industry. They influenced the heavy militarization under Reagan and would resurface with the militarization of the US administration under the second Bush. The Committee on the Present Danger, not unlike the present Project for the New American Century, would play a significant role in increasing US military spending throughout the 1980s, which revived the US economy temporarily, and in committing the administration to military interventions across the world, especially in Central America.

The supposedly closed space of the Communist bloc, particularly that of the USSR, was not out of reach of US and Western European capital. More than US military superiority, the "heavy artillery" of the bourgeoisie, the commodity, "with which it batters down all Chinese walls," as Marx and Engels (1948) put it, found at its other end not only the compulsion but the voluntary willingness of the non-capitalist economies, "on pain of extinction," to integrate into global capital. By 1980, 34 of the world's largest transnational corporations maintained "cooperative agreements" with the Soviet Union, and some 151 corporations maintained offices in Moscow. The Soviet Union, in its turn, upheld some 170 joint ventures in 19 Western countries (Halliday 1983). Not accidentally, there-fore, the integration of the Soviet Union into the world economy coincided with global crises and the inexorable need of Western capital, in particular US capital, to expand the geographical limits for accumulation. Inter-imperialist rivalry of the period between 1870 and 1940, culminated in two world wars that finally opened the economic territories of the rivals to the controlled expansion of each other's capitals. The rivalry of the Cold War amounted to the same general result: the unfolding of an economic integration at a higher level, accompanied, however, by the eventual Third Worldization of the inheritor states of the Soviet Union, with Russia emerging as a "semi-peripheral," yet capitalist rival, that would engage, less than a decade later, in another round of inter-imperialist rivalry (especially in the competition for the control of oil and gas – see Chapter 5).

Inter-imperialist rivalry in the second Cold War

"Deep" globalization of the economy after World War II, and especially since the 1960s, rendered the crises that followed the economic growth of the post-war period global in scale. The rapid growth of the world capitalist economy began to slow down considerably after the early 1970s, although decline was already apparent in the US economy by the middle 1950s. Certainly the economies of the most advanced capitalist countries continued to grow, but at a much slower rate, leaving significant productive capacity unutilized and leading to overaccumulation of idle capital, financial and productive.[30] Despite the post-war industrialization of parts of the Third World, the gap between the developed and the developing world increased as growth in many Third World countries slackened and, in some instances, ceased altogether. By the end of the 1980s, the economies of the former Communist bloc collapsed and after bouts of "restruc-turing" in the 1990s, deteriorated even further. The only region that continued to grow, albeit with uneven geographical and temporal patterns, was East and Southeast Asia. The growth of the Japanese economy and later the economies of the "four tigers" and the "dragons" which followed, was the direct result of Cold War geopolitical calculations, which made these economies recipients of US financial, technological and military support. The emergence on the global market of the most vigorous, the Chinese economy, however, was not. Ironi-cally, as the managed, or mixed, economies of the West came under the attack of the capitalist classes, blaming the state's overspending and labor's high wages for being major causes for the decrease in the profitability of capital investments and the economic recessions that hit the capitalist world, economic growth was proceeding apace in the managed economies of Southeast Asia and in Communist China. The economies of this region would grow over the following three decades to become a major threat to the economic hegemony of the US, intensifying inter-imperialist rivalry while expanding it.

The recessions of the 1970s and resurgence of inter-capitalist competition were the result of the two decades of economic growth and apparent stability after World War II, underlining the continuities of post-war capitalism with modern imperialism and inter-imperialist rivalry. Post-war capitalism failed to transcend the contradictions of imperialism because it failed to transcend the contradictions of capital.

The development of large-scale, capital-intensive industry in the core countries of the capitalist world and its geographical extension into parts of the Third World, resulted in a combination of falling rates of profit in the more developed capitalist economies (from around 24 percent to 12 percent in the US between the middle 1960s and early 1980s; Duménil and Lévy 2004; see also Brenner 1998), increase in unemployment (from 1.5 percent to 11 percent in Western Europe between 1960 and 1993; Hobsbawm 1994), and saturation of the world market. Decline in profitability led to decline in investment and in technological development, leading to further decline in profits but also to several rounds of capitalist centralization, particularly in the middle 1980s and the middle 1990s. Under compulsion of intensifying competition, decline in the metropolitan economies prompted the export of capital from the most developed regions to others where more profitable investments could be made, i.e. more surplus value could be *extracted* from (low-paid) workers. Within the most developed economies, capital migrated also into labor-intensive branches of industry with higher rates of exploitation than manufacturing, such as the service industry and agriculture (hence the "green revolution"). Capital also moved across the most advanced capitalist economies with the attempt of rival factions of capital to compete with each other in their own markets – most foreign investment remains across the most developed countries of the North, despite a surge of foreign investment from less developed countries into the metropolitan economies. As this did not solve the problem of the *realization* of surplus value, it only exacerbated the problem of overaccumulation and overproduction and led to a resurgence of protectionist policies in the advanced capitalist countries at the same time that transnational corporations, from the US particularly, expanded their reach over the globe.

Despite relative decline in the hegemony of US capital, the US remained the biggest producer and exporter of manufactured goods in the world in the three decades following World War II – a position it still enjoys today. US markets, however, were increasingly flooded by the more competitive and profitable products of German and Japanese industries and, by the mid-1980s, by cheaper products from the Third World. The result was a generalization of the decline in the profitability of manufacturing industry, beginning in the US but spreading, through the competitive struggle and the enactment of protectionist and interventionist policies, throughout the global capitalist economy. As mentioned above, protectionist policies against Japanese and Third World exports were already in place by the early 1970s, beginning with the devaluation of the US dollar in 1971 and the abrogation of the Bretton Woods regime (of fixed exchange rates) by the Nixon administration. The liberalization of financial markets accelerated the expansion of transnational investments already in progress with the expansion of transnational corporations. The devaluation of the dollar made US exports more competitive in the world market; it also resulted in the relative revaluation of the Deutschmark and Japanese yen. Making the dollar non-convertible against gold put a stop to the drain of the coffers of Fort Knox by European countries (especially France) that, expecting eventual devaluation of the US dollar as a result of the Vietnam War and financial crises of the late 1960s, returned the piles of US dollars accumulating in European banks to the US for gold. Dollar reserves held abroad by foreign governments were furthermore depreciated with the devaluation of the US dollar. Aggressive protectionism mixed with financial market liberalization and surges in mergers and acquisitions, as well as expansion of foreign direct investment, continued throughout the 1980s and 1990s, especially in the US throughout the administrations of Reagan, Bush *père*, Clinton, and Bush *fils*. (Periodic) economic growth in the most advanced capitalist countries became increasingly dependent on non-market mechanisms – manipulation of taxes, interest rates, and prices; currency devaluations; inflationary practices coupled with freezes on real wages; and unproductive state spending, not in the least on rearmament and war – the "artificial stimuli" necessary for growth under monopoly conditions, all of which depend on the strong (bourgeois) state (see Mandel 1995).

The return to protectionism and the expansion of capital exports, primarily among the most advanced capitalist countries, confirmed the maturity of inter-imperialist competitive struggles gestating in peaceful economic growth since the end of World War II. Militarization of the US economy and foreign policy during the post-war period gained momentum during the Reagan administration, which aimed at regaining the competitiveness of US industrial capital and preventing the development of a worldwide crisis in a global economy that had become structurally dependent on the US market. Enormous increases in military spending combined with tax cuts for the rich and subsidized by growing deficit – deficit financed by Japanese, and later Chinese, credit – needed political support and, therefore, justification. The Soviet invasion of Afghanistan in 1979 and subsequent (disastrous) Soviet interventions in other parts of the Third World in the 1980s, were ample evidence of (presumed) strident expansion of Soviet military power and sufficient reason to plunge the US into another arms race.

By some geographical warp, the Soviet invasion of Afghanistan appeared in Washington [DC] as an advance towards US oil interests in the Persian Gulf at a time when the "friendly regime" of the Iranian Shah, which the CIA put in place in 1953, fell to another brand of enemy that immediately removed Iran, one of the two "pillars" supporting US interests in the region, from its sphere of influence. Such crises, in addition to the voluntary entry of China into the global market economy as a potential competitor, inaugurated the coming to power of the neoliberal conservative governments in the US, Britain, and Germany. Intensifying inter-capitalist competition, in times of economic recession, went hand in hand with renewed military aggression in the Third World, which the US still carried out on behalf of its capitalist allies. The massive arms race of the 1980s was detrimental to the Soviet Union, which, not unlike other semi-peripheral states, had already accumulated foreign debt; but it stimulated (short-lived) economic recovery in the US. "Defense" spending would only grow over the next two decades, despite the demise of the Soviet Union, and would find justification in new enemies and new threats. However, it would also reproduce the contradiction between US super-imperialism and capitalist ultra-imperialism by assigning the US, in the division of labor among the advanced capitalist countries, the task of expanding capitalism, by military force, into the "pores of the globe economy" but also upholding its waning hegemony over its rival allies in Europe and Asia. The decline of US economic hegemony during the 1970s was only relative. The US retained its position as the world's largest manufacturer and exporter and its preponderance in terms of the strength of its nuclear and conventional weapons which, in addition to providing it with the strongest military force, helped maintain a positive balance of payments with its European trading partners (although it ran a trade deficit with Japan). The rising militarism of the US contrasted with the decline of the economic hegemony of US capital as the aggressive expansion of capital in general came into conflict with the expansion of its constituent, rival factions. The neoliberal project came into being out of inter-capitalist contradictions, on the one hand as a project to restore US super-imperialism and, on the other hand, as a political project aimed at reproducing the North–South divide. As another phase in the development of monopoly capital, it will come to depend on the further development of capitalist militarism.

Neoliberal imperialism

Despite European opposition, the post-war capitalist economy developed to become centered on the economy of the US. The power of the US bourgeoisie in the global economy did not depend so much on the control and ownership of global capital – no matter how much this did actually grow in the post-war period – but on the dependence of global capital on the "health" of the US economy. A common interest in the growth of the US economy sent capital, industrial capital and financial capital in the form of credit, to the US as US capital left the country in the search of higher profits elsewhere. As the economic hegemony of US capital relative to its European and Asian counterparts declined further beginning in the 1970s, US imperialism grew not only by the export of capital but, more critically, by its import. Increasing economic interdependence and integration grew with intensifying competition and rising protectionism. Major capitalist rivals, whose export-oriented industries and the "health" of their economies depended on the US market, became susceptible to accepting US foreign policy, if not endorsing it, despite the relative decline of the power of US capital in the global economy. The relative autonomization of the power of the US state from US capital, exercised increasingly in military and militaristic terms (financed by foreign credit), exacerbated the contradictions between states and transnational corporations of the former Cold War allies, as those states were expected to perform contradictory functions, i.e. to manage the expansion of global capital and to support the global expansion of their companies yet "pressure" them at times to coincide with the interests of US foreign policy (the case of US sanctions on Iran, discussed in Chapter 6, is one demonstration of the development of these entangled contradictions). The governments of countries where the economic power of the dominant faction of the bourgeoisie was not directly dependent on the US market could still exercise some political independence and compete with the US in the global political arena, but only within the limits of their dependence on the global economy or, more precisely, on their dependence on the dependence of the global economy on US capital. But even companies from countries whose economies are dependent on the US and the global economy have to yield under the heavy weight of inter-capitalist competition to the motion of capital accumulation, such as in the case of Japanese companies investing in Iran against threats by the US, China's military and economic expansion, etc. Variation in the power of different factions of capital and their dominance in different places affects the variation in the relationships among the rivals. For example, although the US has so far failed to prevent European and Asian oil companies from investing in Iran and to prevent trade relations between Iran and major European countries, especially Germany, it has proved more successful in exercising power over transnational banks as those are more dependent on the US financial system than their industrial and commercial counterparts. Thus, in the context of increasing interdependence, the geometry of power shifts constantly and inter-capitalist competition acquires new forms that nevertheless reproduce the geographical contradictions of imperialism.

Globalization of capital in its neoliberal guise has so far failed to transcend the contradictions of capitalist imperialism and has, instead, exacerbated and reproduced them at an expanded scale. The common interest of the global bourgeoisie in an ultra-imperialism that manages, if not eliminates, the conflicts among the different factions by elevating them to a higher plane and taking them elsewhere has reproduced the North–South divide in a "collective" economic war on the peoples of the global South. Inter-imperialist rivalry did not abate, however, as new rivals from the less developed countries have risen to compete in the global economy and as the global hegemonic projects of old rivals still compete with US globalism from within the collective imperialism of the North. The latter is most prominently visible in the ongoing bickering between the US and the EU in the WTO over protectionist policies (especially regarding their respective subsidies to Boeing and Airbus) and over conflicting approaches to military interventions and dealing with new threats and enemies, rogue states and failed states, terrorists and weapons of mass destruction, insurgencies and Chinese militarism – and this itself is pregnant with the most glaring contradictions. To state but two recent examples: as Germany opposed the US invasion of Iraq in 2003, German intelligence provided the US Defense Intelligence Agency with Iraq's military plans to defend Baghdad and with information on the location of police and military units in Baghdad, and continued to cooperate regularly and systematically with US intelligence throughout the invasion; as European countries endorse heavier UN sanctions on Iran to keep it from developing its nuclear power program, they keep ignoring US sanctions on Iran, and threats of US sanctions on European companies, especially banks, and continue to trade with, extend export credit to, and invest in Iran.

The rise of transnational companies and industrial economies from the periphery to compete in the global economy has gradually transformed the economic war on the South into an economic war with the South. The ongoing protectionist assault on Chinese industry is a case in point. US Senators from both sides of the aisle have accused China of "unfair trade," paradoxically because China has pegged its currency to the US dollar, and, as China's trade surplus with the US grew, threatened to repeal normal trade relations with China and impose a 27 percent tariff on Chinese imports should China fail to float its currency. This protectionist stridency is, on the one hand, anachronistic – around 60 percent of Chinese exports to the US are by foreign-owned companies producing in China – but also contradictory, for the US actually registered a trade surplus with China in services. The contradictions run deeper than trade, into the centralization of capital under the control of companies from the periphery. Cases abound – China National Offshore Oil Corporation's botched attempt to acquire Unocal (US) in 2005 is a case in point. This resulted, in 2007, in legislation preventing foreign companies from acquiring US oil and other energy-related companies. This legislation is, in fact, an extension of the purpose and function of the Committee on Foreign Investment in the United States, an interagency commission established in 1975 to ensure that takeover of US assets by foreign companies with ties to their governments do not compromise "national security." The acquisition of the British port operator Peninsular and Oriental Steam Navigation (P&O), which controls operations in major port terminals in the US, by DP World of Dubai (after competition with PSA International [Singapore]) is another case that specifically embodies contradictions representative of the neoliberal imperialist moment. A protracted political campaign and public outcry in the US followed the acquisition of the British firm by DP World (after PSA International withdrew in February 2006) which was alleged to have ties to the September 11 hijackers and which, therefore, made the marine industry in the US "vulnerable to terrorism." Questions of national security mixed with a nationalistic uproar over foreign takeovers of US assets, reminiscent of that of the 1980s against Japanese acquisitions in the US. The campaign against the foreign takeover, however, began in late January (before DP World won the deal) when Eller & Co, a Florida stevedoring firm based in Fort Lauderdale and a partner of P&O in the port of Miami, feared that the takeover would harm its business interests in the US. Hence, Eller & Co promptly began lobbying Congress after the objections it raised to British courts were dismissed. Although Eller & Co's concerns were for reasons unrelated to questions of national security, their lobbyists on Capitol Hill framed the campaign in jingoistic terms, describing it as a campaign against "foreign control over critical infrastructure during wartime," a theme which was later picked up by both Democrats and Republicans in the House and Senate. (Note that 60 percent of US port operations are controlled by foreign firms.) By early March, after DP World was coerced into requesting from Congress a 45-day review of the takeover, a House panel succeeded almost unanimously in blocking DP World from taking over control of operations in US ports, and the Dubai firm eventually divested itself of all US holdings. Notwithstanding threats to "national security," Dubai, a major destination of US investment, some of it from pension funds, has recently become the home for the headquarters of Halliburton.

The expansion of inter-imperialist rivalry not only reproduced but also fused the two interrelated aspects of imperialism that Luxemburg identified into one global inter-capitalist rivalry, without transcending their duality, and reproduced the geographical contradictions of imperialism in the three forms we identified in the beginning as inter-imperialist rivalry sprang from the contradictions between "American Empire" and the "Empire of capital," US super-imperialism and the ultra-imperialism of global capital. The neoliberal globalization of capital is only the latest phase in the development of inter-imperialist rivalry, determined by an expanding global inter-capitalist competition no longer confined to the advanced capitalist economies and continued (economic and military) aggression, "lawlessness and violence," by capital against the less developed regions of space and society – not simply the less developed *countries*.

The shift from the global Keynesianism of the post-war era to the neoliberal globalization of the 1980s sought to restore the political power of the capitalist class as a whole, as Harvey (2005) argued, and to expand the power of the capitalist classes in the North over the peoples of, and against rising counter-hegemonic struggles in, the South (Amin 2004; Slater 2004; Peet 2007). But the neoliberal project is also an attempt to counter the decline of US hegemony in relation to its old and new rivals in the context of developing inter-imperialist tensions. The neoliberal project is, therefore, a profoundly contradictory project that aims at restoring the hegemony of US capital over its rivals, the hegemony of Western capital (the North) over its rivals in the South, and to establish the hegemonic power of global capital in general. As such, it is destined to come up against internal contradictions as much as growing external opposition, despite the hyper globalism that the proponents of neoliberal capital never tire from imagining as the reality of "really existing capitalism," i.e. globalism free from contradictions, dwelling beyond geography, in the ethereal universe and "flat world" of fictitious capital and cyber capitalism.

Neoliberalism is, therefore, also profoundly a political and geopolitical project. The neoliberal project matured during the second Cold War, but in important ways it emerged from the inter-capitalist rivalry of the second Cold War (see above). One of the main objectives of neoliberal transformations in the Reagan years was to restore the competitiveness of US capital against its allies and to revive the US economy by curbing inflation and shaking out non-competitive industries. There is near consensus today on the effect of such policies on the relative power of different factions of capital in relation to each other – in particular the ascendance of financial capital – and the relative weakening of the economic power of the state, both in the North and the South, through a process of privatization that redistributed control over the production process back to the private sector (including military-related industries). Accordingly, the financialization of the global capitalist economy had an effect on the form of globalization and the place of the state in it. The responsibility of the neoliberal state concentrated in the creation of a favorable "business climate" for global capital, which accelerated the concentration of state power in the executive and away from the democratic process as it generalized it across a wider geography. Third World countries, buckling under chronic debt to banks in the US and Europe, were especially susceptible to the dictates of creditors regarding the restructuring of economy and political government. As private debt became public, with the intervention of the IMF, power transferred up to the global governance institutions. From an active destruction of Keynesian and developmental states emerged the process of an active (re)construction of strong authoritarian states, combining expanded police power and technocratic, economic management along lines formulated in Washington [DC] and New York. The success of this process depended on the voluntary and active adoption of neoliberal economic policy, ideology, and rhetoric by Third World governments rather than a simple, mechanical imposition from above on the countries of the Third World (as much as the adoption of the "war on terror" rhetoric and practice makes Third World ruling classes eligible for US military aid and political support). Neoliberal states, in this second incarnation, had to be interventionist, compelled to perform the contradictory process of carrying out interventionist policies in order to create free markets while restructuring and downsizing – "streamlining" – themselves in the process (see Peck 2001; 2004; Peck and Tickell 2002).

Although the power of specific governments vis-à-vis global capital and the domestic bourgeoisie varies across geographical space, the neoliberal state, contrary to the hegemonic rhetoric, is generally a *strong* state, marked by an elite and technocratic managerial form of government – literally, as governments come to be managed as if they were companies, by actual executives who are not accustomed to notions of accountability, etc. – authoritarian aversion to the democratic process, participatory and otherwise, and dependence on the technologies of policing and physical force to ensure consensus. The shift to neoliberal technologies of government transforms the political process into a prolonged act of violence, expressed in many forms and at several levels. Instead of seeing "terrorist attacks" (i.e. any attack against the vital interests of [US] capital) and the perpetual "war on terror" (i.e. the expansion of the domain of capitalist control) as processes taking place outside of politics, we might as well see them as acts of politics, as expressions of the form of politics under neoliberal capitalism. As the Keynesian states gave way to the neoliberal state, the conflictive compromise between national capital, government, and the national working classes transformed into an expanded power of a transnational capitalist class over the mass of workers at the global scale, aided and legitimized by the most repressive and coercive means.

The neoliberal globalization of capital did not transcend inter-capitalist contradictions, but reproduced the contradiction between capital in general and individual factions of capital at an enlarged scale. The general subordination of the state to the dictates of global capital in a protracted war against the working classes did not include, nor lead to, the weakening of the state in relation to competing factions of capital, for the neoliberal state, *qua* capitalist state, must also perform the necessary function of protecting factions of the bourgeoisie against each other. Transnational violence exercised on the global working class, or the global "multitude," does not preclude the violence of capitalists against each other. This is practiced not only in terms of protectionist measures, takeovers and acquisitions, but in an increasingly militaristic form and also in war – the decisive means by which inter-capitalist competition is settled. Intensification of inter-capitalist contradictions finds expression in the expansion of military interventions and the expansion of military(-related) industry (and the arms market). The capitalist contradiction in this context takes the form of a contradiction of the continuous militarization of US foreign policy as an aspect of neoliberal capitalist expansion, as the US must perform the dual role of advancing and protecting the interests of global capital (a role it has "accepted" since World War II, but actually practiced since 1919) and protecting the interest of US capital against rival factions of capital, a role the US has assumed and practiced since its formation.

Permanent war

> Only the unlimited accumulation of material power could bring about the unlimited accumulation of capital. [But] power left to itself can achieve nothing but more power, and violence administered for power's ... sake turns into a destructive principle that will not stop until there is nothing left to violate.
>
> (Arendt 1951: 137)

Neoliberal globalization is one moment in the expansion and restructuring of geographical space for the continued accumulation of monopoly capital under conditions of intensifying inter-capitalist rivalry. The ascendance of financial capital and the increasing financialization of the global economy did not bring peace with it or erode the political power of the state but rendered capital more dependent on "material power" – the military strength of the bourgeois state. Here the distinction between financial capital and productive capital in relation to the nature of globalization becomes limited, if not altogether misleading. Under monopoly capital (as we observed above), productive enterprises become financial enterprises with the overaccumulation of money from profits that capitalists deliberately abstain from reinvesting in production in order not erode their monopoly privileges. So is the case with the distinction usually made between the dominant "peaceful" geoeconomic tendencies of the Clinton administrations and the warmongering and territorial tendencies of the Bush administrations, which ignores the expansion of the US military and military interventionism under the apparent multilateralism of the Clinton administrations. The image of a "peaceful" expansion of capital is wishful thinking and neoliberal globalization, because of, not despite, its financialization, is essentially militaristic in so far as it remains a moment in the development of capitalist imperialism. As Arendt (1951) observed in her analysis of classical imperialism, the export of material power follows the trail of the export of money capital (to protect large investments). But we must reformulate this formula to get the complete picture, for on the one hand, the export of capital follows and depends on the export of material power. But, and this underlines the importance of war for capitalism, the export of material power *is* the export of money capital and is an aspect of the circulation of monopoly capital, not only in terms of the circulation of value in the economy through the absorption of surplus in military and military-related industries, but through the expansion of the market of military and military-related products and through the destruction of value in the act of war. As Harvey (1999: 445) aptly put it: "not only must weapons be bought and paid for out of surpluses of capital and labor, but they must also be put to use." M-C-M' becomes M-destC-M', where destC is the physical destruction rather than the creation of commodities. Capital circulates and expands in the actual destruction of commodities – the underside of the mass production of value is the destruction of value at a more massive scale. In the process of destruction, profit is made and accumulated for further rounds of destruction.

Militarism is a moment in the expansion of capital indissociable from imperialism. Not only are they related, but they are two aspects of the same process.[31] The accumulation of capital is realized in periodic acts of destruction and is dependent on war in two other important respects: to expand accumulation by creating and expanding the space for the establishment of political "order" and "stability," i.e. control over geographical space to provide for the safe expansion and accumulation of capital, paradoxically through the creation of conflict and chaos. Thus, the "war on terror" is not simply an imperialist war for the control of resources, such as oil in the Middle East, but is an open-ended war for the permanent reproduction of order in its paradoxical neoliberal sense. The "war on terror" is the ultimate neoliberal war of extending the technologies of police deeper into the pores of the global economy, material, social, and spatial, for the expansion of monopoly capital accumulation. As E. M. Wood (2003) remarked, the current global war is a war without end in both ways: it does not have a specific (declared) objective (or, as Žižek [2003] observed in relation to the invasion of Iraq: it has too many contradictory objectives) and it does not have a specific end in time, making it conveniently malleable to changing circumstances and conveniently permanent, i.e. a permanent state of exception that concentrates political power in the ruling classes and provides inexhaustible markets for the products of the military–industrial complex.

If "accumulation for accumulation's sake" became with "classical imperialism" the equally absurd "expansion for expansion's sake," then, with neoliberal capitalism, it has become a process of "war for war's sake." For war is itself a lucrative growth industry with effects on the economy in general. Hence the second importance of war for monopoly capital, as an "artificial stimulus" to an economy endemically prone to stagnation. Complete analysis of the economic significance of war – preparation for war and war itself – is beyond the scope of this study, so we must confine this brief analysis to elements relating directly to the issues under consideration, namely the development of inter-imperialist rivalry under the contradictory conditions of neoliberal capitalism, i.e. the contradiction between the empire of capital and US super-imperialism.

Contrary to neoconservative critiques, US militarization proceeded unabated throughout the Clinton administrations. Military interventions and engagement in military conflicts – misleadingly called "crisis response activities" – have only increased with the collapse of the Soviet Union. Such military interventions, as with imperialist interventions in general, did not always have immediate economic gains or economic objectives defined in a narrow sense (control of this or that oil region), but served to expand the military reach of the US for what appears to be anticipatory and preventive purposes, as Sweezy (1942; see also Bukharin 1929) described territorial aggrandizement during the era of classical imperialism. As such, US military interventions did not have, and do not have, to be construed around a specific enemy embodied in one nation-state or a combination of nation-states in the here and now. As Bacevich (2002) observes, since the 1990s, US grand strategy did not rest on constructing a "strong military" but aimed at establishing military capabilities strong enough to allow the US to "prevail over any conceivable combination of adversaries." This is often reflected in a military budget equivalent to the combined military budgets of all major powers, be they allies or potential adversaries. Military budgets measured in quantitative military terms, however, conceal two essential sources of military strength, and can therefore be misleading: regional alliances augment the material power of the allies and technological development of arms and weapons allows cuts in military spending without decline in the accumulation of material power.[32] (Reliance on allies and proxies can, in addition, augment military spending by revenues from arms sales.) Relative decline in military spending in the US in the 1990s since the all-time high of 1987, therefore, conceals improvement in the efficacy of new generations of weapons, i.e. their destructive power, that are applied in "asymmetrical" wars to showcase the improvements of new models to potential buyers and to demonstrate their destructiveness to potential adversaries watching from the sidelines.

Military spending and planning in the US has come to be determined by a perpetual preparation for war rather than the means to prevent it. Apparent Cold War strategies of containment and deterrence gave way to more explicit strategies of "extraordinary power projection" and the active shaping of the "international environment" to meet US vital interests in the context of "new strategic realities" and, ultimately, to further the global expansion of capital under the banner of liberal democracy and international security. The Bush doctrine of "pre-emptive attacks" takes this strategy further by transforming every adversary into a potential enemy and, more importantly, makes potential military crises a present actuality. Potential military threats of the future, no matter how improbable they may be, become part of the present strategic environment. (Note the "nuclear crisis" with Iran and the talk about Iran as if it already possesses nuclear military capabilities.) Military planning, which by its very nature is anticipatory, must deal with *all* imagined future crises as possible present realities. Current US military strategy, therefore, assumes a collective adversary comprising all potential adversaries and then treats the potentiality of such confrontation as already an actuality.

Consequently, it is futile to try to identify this or that entity as the present enemy of the US for two reasons. First, despite the shifts in the geometry of power after the collapse of the Soviet Union and the re-emergence of inter-capitalist rivalry, especially with the entry of China and Russia into the club of great capitalist powers, US military interventions could still be explained as being involved in the expansion of capital in general rather than US economic interests in a narrow sense. The doctrines of "forward defense" or "defense in depth," which developed in the 1940s, expanded the global military reach of the US in defense of *capitalism*, not so much out of a political or ideological commitment to liberal democracy, one must add. No matter how much capital expansion was centered on the interests of the US, the expansion of capitalism was the only means to curb the loss of territory to Communism or any socialist variation in the Third World that closed space for capital as a whole. This was often carried out not by direct military expansion, but by military support of ruling classes in Third World countries (see below). We can still discern the same impulse in the plans of subsequent US administrations to spread liberal democracy to the rest of the world as an attempt to expand the capitalist free market and not only US capital, despite its centrality to the neoliberal project. Certainly, it is important that US capital retain a hegemonic and decisive role in this process. However, at a fundamental level, it is a process of what Smith (2003) described as eliminating, or filling, the "interstices of globalization" – geographical entities of all scales that threaten the total expansion of (US-led) capitalism – or what Barnett (2004), from a rather different perspective, called the "non-integrating gaps" – countries and regions outside the "functioning core," not integrated and harmonized with the global economy. On this basis, US globalism (US super-imperialism) could be conflated with the globalism of capital (ultra-imperialism or Empire), the interest of the US with the interests of global capital, expressed in the rhetoric of the White House and Department of State as the universal interests of humankind. In this case, the new enemy cannot be identified as this or that nation-state, but forces residing in the cracks of the global economy that have resisted the expansion of capital under US hegemony.

This process is, of course, not free of contradictions precisely because of the persistence of inter-imperialist struggles that have not only prevented the full conflation of US capital with capitalism but also shifted its geographical scale. This could already be discerned in the contradictory relations between US capital and an integrated Europe after World War II: a necessity to prevent the rise of a hostile German rival and prevent recourse to French and British imperialism that, nevertheless, presented US capital with the danger of the rise of an independent European continental rival. Geopolitical anxiety over a German–Russian dominance over the Eurasian landmass of the prewar period, and Soviet dominance during the Cold War, resurfaced in the post-Cold War era as anxiety over a potential Eurasian alliance including not only major European powers hostile to the US, namely France and Germany, but extending through Russia and all the way East to China, with the gradual transformation of Russia and China from Communist rivals to capitalist competitors. From Kennan and Spykman to Kissinger and Brzezinski, it has become a central tenet of US foreign policy that the control of the Eurasian landmass by any single power or combination of powers hostile to US interests should represent a direct threat to the military and economic security of the US and must, therefore, be contained by a counter-expansion of US ideological, political, and economic influence, and, if necessary, by direct territorial and military control. A potential threat from a continental rival – one that does not yet exist – provides the second dimension of current geopolitical rivalry that makes it difficult to name one arch rival and pin it down geographically.

The core argument of the Project for the New American Century's (PNAC) 2000 report, *Rebuilding America's Defenses*, sums up the structural changes and contradictions in contemporary geopolitical rivalry. Calling for an increase in defense spending from 3.5 to 3.8 percent of GNP, with an annual increase of $15–20 billion to total defense spending, the PNAC argued for asserting US military pre-eminence in the opportune strategic environment of the post-Cold War era:

> At present the United States faces no global rival. America's grand strategy should aim to preserve and extend this advantageous position as far into the future as possible. There are, however, potentially powerful states dissatisfied with the current situation and eager to change it, if they can, in directions that endanger the relatively peaceful, prosperous and free condition the world enjoys today.
>
> (PNAC 2000: i)

There is currently no rival power immediately present to threaten US pre-eminence. Yet, there is the ever-present threat of such a great power rival rising in the near future and the US must be prepared not only to cope with such an event, but prevent it altogether. The dual mission of US military forces is to "secure and expand zones of democratic peace," i.e. "Pax Americana," and to deter or preclude the rise of a great power rival. Of course these are two aspects of the same process that, significantly, is unlimited in time and space. The major military threats of the new century are "potential theater wars spread across the globe," with strategic focus in East Asia. Although China is the implicit contender for the position of great power rival, the PNAC refused to limit defense requirements to such assumptions. The quantitative expansion and modernization of the military aims not only at maintaining conventional and nuclear military superiority under present conditions but must be accompanied by a qualitative geographical restructuring: US forces must be repositioned "to respond to twenty-first century strategic realities by shifting permanently-based forces to Southeast Europe and Southeast Asia, and by changing naval deployment patterns to reflect growing US strategic concerns in East Asia" (PNAC 2000: iv). Moreover, US military control must not be confined to Asia, or indeed to the planet, but must expand to control "the new 'international commons' of space and 'cyberspace.'"

On planet earth, and in physical space, there has indeed been a shift in the "global footprint" of the US military, which, as with the activist interventionism of the Clinton administration, is unrecognized, or simply ignored, by the PNAC. Since the middle 1990s, and to the consternation of Russia and China, there has been a shift of US deployments from the edges of Eurasia – Western Europe and East Asia – to the former Soviet Republics in Eastern Europe, the South Caucasus, and particularly Central Asia. Direct military assistance to Central Asian republics and ongoing plans by the US to erect a missile defense system in Eastern Europe, have accompanied the eastward expansion of US and NATO military forces and establishment of permanent military bases in Central Asia and the Southern Caucasus, especially Georgia. This process expanded after 2001, but it had already begun in the middle 1990s through NATO-sponsored programs such as the Partnership for Peace program (PfP), and the associated Central Asian Battalion (CENTRASBAT). The Partnership for Peace program was adopted at the NATO summit in January 1994. It is primarily a US initiative, deliberately designed to expand NATO while avoiding "early decisions" on its enlargement, and to provide NATO with a "flexible system of halfway houses" that allow for its expansion without requiring an expansion of membership (Borawski 1995). The Central Asian Battalion, on the other hand, was formed in 1995 by an agreement between Kazakhstan, Kyrgyzstan, and Uzbekistan, to operate under the auspices of the United Nations for the purposes of "peacekeeping" and preventing conflict in volatile areas (Olcott 2000). But CENTRASBAT quickly became the focus of major military exercises sponsored by the PfP. Moreover, the sponsorship of CENTRASBAT shifted from Atlantic Command to Central Command following the modification of the Unified Command Plan to include Central Asia in Central Command's "area of responsibility," an area, most of which, is significantly riddled with "ethnic" and "religious" conflict. This territory spans Kenya, Sudan, and Egypt in the west all the way northeast through the horn of Africa to the five republics of Central Asia, including the Arab Peninsula, the countries surrounding the Persian Gulf, Afghanistan, and Pakistan, and bisecting an "arc of crisis" or "arc of instability" (an area of possible US intervention) that stretches from the Balkans to China and, by some accounts, from Northwest Africa to Southeast Asia.

Both geopolitical dimensions outlined above – expansion into the pores of the global economy and the prevention of the rise of a Eurasian power rival – appear to have reshaped the "global footprint" of the US military to reflect "new strategic realities." The geographical migration of US military facilities and personnel from US bases in Germany, Japan, and South Korea that were designed to contain Communist expansion during the Cold War is part of a military strategy that aims at creating a global "web of far-flung, austere forward operations bases ... to adapt quickly to suddenly appearing military needs" ... a "patchwork of ... 'lily-pads' ... throughout the 'arc of instability' running along southern Eurasia" (Cornell 2004). The great potential for "instability" in these republics that combine weak, yet authoritarian regimes – all supported by the US – with feeble economies and predominantly Muslim populations makes them especially susceptible to influences from radical Islamic movements in the South, especially the radical Islamic republicanism of Iran. Central Asia's geographical location lends it increased strategic importance as it sits between three developing capitalist regional powers, Russia, China, and India, that have their own, often conflicting, strategic plans for Central Asia and which, together with Iran, have been trying to strengthen and establish new economic, political, and military ties with the former Soviet Republics. This makes Central Asia crucial for both the further globalization of capital and the formation of intercontinental rivalry.

US military expansion has not always been exercised directly, however, and has increasingly come to depend on several layers of proxies and allies. Indeed, as Slater (2004; see also Smith 2005) argues, rule by proxy rather than direct colonial administration is a hallmark of US imperialism distinguishing it from its European counterpart, especially with the decolonization of the Third World after World War II. (It does not mean that European and other imperialist powers did not resort to similar indirect military and political interventions – see Johnson [2004].) The distinguishing element of the present rule by proxy is the thickening mediation through private contractors. The advantages of expanding power through erecting and supporting proxy governments and military/police forces mediated by private service providers are both political and economic.[33] First, it is "cheaper" as it minimizes *apparent* and *direct* military expenditure at the same time that it promotes military assistance, arms sales, "training" programs, and the hiring of private contractors, all of which amount to a transfer of public funds to private firms in the name of defense and national security. Power expansion by proxy also avoids the politically treacherous task of having to account for casualties: "native" and nameless casualties are easier to stomach at home, including the death of civilians as "collateral damage." On the other hand, the death of private contractors and hired civilians can easily be absorbed into the neoliberal discourse of "business risk" and "individual responsibility."

Military "training" programs amount to nothing more than the perfection of the techniques of police and state terrorism in support of allied ruling classes, dictators, and repressive regimes, in the less developed countries against actual or potential popular opposition. Justification of such programs depends on the creation of enough chaos and disorder to make political repression plausible and necessary – especially if this threatens to destabilize the immediate region or global security. In most places, violence and disorder could conveniently be attributed to local ethnic and religious conflicts (as if European colonialism never happened) that can only be eradicated by the expansion of liberal democracy and free markets, buttressed by military aid and military training programs, followed by commercial contracts for arms sales. Thus the State Department's view of what is essentially a political struggle for power in Lebanon between a pro-US governing coalition and an opposition largely supported by Syria and Iran – both comprising a wide and rather similar variety of religious and ideological positions – is a conflict between Sunnis, Druze, and Christians (i.e. Maronites) on one side, and Shiites on the other. Its idea to stabilize this conflict is by extending a $1 billion military "aid" to the government for its security forces, with the participation of Saudi Arabia and France. In a different context, the eastward expansion of NATO and the US military presence in Central Asia and the Caucasus provoked very "hostile" reactions by Russia and an assertion of Russian nationalism that became the very basis of justifying the expansion of the US in the region to support the former Soviet republics against resurgent Russian imperialism.

Military-to-military contracts and assistance programs have been concentrated in agencies tied directly to the Pentagon and the State Department, often with ties to intelligence agencies, and to private military contractors.[34] But the proliferation of private military contractors has gone hand-in-hand with the militarism of what Mann (2003) describes as the "neoconservative chicken-hawk coup" that has increasingly removed the military from civilian control and which continues to blur the division of labor between elected government officials, military professionals, and representatives and lobbyists of the arms industry in what Johnson (2004) calls the "circulation of elites" between the three nodes: military officers retire to the private military firms, while executives from such firms and military think tanks are appointed to high-ranking positions in the Pentagon and the White House.[35]

The concentration of political power in this triadic nexus has proceeded in parallel with its relative autonomization, which is only reinforced by its increasing privatization. The privatization of the US military, subcontracting operations to private firms including military training programs provided to allies and proxies, has increased the autonomy of military operations – or, as I offered above, militarized politics – by allowing military activities to circumvent "outside scrutiny" and at the same time operate outside the rigid and hierarchical chain of command of the military. Contractors are not accountable to Congress, thus expanding the scope of military actions. As Bacevich (2002) put it: "hired guns could do things that remained off limits to soldiers." At first glance this may seem little more than an idealization of professional soldiers and military conduct, for nothing is really off limits to soldiers on the front. Yet, the operations of private military contractors are regarded as "proprietary information," which allows for high levels of secrecy. The flexibility of hired help in military operations derives from its operation outside the military chain of command and public scrutiny in so far as this is determined, and must be justified, by plausible national interest. Nothing prevents private contractors from offering their services to both parties in a conflict as they are solely motivated by profit-making. They also allow the extension of military contacts to governments with bad human rights records – an exchange that would otherwise be difficult to pass Congress. Private contractors that train foreign allies are mostly hired by the US government, but they can be directly hired by foreign governments with approval from the Pentagon and the State Department. However, they are also hired by the US government to provide every conceivable type of service, including the maintenance of military bases and camps. As the network of far-flung military bases expands, the market for services of private military contractors expands, expanding their revenues, jobs, and expenditures in the US market.

Military-to-military training exercises have not only increased military and police control by proxy but have also expanded the arms trade, sometimes financed by loans and assistance from the Pentagon and Department of State. The arms market, which is still dominated by US companies (accounting for around 49 percent of the world's arms trade) and often subsidized by loans from the US government (approximately $3 billion annually), thus grew in tandem with the expansion of military intervention and military spending, especially after 2001. Commercial sales of arms weapons go directly through the Pentagon, but private companies can sell them directly to customers with proper authorization from the State Department's Office of Defense Trade Controls. Indeed, the arms industry has undergone transformations similar to many other industries with the liberalization of markets and globalization of production. Despite the preponderance of US arms manufacturers, as with any capitalist market, the expansion of the arms market after the end of the Cold War has led to intense competition, protectionism, and a round of centralization and outsourcing that placed arms production under the control of a few large producers as it expanded their global reach.

For most of the twentieth century, arms production was intimately linked to the state and to the strategic "needs" of its armed forces. As we saw, this link had its origin in the development of inter-imperialist rivalry at the turn of the twentieth century, which forced states to keep national arms production active and profitable during times of peace, in a perpetual preparation for imperialist wars of division and re-division. In the post-war period, arms production and transfers served to cultivate strategic allies on both sides of the Cold War and had, therefore, to meet the strategic "needs" not only of the state but its allies. The development of the war industry in the post-war period, as we saw above, had more than a military strategic function and was part of the Keynesian compromise between state, capital, and organized labor. With direct and indirect support of the state, from defense budget allocations to finance research and design in universities, the arms industry absorbed large factions of the working class in relatively high-paying jobs and provided work in other related industries. In fact, the development of large, high-tech industry could not have proceeded without the power of the state to make available large sums of capital that could not have concentrated in any single private enterprise. Competition with the Soviet Union forced arms production in the capitalist countries, the US especially, to keep pace with technical progress not determined by maximum utilization and full valorization of capital invested in production. This led to a deepening of dependence on the state for socializing the costs of investments, including research, and concentrating large amounts of social capital in the military industry. Demand for arms to meet the strategic needs of the Cold War kept the large concentration of capital in the military industry productive.

The capitalist states' strategic needs changed with the collapse of the Soviet Union, however, which reduced the global demand for arms and related military products and afflicted the industry, already burdened with overcapacity, with shrinking government budgets, shrinking markets, and declining profit rates. This led to a dual process of consolidation of the industry through mergers of already huge corporations into, and the acquisition of smaller ones by, larger conglomerates (e.g. Lockheed Martin and Northrop Grumman) and to attempt to expand global markets through "strategic partnerships," joint ventures, licensed production, and cooperative programs. Very few and large companies dominate global arms markets, which makes for very intense competition, especially as the national markets of the largest producers, the US in particular, are closed to each other.[36] Certain large (European) producers, such as BAE Systems (UK) and Thales (France), have subsidiaries in the US or South Korea and Australia (respectively) and have set up joint ventures in transnational projects or merged with other (European) companies (such as MBDA). Yet, the transnationalization of arms production has its limits in the (strategic) nature of the industry and the continued dependence of large manufacturers on the state, not only for lucrative contracts, subsidies, and protection in a tight market, as well as the provision of loans and military aids to finance foreign sales to other states, but also for creating the strategic "need" for the products of the industry. Most requests for military budgets made in US Congress by representatives of states where arms and weapons are manufactured (California, Texas, Connecticut, etc.) to finance specific projects do not have immediate or justifiable need (see Johnson 2004). Arms producers must, therefore, influence government policy on defining threats to national security and strategic needs, and they do, as long as the state depends on arms sales and military aid to cultivate "diplomatic" relations and alliances (and as long as arms manufacturers can close shop and move elsewhere). The "dual containment" policy of the Clinton administration transferred arms to US allies neighboring Iran and Iraq, i.e. Turkey, Israel, Egypt, and Saudi Arabia (see Tirman 1997). The current "war on terror," by freeing security threats from any one specific geographical location, expands arms transfers further by projecting security threats at the scale of the whole globe and allowing for the definition of any conflict as a potential threat to international peace or, what amounts to the same effect, US vital interests and national security.

The arms industry wields tremendous political power in the global economy compared to its rather small share of national GNPs and employment. Its strategic significance lies in the decisive part it plays in *inter-imperialist* wars: in the reproduction of the global capitalist economy and the expansion of the domain for capital accumulation and in the preservation and reproduction of rival factions of capital. Our excursion into this brief sketch is to reiterate the contradiction between individual factions of capital and capital as a whole, which is at the root of imperialist rivalry and the production of contradictory geography. The arms industry embodies and expresses this contradiction in that it is another faction of capital necessary to the existence of capital in general, and representative of the interests of the capitalist class in producing the means of destruction whose interests conflict with other factions of capital in the competition for profit. That this contradiction has increasingly taken militaristic forms, expressed in expanding arms production and expanding wars, is one indication of the intensification of inter-imperialist rivalry in the neoliberal moment of monopoly capital and its continuity with the rivalry developing since the end of the nineteenth century.

The privatization of war has proceeded with the militarization of private enterprise. Governments do not go to war because of surpluses and decline in profitability in their arms industry; nor do conflicts leading to war arise simply from conflicts over the control of resources. Both are part of a more general inter-capitalist rivalry specific to the development of monopoly capital. Modern military interventions, indissociable from imperialism, have, as their objective, the functioning of the global capitalist economy as a whole under conditions of uneven development that lead to competitive struggles either to uphold the asymmetries in the geometry of power – among the more developed rivals, between the more developed parts of the world and the Global South – or to erode these asymmetries and transform the patterns of uneven geographical development. In the process, a contradictory geographical space is produced and reproduced at many levels and in different forms depending on the specific circumstances of the struggle among different factions of capital for the appropriation of global surplus value (and the expropriation of each other). The competition for oil is one instance of this struggle, which occupies a special place given the strategic nature of the raw material and the significance of the industry to capital as a whole. But the competition for oil, as I shall show in the following chapters, is, nevertheless, an expression of the contradiction between the interests of global capital as a whole and the conflicting interests of competing factions of capital, including, and centered on, the contradictions between transnational oil companies and resource-owning states acting as rival factions of capital. If there will ever be "resource wars," as many have so far predicted, they will not be wars for resources, oil and otherwise, but part of an ongoing capitalist war of expropriation of capitalists by one another.

4 Oil in the development and decline of the Soviet Union

The demise of the Soviet Union in 1991 marked the climax of what Eric Hobsbawm (1994) called the crisis decades, beginning in the late 1970s after three decades of unprecedented economic growth in the global economy. The "great transformation" of the global economy did not spare the fragile project of "socialism in one country," built on the industrialization of the Soviet Union in seeming seclusion from the capitalist world economy and, with the implosion of the Soviet Union, brought to a conclusion the apparent geographical contradiction between capitalism and socialism, paving the way for the full realization of capitalism at a world scale. Far from confirming the victory of capitalism and its expansion into new geographical territory, however, the collapse of the socialist economies of Eastern Europe and the Soviet Union confirmed the falsity of their independence and seclusion from the global economy, and revealed the global extent of the political and economic crises developing in the world economy as a whole. It also revealed the crucial role that oil had played in the integration of the Soviet economy into the world system and in its eventual demise.

The voluntary integration of Soviet oil production into the world market was fundamental for the industrialization of the Soviet Union from the beginning. It developed throughout the successive Five-Year Plans to become largely irreversible in the early 1970s and intensified further throughout the next two decades. The mixture of vast resources, a rigid domestic economic system, and a global oil crisis that quadrupled oil prices almost overnight transformed the Soviet Union from a relatively advanced industrial economy, potentially equal in its industrial capacity to the industrialized West, into a resource-exporting, peripheral dependency, such that, by the middle 1980s, the US administration could debilitate the Soviet economy by persuading Saudi Arabia to flood the oil market, sinking together world oil prices and Soviet external revenues.[1] The windfall from the oil crises of the 1970s may have postponed the collapse of the Soviet economy till 1991, only to reveal, however, the extent to which its development, or perhaps survival, had become dependent on revenues from oil (and gas) exports.

The focus of the Soviet planners on carbon fuels in forging a path of economic development "independent" of the capitalist West, produced a fundamental contradiction in that it could have been achieved only through its own negation, its dependence on its opposite: the integration of the Soviet economy into the world market through a structural dependence on the export of oil. The possession of vast reserves of strategic resources was necessary to provide the basis for economic development but not in itself sufficient to put it in motion, for the valuation of a vast array of diverse resources depended on capital that the Soviet Union lacked and which, therefore, had to come from abroad. In the following, I examine the development of the oil industry of the Soviet Union to shed light on two fundamental and related aspects of the development of the oil industry over the twentieth century. First, the problem of the abundance of oil: there has always been too much of it that threatened market prices and the profitability of major oil producers unless a way was found to control it. The problem of Soviet oil was that it was not open to foreign transnational oil companies. Although they could obtain it commercially, oil reserves and oil supply on the market lay beyond their reach. This, as we shall see, did not prevent oil companies from trying to penetrate the Soviet oil industry, but they ultimately had to rely on other measures to control Soviet oil on the world market. The problem of oil's abundance was exacerbated by the fact that Soviet oil production did not operate according to the capitalistic logic of profitability but according to quotas determined by the quantitative logic of Five-Year Plans, which were insensitive to market dynamics. This ultimately led to the development of wasteful extraction technologies, damage to reserves and early depletion, and, most critically, chronic overproduction that had to find its way to the market. Just like a giant corporation, the Soviet Union had to find outlets abroad to dispose of its surplus oil. Second, the development of the Soviet oil industry represents the fundamental contradiction between integration and fragmentation emanating from the contradictory dependence of resource owners on the expansion of capital into the production of the resource while retaining control over the resource against the predation of capital – a contradiction we shall see reproduced in the case of contemporary Russia and Iran. The Soviet Union represents the interconnectedness of this contradiction and the problem of oil abundance, for its independent economic development was dependent on the quantitative growth of the Soviet oil industry and the integration of Soviet oil in the world market.

Oil in the command economy: the rise

After the Revolution of 1917, the Bolshevik government found itself in command of a backward economy whose only promising sector was an inoperative oil industry, lagging significantly in technological capacity and in need of substantial investment in order to get back on line. Obtaining the necessary oilfield technology for the development of the Soviet oil industry could have come only from technologically advanced Western oil companies. Moreover, the Soviet Union's vast oil resources appeared to the Bolshevik government as a potential lever with which to bargain with hostile Western capitalist countries for both economic assistance and diplomatic recognition. Lenin's New Economic Policy (NEP) of 1921, proposed to open the Soviet economy to foreign capital, and went as far as to permit granting concessions to foreign investors in order to develop Russia's natural resources and eventually to revitalize its war-ravaged industries. Foreign, especially US, capital investment would accordingly lead to normalized relations with the Western world. The Soviet government approached a group of major international oil companies, including Standard Oil of New Jersey, and proposed the formation of a single company to develop the Russian oilfields, but the proposed deal failed because Royal Dutch Shell and Standard Oil refused to participate. Royal Dutch Shell had purchased the Rothschilds' oil interests in Russia before World War I, only to lose them after the Soviets nationalized the oil industry in 1918. Standard Oil of New Jersey also purchased from the Nobel brothers the property rights of their oil interests in the Caucasus (for a mere $6.5 million) in July 1920, after they had been already nationalized. Sir Henry Deterding, president of Royal Dutch Shell, refused to let the Soviets sell to Western oil companies, let alone his own company, oil which he regarded as rightfully belonging to his enterprise.[2] Thus, the Western oil companies refused to invest in the nationalized oil industry in the hope, and expectation, that the existence of the Communist government would be temporary. The defeat of the Bolsheviks, the companies speculated, would make them the legitimate owners of the Russian oil properties they had purchased from their former foreign owners. The Bolshevik government survived the attempt of hostile capitalist allies to strangle infant Bolshevism in its cradle, as Churchill put it, but failed to attract the necessary foreign investment into the oil industry without the participation of major oil corporations.

The refusal of major oil companies to invest in Russia did not deter smaller enterprises from exploring investment possibilities in the Soviet resource industry. Lenin hoped to awaken US economic interest in the Soviet Union and facilitate future investment of capital and transfer of technology with an asbestos concession, and eventually enhance national security by improving political relations with the US as a counterweight to belligerent Britain. In 1921, and with the help of his family connections in Russia, a rather young Armand Hammer (later to establish a major mining company, Occidental), won a concession to develop asbestos in the Urals and, between 1920 and 1923, two small oil companies from the US, International Barnsdall Corporation and Sinclair Consolidated Oil Company, won concessions to develop Russian oil and explore for new fields (see Gillette 1973, 1981). Small oil enterprises, however, were constrained by pressure from the US State Department and major oil corporations not to invest in any "stolen property" – property nationalized by the Soviets – and by the unwillingness of the Soviet government to grant large-scale concessions. Thus, foreign investment in Soviet oil was over by 1924.

The Soviet government was no longer interested in soliciting direct investment from the West. It abandoned the granting of concessions and transferred US enterprises, through negotiations with the owners, to the Soviet government, and opted instead for the purchase of technology and know-how on the market. Oil companies that refused and prevented investment in the Russian oil industry, on the other hand, could not resist the purchase of cheap Russian oil to sell in their markers. The devastated post-war economy had significantly reduced the domestic demand for oil and made larger quantities of oil available for export to already existing, but not yet saturated, world oil markets. The Soviet Naphtha Syndicate embarked on rebuilding the war-devastated export apparatus and establishing an independent distribution network in Europe. The Syndicate, which had set up offices in Berlin and London by 1922, set up its own subsidiary in England, Russian Oil Products Ltd., and began to flood established oil markets, i.e. markets divided among the few large corporations, with Russian oil far below market price. Under the leadership of Royal Dutch Shell, Western oil companies launched a campaign to boycott Soviet oil, in order to force the Soviet government to restore confiscated property. But not wanting to miss out on the availability of cheap Soviet oil, they embarked on clandestine purchases to compete with each other in their own markets. Standard Oil of New York and Vacuum Oil Company (later to merge into Socony Vacuum) bought cheaper kerosene from the Soviets to compete with Royal Dutch Shell's Rumanian oil in markets in Egypt and India. Royal Dutch Shell, in turn, sold cheap Russian kerosene in its markets in the Far East. Russian Oil Products Ltd. continued to compete with the major oil companies in the British market, however, until an understanding among major oil companies was reached in 1929 granting the Soviet Naphtha Syndicate a share of the British market and allowing it to increase its share in proportion to growing demand. Thus, by the end of the 1920s, although not yet officially recognized as a legitimate state in the international system, the Soviet Union was recognized as a major oil producer with a reserved place in the world market.

The agreement of 1929, however, coincided with a great market slump. In the face of a sharp drop in demand and prices of oil, the Soviets pumped even larger quantities of oil into the depressed market, raising the Soviet Union's share of world oil exports from 4.7 to 9.1 percent between 1929 and 1932, and bringing on themselves accusations of dumping oil in pursuit of a "diabolical plan" to break the capitalist economy (see Heymann 1948). To stabilize the oil market and fend off Soviet competition, Western oil companies invited the Soviets to an international oil conference in New York in 1932, in which Standard Oil of New Jersey offered to buy all Soviet oil exports for ten years. In return, the Soviets would liquidate their distribution networks abroad. The conference failed, and produced, instead, another "gentlemen's agreement" among Western oil companies to boycott Soviet oil.

Far from using oil as part of a strategic attack on the capitalist world, however, the Soviets kept their oil exports at high levels primarily to obtain the foreign exchange needed to meet the targets of the first Five-Year Plan (1928–1932). The export of oil at high volume and at prices below market price during the first Five-Year Plan was forced by the need of the Soviet Union for imported technological goods.[3] The subsequent Five-Year Plans, which replaced the New Economic Policy, set the Soviet economy on a path of development whose immediate priority was the creation of basic heavy industries and energy production. The wealth of the Soviet Union in natural resources made this logical and possible, and a rapid process of modernizing the oil industry began with the first Five-Year Plan, and continued especially in the late Plan years of the early 1930s. During the early stages of modernizing the Soviet economy, oil production, determined by targets set by the Plan rather than by domestic industrial or individual consumption needs, increased much faster than the slowly expanding domestic economy could absorb, allowing – almost forcing – surpluses for export, which increased steadily until 1932.

The drive for large-scale industrialization, motorization, and especially the mechanization of agriculture under the second Five-Year Plan (1933–1937),[4] stimulated domestic consumption and slowed down the export of oil, so that by the early 1950s exports practically ceased (Hassmann 1953). Growing oil consumption, and increased demand for refined products, was accompanied by expansion in refining capacity and advances in refining technology. In the 1920s, most crude oil was burnt as fuel in furnaces, but modern cracking techniques were applied more widely in the 1930s, increasing the total yield of refined products (see Lamet 1952). In the third Five-Year Plan (1938–1942), refinery capacity was increased further at the same time that refining activity was progressively relocated from the South Caucasus to the newly developing region of oil production in the Volga-Ural Mountains, north of Kazakhstan. Despite the progressive technological modernization of the oil industry, however, and the improvement of extraction and refining methods during the 1930s, Soviet oilfield technology remained relatively underdeveloped compared to the production technologies employed by major oil corporations. Increases in production did not come from a development in social productivity, but from the geographical shifts to newer fields with higher natural productivity.

Abundant and productive oil reserves contributed to the modernization and industrialization of the Soviet economy by generating foreign exchange and by establishing the Soviet Union as a creditworthy trader in the world market. The export of oil allowed the Soviet Union to obtain the advanced technologies necessary for industrial development, including the development of the oil industry itself. The export of large quantities of oil during the early years of Soviet industrial growth was buttressed by the abundant supply of coal. Notwithstanding the development of oil production and refining methods, growing domestic demand and decline in oil exports, the growth of Soviet industrial production until the middle 1950s was largely fueled by coal. Although it did not always meet planned targets, the production of coal expanded nearly five-fold between 1928 and 1940. Oil production, however, did not grow with the same consistency – output doubled in the first Five-Year Plan (1928–1932), increased by 30 percent in the second (1933–1937), and did not increase at all in the third (1938–1942).[5] It was not until after 1950 that domestic demand for oil grew rapidly with the expansion of road transport, the switching of railway transport from coal to diesel for about half its motive power, and the development of the petrochemical industry. Exports, however, continued to grow again, to countries of Eastern Europe, with the establishment of the

Council for Mutual Economic Assistance (COMECON) in 1949, and to countries in Western Europe.

The thrust eastward

The more West the Soviet Union looked for markets for its oil exports, the further East it looked for new oil reserves to feed growing production. The expansion of Soviet industry after World War II was accompanied by a geographical redistribution eastward, especially of oil extraction with the discovery of new oilfields. Between 1940 and 1955, plants were dismantled and transported, with the requisite skilled labor, deep into the Soviet interior and by 1965, the Volga-Urals region and Western Siberia had become major centers of industrial development (see Dienes 1971; 1972; Rodgers 1974). The major shift eastwards in the immediate aftermath of the war was motivated by strategic planning, namely to protect the most developed industries from future German invasion. But the continued "thrust eastward" well into the 1960s, cannot be explained solely by the relocation of manufacturing industries to the more strategically located and naturally protected interior. It was motivated by the actual expansion of the Soviet economy and its extension into regions rich in natural resources and not yet fully integrated into the (national) economy. The location of large and unexploited reserves of oil meant immediate production at high volumes with available technology and without considerable increase in cost. Increase in oil output to meet the quantities dictated by the Plan could be achieved by relying on the higher natural productivity of large oilfields not yet exhausted. Thus, Soviet industrial "capital," so to speak, moved East to develop the resources of underdeveloped regions, where the relative amount of oil output to the share of capital investment was much higher than in other regions. The high costs and technological complexity of exploiting the deeper strata of the old Baku fields inhibited the further development of oil extraction in the Caucasus. The development of the Volga-Urals oil industry thus proceeded in the post-war period, as the significance of the Caucasus for Soviet oil industry declined and the infrastructure fell into disrepair.[6] The Soviet oil industry kept moving East with discoveries of more and bigger reserves of oil (and gas) until the late 1970s when large discoveries in Kazakhstan brought it back West.

As more and larger reserves were discovered in the late 1950s, and as more emphasis was put on reducing the dependence on coal and on expanding the petrochemical industry, Soviet oil output doubled in the period between 1955 and 1960. The 15-year oil plan (1958–1972), which replaced the aborted ten-year plan of 1951–1960, aimed at increasing oil output further by four times over its 1958 level.[7] The discovery of abundant reserves, which extended further into Siberia, met the increase in planned targets but postponed, indefinitely, the technological development of inefficient and wasteful oil production. The effects were not confined to the oil and gas industry, but had their repercussions on the whole of the Soviet economy. More investment was poured into the production of oil and other resources to the detriment of other industries, which, paradoxically, exacerbated the unevenness in the development of resource extraction and the underdevelopment of manufacturing industries, distorting further the difference in supply of, and (domestic) demand for, energy and raw material. Oil surpluses grew and needed foreign outlets,[8] but as manufacturing lagged behind extractive industry, the need for, and dependence on, advanced foreign technology to maintain production levels also grew (see North 1972; Luke 1985).

The first Cold War: the great leap into the world market

The expansion of the Soviet oil industry in the two decades following World War II allowed the Soviet Union to resume its exports of cheap oil to Western Europe at a commercial scale, becoming, by 1970, a net exporter of oil. The expansion of Soviet oil exports appeared to Washington [DC] as another deliberate "economic offensive" directed at undercutting US companies in Western European markets. Indeed, in the ideological context of the Cold War, increased exports of Soviet oil to countries in Western Europe (and later the Third World) were perceived in the US as a strategic means to undermine the whole "free world" by making NATO members dependent on Soviet oil. The Soviet Union could then use this dependency to dictate foreign policy to its trade partners. This charge, however, not unlike its predecessor in the early 1930s, was rather exaggerated. The expansion of Soviet oil exports was determined by differential rates of growth in oil production and domestic demand, creating chronic surpluses that needed outlets in foreign markets, rather than geopolitical calculations.

Soviet oil exports to the Eastern bloc (and China before the rupture), Western Europe, and the Third World did increase in the post-war period. With large reserves in Northwest Siberia entering production, Soviet oil remained abundant and cheap, yet not in comparison with Middle Eastern oil. It would have cost the Soviet Union less to import oil from the Middle East than to produce it at home – which the Soviet Union, in a manner, did. Trade expanded with Western Europe, beginning with "neutral" states but soon including NATO members. In the early 1960s, the Soviet Union was trading with Germany, France, Italy, Sweden, Denmark, Iceland, Egypt, Pakistan, Tunisia, and Argentina. The Soviet Union offered oil-rich Third World allies (Iraq) technical and financial assistance in the oil industry in addition to exports of manufactured goods from Eastern Europe, in exchange for oil exports to Eastern Europe that helped the Soviet Union shift some of its own oil exports to Western Europe. Trade with the West generated more income than the exchange of underpriced Soviet oil for overpriced manufactures from Eastern Europe, although most of it did not generate foreign exchange, as oil deals were arranged on a bilateral barter basis. Moreover, Soviet oil exports were too scattered and of magnitudes smaller than could provide the Soviet Union with any effective geopolitical tool to launch an economic offensive against the West, and no one trade partner risked becoming dependent on Soviet oil to the extent of endangering its economic security. Nevertheless, the US pressured its NATO allies during the early 1960s to cut their imports of Soviet oil and to embargo the export of oil and pipeline technologies to the Soviet Union. The IMF and World Bank, in their turn, tried to "persuade" developing countries not to trade with the Communist bloc (see Bromley 1991).

Trade between the Soviet Union and the Western capitalist countries, including Japan, continued to grow throughout the 1970s, however, as did the Soviet economy and especially the production of oil. The number of proven oil and gas fields had increased enormously by the early 1970s, which compensated further for the low productivity of older oil- and gas-producing regions and lagging Soviet oil technology. But the technological lag was also to be well compensated for by the unexpected windfalls from the first "oil crisis." The increased revenues from the sale of oil permitted the Soviet Union, once more, to turn to the West for technological assistance in the modernization of its oil and gas industry. In the context of oncoming détente, major transnational oil companies, which had hitherto obtained Soviet oil by purchasing it on the market and which had, since the late 1960s, attempted to make inroads into the Soviet economy, saw a potential opening for direct access to Soviet oil through direct investment in its production. The Soviet oil industry provided a vast, relatively undeveloped, oil frontier at a time when the nationalization of the oil industry in Third World countries, and the closing of the Middle East to US companies, deprived foreign companies of access to upstream production. Foreign oil companies could not only satisfy the needs of Western industrial countries, but also vast markets in Russia and other Soviet Republics. But there were no production sharing agreements on offer, however, which would have guaranteed foreign investors a share of the produced resource. The Soviet Union offered, instead, "cooperative ventures" consisting primarily of exchange of know-how, technology, and licenses for a fee (including payment in oil and gas), i.e. contracts akin to Risk Service Agreements (RSAs) that guarded foreign investors within the safe space of technical provider (see Chapter 6 for further discussion of RSAs and other types of contracts).

The promise of great investment opportunities was clouded further by skepticism about the prospects of Soviet resources on one hand, and the Soviet Union's support for the Arab countries in the Arab–Israeli war on the other. The bulk of the Soviet Union's undeveloped mineral resources lay in East Siberia, as nothing more than a mere "geological potential" that remained to be realized. The development of Siberian resources for export would take years, which meant that until this happened, the Soviet Union would be able to purchase foreign technology with money or credit, rather than oil and gas. The provision of technical "aid" for the development of Soviet oil and gas appeared even more absurd in the context of the Soviet Union's support for the Arabs who had just used their oil as a political weapon against the US. Foreign investment in the development of the Soviet oil and gas industry would only help the Soviet Union to gain more control in the world oil market and to develop the potential to follow the Arabs' suit and use the "oil weapon" in the Cold War with the US. Instead of using its abundant hydrocarbon resources to create dependencies in Western Europe and to dominate the world market, however, the Soviet Union appeared to be moving in the opposite direction by becoming increasingly dependent on Western European countries for the export of its surplus oil and for the very technologies necessary to develop the oil and gas industry. The Soviet Union was becoming more dependent on, and integrated with, the market, and this dependence would slowly erode the political power of the Soviet Union in the international system.

The Soviet oil crisis and the second Cold War

The coming of détente between the Soviet Union and the US promised techno-logical and economic development on one side, and an "unlimited market" on the other for overaccumulated capital facing an imminent crisis and in desperate need of expansion. Over the decade, the Soviet oil and gas industry would absorb greater and greater shares of investment in the Soviet Union, most of which, given the technological state of its industries, were to maintain existing output levels and to open up new regions for resource exploitation. Oil production increased by around two-thirds, and gas production would more than double. Transnational oil companies kept their interest in investing in Soviet oil and gas alight, seeking joint ventures to explore in the Arctic Circle, the Caspian Sea, and Siberia. Yet, renewed tensions between the US and the Soviet Union, beginning in 1975 and culminating with the Soviet invasion of Afghanistan in 1979 – the oncoming of the so-called "second Cold War," to last until the middle 1980s – slowed down the economic exchanges between the Soviet Union and the West, and, with it, the economic growth that the Soviet Union was beginning to enjoy. The Soviet Union seemed to be heading towards an energy crisis as its oil and gas industry was not developing enough to meet its domestic and export needs. To make things worse, most of the oil revenues were now drained into wars fought in the Third World and an expensive arms race with the US.

In 1977, the CIA published two reports predicting a decline in Soviet oil pro-duction beginning in 1980, and a consequent energy crisis in the Soviet Union to reach its height by the middle of the 1980s. Incidentally, the Soviet Union during this time was importing oil from Libya and Iraq in exchange for techno-logical assistance in their oil industries, and had offered Iran electric power in exchange for oil. The Soviet Union had also begun to employ more nuclear energy and electricity in domestic consumption in order to free more oil for foreign export. By the end of the 1970s, it appeared that the Soviet Union would not be able to exploit its vast oil reserves, or discover larger ones, quickly enough to prevent the imminent decline in oil production. Whereas oil and other foreign companies with technological services on offer saw an opportunity for further "technological cooperation" with the Soviet Union, and perhaps direct investment in oil production, the military planners in the US saw a different picture. Decline in Soviet oil production was enough motivation to drive the Soviet Union into the Middle East, i.e a domestic oil crisis would compel the Soviet Union to advance closer to the Persian Gulf rather than seek techno-logical cooperation with Western enterprises. As if to confirm such a scenario, the Soviet Union invaded Afghanistan in 1979. The invasion of Afghanistan, it seemed by virtue of geographical ignorance, put the Soviet Union on the way to the oilfields of the Persian Gulf, thus creating a direct threat to the "vital interests" and security of the US. Although the CIA had reversed its predictions in another report in 1981 showing that the Soviet Union was, after all, able to meet its oil needs without having to import any oil from abroad or conquer foreign oil-producing countries, the defense of US interests in the Middle East and the renewed arms race were on their way.

The expected severe oil crisis did not happen, and the Soviet Union did not invade the Persian Gulf. The growth rate of oil production in the Soviet Union did fall in relative terms but, in fact, oil production kept growing in absolute terms throughout the 1980s.[9] US geopolitical concerns shifted again to Western Europe as the Soviet Union embarked on increasing its oil and gas exports to the West in order to augment foreign exchange. In 1985, the Reagan administration tried to stop the expansion of Western European imports of natural gas from the Soviet Union on the grounds that an increase in the Soviet Union's hard currency earnings would strengthen its military power and give it "political leverage over Europe." With direct intervention by [Margaret] Thatcher, the Reagan administration compromised and allowed Western European countries to import no more than 30 percent of their total gas from the Soviet Union as they developed alternative gas resources within NATO's reach. Despite opposition from Western European countries, the US managed to ban the export of any US equipment, or European equipment containing US technology, for the development of Soviet gas projects.

Commercial exchange between the Soviet Union and Europe did not grant the Soviet Union diplomatic or political leverage over Western Europe. If any such dependence developed from the export of Soviet oil and gas to Western Europe, it was that these commercial ties granted Western European capital more leverage over the Soviet Union, since the fixing of huge investments in a pipeline network left the Soviet Union with little choice as to where to export its oil and gas (see Gustafson 1982). The export of Soviet oil and gas did not augment Soviet geopolitical power; on the contrary, it contributed, with the congealing rigidity of the command economy, in bringing about the demise of the Soviet economy and, with it, Soviet power altogether.

Oil in the command economy: the fall

Despite its inefficiency, the command economy transformed the Soviet Union in a little more than a decade from a backward, peripheral economy into an industrial power equal to the developed capitalist West. The early development of the Soviet economy depended on the "technical assistance" of Western, especially US, enterprises in sectors such as the steel industry, car (and tractor) production, electrification, and gold and coal mining (see Naleszkiewicz 1966). The export of oil helped the Soviet Union purchase Western technical "assistance," in addition to machines and tools. Whereas pre-Soviet Russian industrial production, including the oil industry, was dependent on foreign investment, Soviet industrialization was, from its beginning, dependent on the import of Western technologies and, therefore, on favorable terms of trade with the advanced industrialized economies of the West which the Soviet Union could only achieve by exporting oil, minerals, ores, and other industrial raw materials to those countries – trade relations characteristic of peripheral, semi-colonies (see Luke 1985). Dependence on the export of raw materials made the Soviet Union dependent on the expansion of its resource base, especially its oil and gas reserves, to meet (but sometimes exceed) the quantities determined by the Five-Year Plans. But increase in production was not always a result of increase in exports. Between 1933 and World War II, while oil production increased, exports continued to decline until the new discoveries of the 1950s. Oil exports, beginning in the 1950s, were forced by accumulating surpluses that could not be absorbed domestically, despite the increasing domestic demand for oil products. The situation changed again in the 1970s, however, when crises developing in the command economy began to slow it down, only to be compounded by a severe failure of global wheat harvests that forced the Soviet Union to turn to the world market for wheat.

The command economy embodied no built-in mechanisms, or reasons, for technological innovation and the elimination of waste. It was not determined by considerations of profitability, but by the quantity of the physical output. The inefficient and wasteful nature of the Soviet resource industry, as with the economy in general, was due to the immense task of managing the centrally planned economy. Some of the tasks were never completed and the Plans were continuously altered. Output targets often failed, while at other times, due to lack of coordination among the different segments of the economy, the achievements of one segment negated those of another. As with other sectors of the economy, the energy sector suffered from underinvestment in technological development while the objective remained to increase the physical output, a great part of which was intended for export. The abundance of resources concealed the deteriorating conditions and the wasteful nature of the industry – energy consumption *within* the energy sector accounted for one-third of total energy consumption. This was coupled with the tendency to start projects that often could not be completed.[10] With the drop of oil prices in the 1980s, exports had to increase in order to generate much-needed hard currency, making the systemic problems of the command economy more prominent. Attempts at reform had been made during the latter half of the 1960s, mainly to make the system more flexible by giving enterprises more freedom in making decisions about resource use and outputs. Yet, no significant departures from the structure of the command economy occurred (see R. Campbell 1968). However, it was clear that from then on there would be no return to the command economy. A process had begun in the late 1960s that was now difficult, if not impossible, to reverse. The planned economy that rapidly transformed the Soviet Union into a superpower, no matter how dependent on its hostile opponents, became, by the end of the 1960s, the very obstacle to economic development, incapable of coping with its own scale and complexity. With this economy the Soviet Union plunged deeper into an already troubled and unstable world market.

The irreversible demise of the Soviet Union began with the integration of the Soviet economy into the world market, marked by the Soviet–US wheat deal of 1972, which was only reinforced by the "positive" impacts of the oil crises of the 1970s. The increase in oil prices in the 1970s had two major effects on the economy of the Soviet Union and the Eastern bloc. As with other developing countries, loans with low interest rates were made available to socialist countries, especially Poland and Hungary, from the surplus of petrodollars accumulating in US and Western European banks, which mushroomed in the 1980s after interest rates soared, plunging borrowers into chronic foreign debt. The more immediate effect of the increase in oil prices on the economy of the Soviet Union, in particular, was the increase in hard currency earnings from oil and gas exports that enabled the Soviet Union to pay for its growing imports of technology from the West and to postpone the restructuring of its failing economy.[11]

The purchase of wheat on the world market plunged the Soviet Union into massive foreign debts whose interest payments alone absorbed much of its foreign earnings from the export of oil. Due largely to "emergency wheat buying," the trade deficit of the Soviet Union grew nine times (to $1.2 billion) between 1971 and 1972 over the previous year. Part of the deficit was covered by the sale of gold, but much of it was offset by the selling of Soviet oil and gas to the US in order to balance payments. Symbolically enough, US wheat destined for the Soviet Union was loaded in Texas directly onto oil tankers that would bring back Soviet oil to the US. The import of technology and food became deeply ingrained in Soviet economic policy by the late 1970s, the result of which was the entry of the Soviet Union into an almost permanent trade deficit with the West. By the early 1980s, with continued poor grain harvests and rising market prices of wheat, the Soviet Union increased its grain imports by around 35 percent from a year earlier at the same time that Western demand for Soviet oil decreased by around 20 percent. Between 1980 and 1981 (June), the Soviet Union's trade deficit with the West doubled to around $3.7 billion. The subsequent restrictions by the US on the export of technology to the Soviet Union did not prevent it from turning toward Western Europe and Japan, to which it primarily sold gas. Also, the US grain embargo – the so-called "Carter embargo" – in 1980, did not deter the Soviet Union from turning to other suppliers such as Argentina, Australia, and Canada (which resumed normal trade with the Soviet Union by late 1980, after it had initially supported the grain embargo).[12]

Gorbachev's perestroika continued the process that had begun in the late 1960s – a reform intended to take the Soviet economy away from the command economy and closer to market socialism. Gorbachev's restructuring, however, destroyed the command economy – centered on the military–industrial complex, with the state as a single client – without establishing any alternative economic organization in its place. Nevertheless, despite fiscal, economic, and political difficulties, companies from the US and Western Europe rushed to establish joint ventures with the Soviet government, especially in the oil and gas industry. The interest of Western companies only matched the eagerness of the Soviet Union to import foreign capital and technology to revitalize the oil and gas industry and increase exports, beginning with downstream operations and petrochemical production soon to be followed by agreements in the upstream sector. Unlike the ventures of the early 1970s, the production agreements of the mid-1980s, for the first time since the 1920s, allowed foreign companies access to reserves and ownership of stakes in the industry, giving them more direct control over the projects they invested in. The Soviet Ministry of Oil Refining and Petrochemical Industries signed its first joint venture with Combustion Engineering (from the US) in November 1987, which involved the modernization of oil and petrochemical facilities. Occidental Petroleum Corporation followed almost a week after, in a consortium with the Italian Montedison and the Japanese Marubeni Corporation, signing an agreement to build a petrochemical plant on the Caspian Sea to process gas and sulfur from the Tengiz field in Kazakhstan. Both Occidental and Combustion Engineering signed two more, separate agreements a year later to build petrochemical complexes in Western Siberia. A Japanese consortium composed of Mitsubishi, Mitsui, and Chiyoda, won an agreement in November 1988 for a feasibility study for another petrochemical complex, after vying for it with Occidental. By 1990, as the Soviet Union was nearing its final demise, production sharing agreements were signed at a frequency of almost one a month. The Soviet market was rapidly becoming part of the inter-capitalist competition developing in the global economy.

Although both production and exports continued to fall between the middle of the 1980s and the end of the decade, the Soviet Union remained the largest oil producer, with 12 million bbl/d, a sixth of world total production, around 10 percent of which went to Western Europe (1.3 million bbl/d) and another 10 percent to Eastern Europe. Before the sharp increase in oil prices in 1990, hard currency earning from oil had fallen from 80 percent to around 40 percent between 1984 and 1990. This prompted the Soviet Union to demand hard currency payment for its oil exports to Eastern Europe, at the world market price, and to divert some of its exports from Eastern to Western Europe. Most remarkably, decline in production and foreign earnings, coupled to a lack of technical and financial means to develop the industry, transformed the "cooperation" between the Soviet Union and Western oil companies from trade of oil surpluses for technologies and goods into direct investment in exploration and production. Foreign companies were now granted exploration and production contracts, and thus, direct access to reserves. The first such "classical" contract was granted by the Soviet Ministry of Oil to Elf Aquitaine in May 1990, giving the French firm access to about 35,000 square kilometers north of the Caspian Sea to explore for oil and gas in exchange for a percentage of the product if commercially viable quantities were found. Negotiations over a joint venture with Chevron, begun in March 1988, won the US company an agreement for exploration, production, and the development of the giant Tengiz oilfield in Kazakhstan. Texaco followed, with an agreement with the Soviet Ministry of Geology in August 1990 for a feasibility study of oil extraction south of the Barents Sea. In September 1990, Amoco Eurasia, a subsidiary of Amoco Corporation signed an accord with the Soviet Union to conduct a feasibility study in Western Siberia, and in June 1991 it won the rights to the Azeri oilfield, offshore from Azerbaijan, in competition with Unocal, British Petroleum, and Statoil.

Gorbachev's opening of the Soviet oil and gas sector to foreign capital investment seemed to realize two goals that transnational oil companies had striven for since Standard Oil speculated on purchasing the Nobel oil properties: the integration of Russian oil into the world economy through direct investment rather than commercial exchange and the collapse of the Bolshevik government. The collapse of the Soviet Union was final, but the integration of Russian oil, accompanied by attempts to open the Russian economy to foreign oil companies, would come across countertendencies of protectionism by the end of the 1990s, as we shall see in the next chapter, which would not halt the integration of Russia into the world economy but rather reproduce the geographical contradiction between integration and isolation in a deeper and more complex fashion.

Conclusion

By August 1991, there were around 3,000 foreign, joint ventures in various sectors of Soviet industries. The Soviet government had, by then, also accumulated a debt of around $52 billion to Western banks. The integration of the Soviet economy into the capitalist world economy as a quasi-dependency whose economic development depended on foreign technology, loans from foreign banks and the export of raw material, was accomplished with the imminent disintegration of the Soviet Union. The Soviet economy appeared to be finally open to the expansion of capital, confirmed by domestic enthusiasm for liberalization, privatization, and membership of the International Monetary Fund and, what was soon to become, the World Trade Organization. A vast, underdeveloped oil frontier seemed open to transnational oil corporations with plenty of cash from rising oil prices triggered by the Gulf War, but little reserves and upstream production open to foreign investment. However, the collapse of the Soviet Union and the opening of the Russian oil industry to foreign capital did not resolve the geographical contradictions that accompanied its development throughout the twentieth century, but rather deepened them as the nature of the contradictory integration of Soviet oil in the world economy transformed, beginning in the 1970s.

The "independent" development of the Soviet Union depended on the development of the oil industry for foreign export to pay for technologies imported from Western countries and consumer goods imported from Eastern European countries. The contradictory dependence on foreign trade arose out of the necessity to bring the technologies necessary for the development of Soviet industries, made possible by low domestic demand, given the relative underdevelopment of Soviet industrial production. By the middle of the century, however, and despite the tremendous industrialization of the Soviet economy and the expansion of transportation, both a source of increase in demand for oil, surpluses of oil continued to accumulate. Between 1955 and 1985, oil exports grew more than production and consumption. Oil exports were no longer determined by the necessity of importing foreign technologies, regardless of its persistence especially in the oil sector, but by the overaccumulation of surpluses that needed an outlet. The integration of Soviet oil in the world economy was now determined not by technological necessity as much as by the abundance of oil. The logic of the plan, which determined abstract quantities with no relation to domestic demand, resulted in chronic overproduction and this, in turn, was only exacerbated by Soviet extraction technology, which, because it left considerable quantities of oil in the ground, depended on the exploration and exploitation of new, more productive oilfields. Abundance, produced by overaccumulation, led to discoveries and more abundant reserves which, in turn, led to new rounds of overaccumulation.

As with any oil producer suffering gluts in its stockpiles, the Soviet Union needed, and found, foreign markets for its (underpriced) oil. The decline in production and exports, coupled with decline in oil prices in the 1980s, forced a turn from trade of oil for foreign technologies to an opening for foreign investment by foreign companies and loans from foreign banks. Ironically, the transformation from integration through trade into integration through capital investment signaled a return to pre-Soviet, Tsarist Russia: dependence on the global economy shifted from dependence on revenues from foreign trade to dependence on foreign capital investment. By opening the upstream sector to foreign capital, the geographical contradiction of the Soviet oil industry moved deeper from the sphere of exchange to the sphere of production, becoming even more complicated by the development of private oil companies and banks in Russia to compete with foreign oil companies and foreign banks for access to Russian oil and gas reserves. The demise of the Soviet Union released intercapitalist competition not only for Russia, but within Russia, among the different factions of capital, including the state. As with Tsarist Russia, post-Soviet Russia is both subject and object in this competition – not only with foreign capital, but also with domestic capital. We develop this question in the next chapter.

5 Geographical contradictions of state and capital in the development of Russian oil

Competition for Russia, competition with Russia

Geopolitical competition for oil has its origin in competition among different factions of capital arising from the progressive accumulation of fixed capital in the oil industry. Competition for raw material develops first in manufacturing industry, causing capital to migrate to extractive industry to ensure the production of cheap raw material at volumes commensurate with the demand in manufacturing industry. Competition for raw material, however, migrated to the extractive sphere with the concentration of fixed capital in the production of raw material. The concentration of capital in extractive industry, historically the consequence of growing demand for raw material (in manufacturing), becomes its primary source. Resource extraction grows in order to valorize capital fixed in extractive industry itself, and the profitability of extractive industry becomes dependent on the quantitative expansion of existing or potential resources. Access to, and control of, available and potential oil reserves becomes necessary to valorize large and growing magnitudes of capital fixed in the production process, including transportation and downstream operations. Expanding natural resources can be achieved through actual geographical expansion to incorporate new reserves into production, or through the application of technologies that enhance the natural productivity of already existing resources. Both geographical expansion and technological development require additional investment in fixed capital and lead to overproduction and overaccumulation, thus threatening the profitability of capital invested in extraction. To expand resources without further investment and to control the production of resources and their availability on the market, capitalists in extractive industry resort to expansion through centralization, i.e. through the merger and acquisition of capital already invested in the production of natural resources.

Resources that cannot be reproduced across space, such as oil, lend their territorial fixity and their ownership crucial importance in the expansion of capital into resource production. The quantitative and geographical expansion of capital into fixed resources comes up against the "external" barrier of landed property, which has the power to withhold from production land containing the non-reproducible resource. In the case of oil reserves which, with the few exceptions of places where the owner of surface land owns the resources beneath, are generally owned or administered by the state, extractive capital comes up against the barrier of the landlord state. The encounter produces a geographical space structured by a contradiction between integration and fragmentation. On one side, states must make resources scarce by withholding them from production, in order to maintain high prices on the market. Yet, the landlord state must allow the extension of extractive capital into hydrocarbon resources to valorize them and produce rent in the form of royalty, tax, share in the profit, etc. The landlord state, as landed capital, must regulate the access of extractive capital to oil resources to negotiate the contradiction between producing scarcity and reaping rent. On the other side, (transnational) oil corporations must overcome political–legal barriers erected by the landlord state in order to gain access to more reserves, but must also uphold the same barriers to protect their monopolistic position against competing capitals. The centralization of capital, the fusion of different factions of capital at national and international scales, becomes the primary mechanism by which the geographical contradiction is negotiated.

The centralization of capital is a process of "primitive accumulation" by which one capital dispossesses another and by which the accumulation of greater capital is accomplished by the combination and elimination of smaller individual capitals. The accumulation and expansion of capital by centralization does not depend on growth in the size of total social capital, but rather on its redistribution between fewer capitalists by the destruction of the individual independence of many smaller capitals and their amalgamation into fewer and larger capitals. The centralization of capital, therefore, accelerates the accumulation process and allows the expansion of capital at a rate and scale higher than its simple concentration. Most importantly, centralization – the amalgamation of different enterprises into one corporation (merger) or the bringing together of different enterprises under the control of one enterprise (acquisition) – allows capitalists to restore profitability without further development of labor productivity and investment in new productive capital, and by reducing production costs through the elimination of "redundant" labor and means of production. It allows fewer corporations to control production and prevent overaccumulation. In extractive industry, particularly in the case of non-reproducible resources such as oil, the centralization of capital has the additional advantage of placing a greater mass of available resources under the control of fewer producers without the necessary development of available resources or the discovery of new ones, while, at the same time, denying access to resources to competitors that may flood the market and push prices and profits down.

Most of the actual growth in the absolute size of oil reserves and volumes of production in recent years has been the result of the application of oil enhancement recovery methods to aging and depleted oilfields to enhance their productivity, rather than the addition of new ones. This has been especially the case in Russia since the late 1990s. Growth in oil production, in the absence of major new discoveries, was largely the result of the entry of foreign oilfield services companies, such as Baker Hamilton, Halliburton, and Schlumberger, in joint ventures with Russian oil companies and the subsequent development of domestic services companies such as PetroAlliance and Integra.[1] The growth of reserves through technological development, however, involves further concentration of fixed capital, making growth through appropriation by mergers and acquisitions crucial to the expansion of the industry without additional investment in fixed capital. Mergers and acquisitions expand reserves under the control of fewer corporations without further investment in exploration or in developing productivity. The "merger madness" that hit the Russian oil industry in the 1990s, expanded the reserves under the control of a few large corporations at a time when Russian oil production was in decline and the Russian oil industry on the verge of collapse. By 2001, the four biggest Russian oil companies controlled 51 percent of Russia's reserves.[2] By 2006, after several rounds of mergers and acquisitions, the four biggest Russian oil and gas companies controlled 82.6 percent of Russia's oil reserves (see Table 5.1). By acquiring Yukos's upstream operations, Rosneft's reserves grew by around six billion barrels of oil-equivalent almost instantaneously, while Gazprom's acquisition of Sibneft automatically increased its reserves by around 4.8 billion barrels. In short, growth by centralization is "bought rather than drilled," i.e. reserves expand and enter the production process by changing ownership, not size or place.

Geographical expansion for the capture of more resources brings capital up against the barrier of state ownership or administration of resources. In the process, however, as we shall see below, the extension of extractive capital into natural resources brings the state into the process of accumulation as another faction of capital in the competition for the control of oil reserves and absorbs the state in the formation of large monopolies comprising industrial and financial capital. This is not a process free of contradictions as the power of the landlord state, deriving from its legal entitlement to the resources within its territory, comes into conflict with its dependence on capital for the economic valorization of resources. Hence, although the politico–legal power of the landlord state depends on the fragmentation of space for the exercise of exclusive territorial control over resources, the economic valorization of the state's legal entitlement is dependent on the opposite – the extension of productive capital into resources and the integration of territory into capital. Both productive capital and the land-

Table 5.1 Monopoly of the four largest corporations over reserves in Russia

	Percent of Russian total,* based on EIA estimate of 60,000 million barrels
LUKoil (2004)	25.8
Rosneft (2005)	24.8
Gazprom (2006)	17.0
TNK-BP (2006)	15.0
Total	82.6

Source: *Companies' websites; US Department of Energy, Energy Information Administration, Office of Energy Markets and End Use.

lord state resort to financial capital to resolve this contradiction, only to internalize the contradiction between financial capital and productive capital in the process. Foreign and Russian banks were instrumental in financing the consolidation of the Russian oil industry throughout the privatization mania of the 1990s. Access to global financial markets made the expansion of production in the Russian oil industry less dependent on Western oil companies and allowed Russian oil companies to compete with, and fend off, takeovers by better-capitalized foreign majors. Investors' capital flowed out of Russia during the crisis of 1998, but returned with the political stability under Putin and high oil prices in the world market. This time, however, foreign financial capital returned to consolidate the Russian oil industry under the control of the state in what appears, on the surface, as a process of reverse privatization – but only on the surface. What in effect took place, is a process of amalgamation of the Russian state, domestic (productive) capital and foreign (financial) capital into hybrid corporations, partly state-owned, partly foreign-owned. Foreign investors entered the Russian oil industry through the state to help it close space further against transnational oil companies and protect the industry from the predation of the domestic oligarchs. In other words, global financial capital became integral to the ongoing competition between the Russian landlord state, Russian financial capital, and Russian and foreign oil companies. The fusion of landed property, the state, financial and productive capital internalized rather than transcended the geographical contradictions of competition among different factions of capital for the control of oil reserves.

The following examines the contradictions of competition for Russian oil in two interrelated parts: the struggle between the state and domestic oil companies through the process of consolidating the Russian oil industry after the collapse of the Soviet Union, and the contradictory process of integrating the Russian oil industry into the global economy while, at the same time, protecting it against foreign capital. Both processes have culminated in the hybrid organizational structure embodied in the partly national oil company, which internalizes the contradiction between integration and fragmentation in the fusion of the Russian state with foreign banks and domestic and foreign oil companies.

Centralization and nationalization of Russian oil capital

During the 1980s, the Soviet Union produced around 11 million barrels of oil per day (bbl/d), as much as Saudi Arabia, due primarily to the discovery and exploitation of new petroleum reserves, mostly concentrated in Western Siberia. Russian oil production, however, fell sharply after the demise of the Soviet Union. The plunge of the Soviet economy into a state of organizational anarchy after Gorbachev dismantled its centralized command structure exacerbated further the decline in oil production. From the 11 million barrels per day of the Soviet era, Russian oil production fell to 7.6 million bbl/d in 1992 and continued its plunge to 5.9 million bbl/d in 1996. Russian oil production, however, started increasing again in 1998, and especially with the recovery of world oil prices after 1999, due to higher levels of investment and technological development coupled with the consolidation of the industry in a few vertically integrated giants. By 2000, oil production rose to about seven million bbl/d, reaching 8.8 million bbl/d in 2004 and 9.7 in 2006 (see Figure 5.1). Crude oil exports increased to around 4.2 million bbl/d in 2000, after they had dropped to about three million bbl/d by 1992, and continued to climb to reach 6.6 million bbl/d in 2006.

The Russian economy is doubly dependent on the development of the oil and gas industry: for the generation of foreign revenue (around 65 percent of total revenue in 2006), and the capture of domestic and foreign capital (mineral extraction accounted for about 19 percent of total investment in 2006 and 43 percent of foreign investment). Not surprisingly, therefore, the Russian government has been keen on increasing the productive capacity of the oil and gas industry by attracting foreign investment and technology, but also, because of its dependence on oil revenues and vulnerability to fluctuation in oil prices, on consolidating its control over the oil and gas industry to protect it from foreign capital. Russia's control of the domestic oil and gas industry, however, is, paradoxically, dependent on foreign capital to finance mergers and acquisitions by state-controlled companies. In other words, both the development of an oil and gas industry independent and protected from control by transnational oil majors depends on its opposite: the integration of Russian oil into the circuits of global

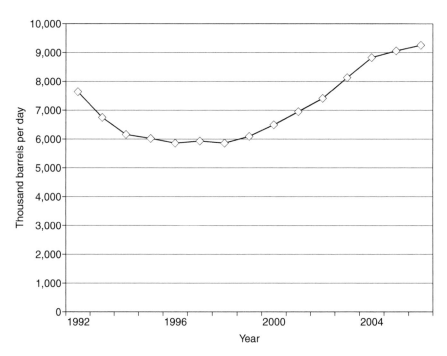

Figure 5.1 Crude oil production in Russia, 1992–2006 (source: US Department of Energy, Energy Information Administration, Office of Energy Markets and End Use).

capital. The latter has proceeded along several lines that we examine below, namely through Production Sharing Agreements, mergers and acquisitions, and, increasingly, through the listing of Russian oil companies on the London Stock Exchange. First, we examine the process of centralization of the oil industry through the two-part process of privatization and "re-nationalization" since the collapse of the Soviet Union.

Amidst the political and economic pandemonium that followed the collapse of the Soviet Union, an orgy of aggressive primitive accumulation transformed the Russian oil industry from an amalgam of fragmented little enterprises to a sector dominated by a handful of large, vertically integrated oil conglomerates. Under Yeltsin, state-owned oil and gas enterprises were sold at bargain prices to the financial oligarchs who were quick to consolidate their control over the industry by centralizing it in a few large corporations. Initially, the industry was structured around 12 vertically integrated companies in which the government retained a controlling interest of 51 percent and in which foreign ownership was limited to 15 percent. Through a controversial "loans-for-shares" scheme, the government offered its shares in the oil companies as collateral to loans it borrowed from the newly privatized banks, then relinquished them to the banks when it defaulted on the loans (Obut *et al.* 1999a; see also Khartukov and Starostina 2000; Khartukov 2002).[3] A few Financial Industrial Groups, controlled by the legendary oligarchs, emerged from the botched loans-for-shares scheme with significant control over the domestic oil industry and promptly embarked on an acquisition spree financed by loans from Russian and foreign banks (Goldman Sachs, Credit Lyonnais, ING Barings, Credit Suisse, First Boston, and Merrill Lynch). Access to global financial markets allowed Russian companies the additional advantage of keeping foreign oil companies out of the industry. The Russian government, as we shall see below, would resort to the same strategy to continue the process of centralization under its control.

Political and economic uncertainty did not deter foreign investment banks such as Goldman Sachs, Merrill Lynch, and Morgan Stanley from taking advantage of the rise in demand for their services and they flocked to Russia to capture the benefits of an impending surge in mergers. The rouble crisis of 1998, however, bankrupted domestic banks and sent foreign investors away, while the decline in world oil prices halted investments by foreign oil companies. Domestic oil companies earning revenues in hard currency benefited temporarily from the devaluation of the rouble, which reduced their production costs and tax debts, until inflation eroded those benefits. Russia was deprived of capital and the attempted sale by the government of more shares in oil companies was only prevented by low oil prices in the oil market. It did not help that the oligarchs divested some of their oil holdings and sent their capital abroad, such that Russia experienced net capital outflows of an estimated $100 billion throughout the 1990s. Windfall profits falling to the oligarchs with the recovery of oil prices in 2000 did not find their way to the domestic industry and were expatriated to avoid high taxes. Thus, Russia was still hemorrhaging capital to offshore banks despite the return of foreign investment: by the beginning of 2004, $9 billion left the country against the $8 billion coming in from abroad. Russia was, therefore, caught in a double bind: it was still dependent on foreign capital for the development of an industry with declining production from dilapidated wells and lagging production technologies, inefficient refineries, export bottlenecks, an aging transport system, etc., whereas its extensively privatized oil companies were becoming vulnerable to the predation of foreign capital as the oligarchs proved they were more willing to sell their assets rather than invest in the domestic industry. Measures had to be taken to reverse this quasi-colonial dependence and protect the economic sovereignty of the country, and this, in turn, depended on reining in the oligarchs.

The "Yukos drama" must be understood in this context. The expropriation of Yukos was practically a pre-emptive intervention by the Russian government to prevent the potential expansion of foreign capital into the Russian oil industry.[4] After a failed attempt in 1998, Yukos and Sibneft planned a merger in the summer of 2003 that would have made the resulting company the largest in Russia. ExxonMobil and ChevronTexaco expressed interest in buying into YukosSibneft in the event of a merger – ExxonMobil offered $25 billion for a 40 percent stake in YukosSibneft – but the arrest of Mikhail Khodorkovsky, CEO of Yukos, halted the merger process and blocked the plans of ExxonMobil and ChevronTexaco to buy into what would have become the largest oil company in the world. The deal would have centralized, in the hands of Exxon-Mobil or ChevronTexaco or both, control over nearly 20 percent of Russia's oil industry. In 2004, Yukos and Sibneft signed a "protocol for demerging." By December 2003, however, despite the confiscation of part of Yukos's assets by the government, ExxonMobil, ChevronTexaco, and Royal Dutch Shell were still interested in acquiring Yukos. Total, on the other hand, offered to acquire Sibneft for $12 billion.

To complete the "Yukos drama," and to strengthen its hold on the oil and gas industry, the Russian government auctioned Yuganskneftegas, the core production unit of Yukos, in Moscow on 19 December 2004. An obscure Baikal Finans Group bought Yuganskneftegas for $9.37 billion (well below the unit's estimated market value of $14 to $22 billion) and four days later sold it to the state-owned Rosneft, with partial financial support of a $6 billion loan from the Chinese National Petroleum Corporation which was to be repaid in oil deliveries. By acquiring Yuganskneftegas, Rosneft acquired control over an additional 11 percent of Russia's total oil production and tripled its output almost overnight. Rosneft, moreover, had outstanding claims against Yukos, which would lead to a further acquisition of Yukos's upstream and downstream assets, again financed by foreign credit (see below). More recently, Rosneft and Gazprom acquired more of Yukos's assets, while an obscure Russian company, Prana, ended the string of sales of Yukos's assets on 11 May by buying the company's headquarters.

The drive to the centralization of the oil industry under state control seemed to reach its apogee in the approval by the government, in March 2005, of a merger between Gazprom and Rosneft. The merger would have transferred the government's 100 percent stake in Rosneft to Gazprom, thus giving the government a majority stake in Gazprom and creating a larger state-controlled company. But the Russian government canceled the merger two months later. Instead, the government opted to increase its control over Gazprom (from 38 percent to a majority share of 51 percent) through the acquisition of stock with credit of $7.5 billion from foreign banks. Gazprom, in turn, prepared to takeover Sibneft for $13 billion, with a foreign loan of $12 billion.

The so-called nationalization of the Russian oil industry under Putin slowed down the privatization process and altered its characteristics rather than reversing it. Nationalization of the oil industry did not in any way lead to its socialization, but moved it towards a form of managed capitalism in which the state became a major partner in this strategic sector of the economy. Thus, what Putin effectively managed to do is to keep the oligarchs in line rather than eliminate them altogether (Lavelle 2004; see also Anderson 2007). In a way, therefore, the Russian government seems to be completing the nationalization process that began in the 1970s, which concentrated the oil industry in a few state-owned national companies (this is also taking place in several countries in Latin America, such as Bolivia and Venezuela). But the Russian government does not seem to be planning for complete nationalization of the energy economy. Instead of erecting one state-owned company (as in the case of OPEC), and without entirely preventing foreign ownership, it has structured the industry around a mixture of private companies, state-owned companies, and partially state-owned companies, or "entrepreneurial" national oil companies (see Collins 2006; Vikas and Ellsworth 2007a). Expanding the government's control of the oil and gas industry would allow it to align investment and export strategies with the state's domestic and foreign policies – the latter is especially crucial if Russia is to compete in the global geopolitical economy with world producers such as Saudi Arabia. However, it would also allow the government to attract foreign investment without relinquishing control over the industry. Rather than the negation of private property, the partial nationalization of the oil industry reasserts it at the level of state, which offers partially or fully state-owned companies as "reliable" partners with foreign companies. The effect on foreign oil companies is that they enter such partnerships as contractors, their role reduced to that of an energy service company with no equity stakes in reserves. (Gazprom, for example, partnered Statoil as a contractor in the Arctic offshore Shtokman fields, while Shell was reduced to a mere operator in Sakhalin after being pressured to sell its controlling stake to Gazprom.) The so-called entrepreneurial national oil company, on the other hand, retains its stock of reserves while enhancing its technological and financial competitiveness, and thus enters the global market on a highly competitive basis compared with both national oil companies (with vast reserves but little capital) and private transnational oil corporations (highly capitalized but lacking reserves). While the partially state-owned company reduces the need for reserve-hungry, yet well-capitalized foreign transnational oil companies, however, and allows the state access to foreign capital without relinquishing control over the industry, its creation, through the acquisition of smaller private companies, has come to depend on the access of the state to foreign financial capital.

Inter-capitalist competition and international centralization of Russian oil

Russia remains one of the world's most attractive oil frontiers, despite politico–legal and economic barriers. Western capital, financial and industrial, which fled after the crises of 1998, is now eagerly returning, drawn by huge undeveloped oil and gas fields and profitable investment opportunities. Foreign banks, in particular, are targeting the lucrative oil and gas industry and most capital flowing East towards Russia is to finance mergers and acquisitions. The Russian government's strategy to raise foreign capital has proceeded in a contradictory manner, at once opening and limiting the scope for foreign capital to invest in the Russian oil industry. Indeed, the opening for financial capital (foreign banks) can be seen as a strategy by the landlord state to guard against productive capital (foreign oil majors) – a move from foreign direct investment by oil companies to indirect foreign investment, a synthesis of money and landed/resource capital, mediated by the state.

The attempt to "liberalize" the Russian economy and to encourage foreign investment in the energy industry dates to the middle 1990s, when the Federal Law on Production Sharing Agreements was passed by the Duma and signed by Yeltsin in December 1995 as an alternative investment mechanism to the existing licensing regime. Under the old licensing regime, Joint Ventures were formed between foreign and Russian companies, which were then granted a license by the state to develop oilfields regulated by the Federal Law of the Subsoil of 1992 – the same law that set the privatization of the oil industry in motion. Under this general subsoil regime, the relationship between the Joint Venture and the state was administrative rather than contractual: the license holder enjoyed the right to use the subsoil under conditions set by the state, which also determined and enforced the obligations under the Joint Venture and could revoke, at will, the license or transfer it to another entity. Rent was paid through a combination of federal taxes including value-added, export, and profit taxes, in addition to local and regional taxes that varied from one locale to another. Production Sharing Agreements, in contrast, were contractual and provided an "enclave of stability" in the relationship between companies and the government. Resources extracted during the operation of a Production Sharing Agreement were to be divided according to conditions agreed upon previously on a case-by-case basis, and that remained unchanged for the duration of the Agreement. In this case, the terms of the contract determined the obligations of the parties involved: Russian companies, foreign companies, and the state. Most importantly, foreign companies and contractors were treated on an equal basis with domestic companies. Except for a profit tax and royalty payment (differential and absolute rent) for the use of the subsoil, whose rate is fixed for the duration of the project, rent is paid to the state as a share of the extracted product or its monetary equivalent, calculated after deducting non-recoverable costs. Otherwise, investors are exempt from all other taxes, such as corporate tax, excise tax, and customs duties.

Almost immediately, opposition to Production Sharing Agreements arose from domestic companies, well stocked with reserves and less dependent on such contracts. Production Sharing Agreements were seen to place too much control of hydrocarbon reserves under foreign companies, which were also granted the right to export 100 percent of their "profit hydrocarbons," and thus prone to developing the industry according to foreign rather than domestic needs. Since most of the oil would probably be exported, Production Sharing Agreements would further delay the development of downstream production and lock the country into a "raw materials dearth." Production Sharing Agreements, moreover, were seen by nationalist groups as nothing but a mechanism to "sell the motherland," threatening the economic sovereignty of the state by potentially opening the hydrocarbon industry to speculative investment, since there was no guarantee that they would only attract "reliable" capital. Opposition increased as Russian oil companies, awash with windfall profits after world oil prices started climbing again at the end of the 1990s, emerged as a competitive investor and lobbied, under the leadership of Yukos, against Production Sharing Agreements to protect their competitive position in the domestic industry. In June 2003, under pressure from Russian oil companies, the Russian government abandoned the Law of Lists that made foreign operations under Production Sharing Agreements possible. Russian legislators, moreover, embarked on formulating amendments to the Law of Underground Resources that would make it even more difficult for foreign oil companies to acquire oil and gas production licenses. Amendments to the law in 2005 placed oilfields and gas deposits, in addition to gold and copper deposits that the state considered to be of "vital strategic importance," beyond the reach of foreign companies.[5]

Foreign oil companies prefer Production Sharing Agreements to other forms of investment since they do not involve investment in assets other than extraction. More importantly, Production Sharing Agreements allow foreign companies independent access to oil and gas reserves. The renewed scramble for investment in the Russian oil industry, however, demonstrates that Production Sharing Agreements are not necessary to encourage foreign investment in the Russian oil and gas industry, and that their absence does not deter foreign companies from investing in exploration and production. Currently, there are only three consortia operating under Production Sharing Agreements: Sakhalin-1, Sakhalin-2, and Kharyaginskoye in the Timan-Pechora Basin, all of which were signed under a decree by Yeltsin in 1993, prior to the Law on Production Sharing Agreements.[6] But even those, justified by their technological complexity, are not immune to takeover by state-owned companies. Most recently, Gazprom bought majority shares from Royal Dutch Shell, Mitsui, and Mitsubishi, hence controlling Sakhalin-2 after the project was blocked by the government on account of violating environmental laws, which, conveniently enough, devalued the share acquired by Gazprom. Shell was kept in the project as "operator," i.e. reduced to service provider.

Foreign transnational companies, however, have found other avenues into Russian reserves, mainly by integrating into Russian capital through mergers and acquisitions. Companies from Western Europe, the US, Japan, and South Korea have invested in several Russian upstream and downstream companies. The largest investment ($6.75 billion) by a single foreign company was accomplished in the summer of 2003, when British Petroleum merged with Alpha Group and Access-Renova to create TNK-BP, which became, after the dissolution of Yukos, the second largest oil-producing company in Russia after LUKoil. British Petroleum had bought a 10 percent stake in Sidanko in 1997, but with the financial crisis in August 1998, Sidanko plunged into insolvency and at an auction that British Petroleum claimed was illegally handled, Tyumen Oil bought Sidanko's upstream assets.[7] In a "peace deal" in August 2001, British Petroleum increased its holdings in Sidanko to 25 percent, assumed management rights of the company, and began negotiations with Access-Renova about a possible merger, which was eventually realized in 2003. British Petroleum brought into the deal its holdings in Sidanko and Rusiya Petroleum, the Sakhalin-5 license and a network of retail gasoline stations in Moscow. The Russian partners contributed their holdings in Tyumen Oil (TNK) and Sidanko, their share of Rusiya Petroleum, their interests in Sakhalin-4 and Sakhalin-5, and their stake in the Rospan gasfield. British Petroleum paid $3 billion for its 50 percent stake in the emerging company, and would pay an annual $1.25 billion worth of its own shares. In addition, Access-Renova and British Petroleum received the European Union's approval, in December 2003, to incorporate Access-Renova's 50 percent interest in Slavneft into TNK-BP ($1.35 billion), thus bringing the investment to more than $8 billion.[8]

US companies have tried but have not, however, been able to secure direct investment in the Russian hydrocarbon industry, with the exception of the participation of ExxonMobil in Sakhalin-1. ConocoPhillips was the first company to invest in a Joint Venture with LUKoil in Russia in the early 1990s, however, and it was later able to accomplish two major direct investments in the Russian oil industry: in September 2004, ConocoPhillips paid $1.99 billion for the Russian government's share (7.59 percent) in LUKoil at a privatization auction and in November ConocoPhillips increased its share, which entitled the company to have an "independent director" on LUKoil's board. In December 2004, ConocoPhillips paid $370 million for a 30 percent stake in Naryanmarnefтеgaz, a subsidiary of LUKoil, thus giving ConocoPhillips joint control over the development of the northern Timan-Pechora, one of Russia's most productive oilfields (notwithstanding the removal of the fields from the list of Production Sharing Agreements). The oil produced is expected to be exported by 2008 through LUKoil's terminal at Varandey on the Barents Sea, which is to be expanded with the financial help of ConocoPhillips. Part of the oil will be transported to the US.

Foreign access to Russian oil has been accomplished by international centralization of capital, after the Russian government made foreign direct access to oil difficult by removing Production Sharing Agreements. But also the process of consolidating the state's control over reserves and production was accomplished by international centralization. The cost of mergers and acquisitions of Russian energy firms in 2003 and 2004 amounted to $20 billion, and is estimated to have risen to $24 billion over 2005, most of which was financed by debt. The government alone spent $30 billion in 2005 buying back oil and gas assets that were privatized only a decade earlier, increasing its control over oil production from 7 percent to around 25 percent. The availability of investment capital was, therefore, instrumental to the centralization of the Russian oil industry under the control of the state, which, accordingly, seems to have opened the space to foreign banks while it tightened it further to foreign oil companies seeking oil and gas reserves. Unlike oil companies, but the same as energy service companies, banks provide their services and reap profits without claims to reserves much coveted by oil companies. The most notable opening to foreign capital is the listing of Russian oil companies on foreign stock exchanges. LUKoil was the first Russian company to have shares listed in the US, on the New York Stock Exchange. But, London seems to have become the destination of current listings. Two independent producers, Novatek, the biggest independent gas producer, and Urals Energy (oil) listed initial public offerings in London in 2005, with Novatek raising $1 billion. Novatek's listing fended off a plan by Total in late 2004 to acquire a 25 percent "blocking minority stake" in the Russian independent estimated at $1 billion. Total's offer to acquire another independent, Sibneft, was also blocked by Gazprom's acquisition of it for around $13 billion financed by a loan of $12 billion from a consortium of Western banks (ABN Amro and Dresdner Kleinwort Wasserstein in the lead, with the participation of Citigroup, Morgan Stanley, Goldman Sachs, and Credit Suisse). Gazprom itself is likely to go on offer after it has been securely brought under the control of the state through the purchase by Rosneft of a share of Gazprom financed by loans from foreign banks. Rosneft, in turn, announced that it would offer as much as 25 percent on the London Stock Exchange in 2006 (enough not to cede state control of the company). The listing, expected to raise $18 billion, went on in July (2007) to the failed objections of Yukos, which claimed that the listing amounted to selling "stolen property." The offering of Rosneft stock was intended to pay the $7.5 billion that Rosneft used to increase the state's share in Gazprom. Rosneft's takeover of Yukos's Yuganskneftegaz, in December 2005, was itself financed by a $6 billion loan from China, and the recent acquisition by Rosneft of Yukos's downstream assets was financed by a $22 billion loan from a consortium of Western banks (ABN Amro, Barclay's, BNP Paribas, Caylon, Citigroup, Goldman Sachs, JPMorgan Chase, and Morgan Stanley).

Conclusion

Intensification of inter-capitalist competition for Russian oil has brought about the amalgamation of state, domestic, and foreign oil companies in hybrid oil companies that have internalized the contradictory interdependence of Russia on global capital for the development of the oil industry. On one hand, the consolidation of state control over large oil enterprises (Rosneft and Gazprom) allowed access by foreign capital to the Russian oil industry and the integration of the latter in the circuits of global capital without the threat of losing control of a strategic sector of the economy to foreign corporations. Yet, state control of the industry, on the other hand, has depended on opening it to foreign capital, primarily financial capital, to finance the merger and acquisition of key oil enterprises under the control of the state, away from the predatory threat of both domestic and transnational oil companies. The result (and the objective) is not the nationalization of the oil industry, as most analysts presume, but the creation of a state-managed oil economy that can negotiate the contradiction between opening the industry to, yet protecting it from, foreign capital – much needed to develop the productivity of the industry and to bring it under state control to make it competitive in the global geopolitical economy of oil. The contradiction is embodied in the hybrid Russian oil company, at once guarded against foreign capital but deeply integrated in it, partially nationalized against rival domestic predators yet competing in the domestic and world market the same as private transnational oil companies. Indeed, this is the strength of the hybrid national oil company: it is essentially structured by the contradictory imperialist policies of expansionism and protectionism, which allows Russia to enter the global economy as a major producer and exporter of crude oil to rival other producing and exporting countries and transnational oil companies alike.

6 Geographical contradictions of Iranian oil
Capital versus the law

Inter-capitalist competition for control of global oil has produced a geographical space structured by a contradiction between the integration of resource-rich territories into the circuits of global capital and their fragmentation through protectionist measures that regulate the extension of foreign capital into the oil industry. The case of Iran expresses this contradiction on two interrelated, yet opposed, levels. On one level, the contradiction is partly the result of the attempt by the US to exclude the Iranian hydrocarbon industry from the circuits of global capital since the Revolution of 1979, intensifying especially with the Iran and Libya Sanctions Act of 1996, coming up against the attempt by Western European countries, Japan, Russia, India, and China to integrate the Iranian economy, especially the oil and gas industry, through trade and direct investment. On another, the contradiction emanates from the attempt by Iran to attract foreign investment within limits on the ownership of, and access to, resources and, more importantly, on the duration and profitability of foreign investment – in summary, to combine the dependence on global capital with national economic independence and national sovereignty over natural resources. The development of Iran's oil and gas industry depends to a large extent on the inflow of foreign capital, financial and productive, for the development of existing oilfields and the exploration of new oil and gas fields to expand Iran's reserves, OPEC quota, exports, and foreign revenues. Iran thus faces the dilemma of how to regulate the influx of foreign capital without relinquishing control over the most strategic sector of its economy. On the part of the US, the problem is reversed: how to isolate Iranian oil from global capital without jeopardizing the ongoing process of global economic integration that depends on European, and, to a certain extent, Russian, Chinese, and Japanese compliance with the US (and vice versa).

In a reversal of traditional imperialist practice defined by the annexation of (economic) territory, US sanctions against Iran have produced what I shall call negative territoriality: that is, the control of (economic) territory by its removal from the circuits of all capital rather than its exclusive incorporation into one. Attempts by US capital to generalize sanctions against Iran at the level of the so-called "international community" have, since the Revolution, been repeatedly met with resistance by rivals from Western Europe and South and East Asia, however, resulting in the opening of the Iranian oil industry to the extension of non-US capital while perpetuating its exclusion from the circuits of US capital. Failed attempts by the US at the exercise of extraterritoriality – the globalization of US legislation – have mostly managed to transform the struggle between the US and Iran into a struggle within the group of most advanced industrial economies, namely the US, Britain, France, Germany, Japan, China, India, and Russia. Iran has contributed to intensifying the struggle by opening its economy further to encourage foreign investment against US sanctions, often inviting US companies to participate in large hydrocarbon projects, only to encounter a persistent obstacle in the limits of Iranian legal and contractual forms, expressed in the buy-back contracts, on the profitability of foreign capital invested in Iranian natural resources. It is often assumed that the shift East in the source of foreign investment flowing to Iran, namely the entry of more Chinese companies into Iran's oil and gas industry, is due to less rigorous demands on profitability by Chinese (or Indian) companies compared to European companies. Ongoing negotiations between Chinese companies, Sinopec and the China National Offshore Oil Corporation with the National Iranian Oil Company (NIOC) have been stalled, however, by demands for higher rates of return by the Chinese companies and by NIOC's inclusion of purchases of large quantities of gas in the contracts. Chinese state companies' refusal of such terms, despite China's massive and growing need for oil and gas, opens a window on the nature of global competition for oil.

International competition for Iranian oil, as is the case of oil in general, is primarily competition among transnational oil companies, national oil companies, and resource-owning states for the control of oil production rather than simply for the product itself. Certainly, oil and, increasingly, gas fuel the global economy, and economic growth results in stronger demand for oil and gas especially to produce energy in various forms, in addition to other industrial raw materials such as minerals and metals. But the supply of oil to industrial and individual consumers, as with other raw material, is mediated by the extractive industry. The competition for oil is primarily competition in the extractive industry for the control of the resource and its production as raw material, for the ultimate goal of producing and realizing high rates of profit resulting from the development of the extractive industry itself, irrespective of demand from other sectors of the economy or demands from individual consumers. Contrary to common belief, oil is an abundant resource and is cheap to produce and unless mechanisms are put in place to control its production, the high concentration of capital in the production of oil leads inevitably to overproduction and decline in profitability.[1] The progressive growth of fixed capital in the oil industry, in absolute terms and in relation to requisite labor, requires larger amounts of oil to valorize it, which yields periodical oversupply in the market, bringing prices down. Oil has low "demand elasticity" (the relation of percentage change in quantity to the relation of percentage change in price) because it cannot be readily substituted with other fuels. A small variation in supply translates into high fluctuation in market price. The US, for example, has a short-term price elasticity of demand for crude oil of –0.0495,[2] which means that a 1 percent increase in price slows down demand by approximately 0.05 percent. But this also means that a 1 percent increase in supply depresses prices by 20 percent and vice versa. Thus, producers have to keep a curb on production to maintain high profit margins, and this requires direct control of the resource and protection against competitors that might enter the market with lower profit margins.

Resource-owning states, moreover, also have to face the prospect of under-supply. Keeping production low leads to an increase in market price and eventually slows down demand and revenues. More critically, high market prices allow the entry of less productive fields and fields in high-cost regions into profitable production, thus effecting a migration of capital into new geographical regions and other energy sectors, creating new competition and potential oversupply in the market. Hence the contradiction for oil producers: making oil artificially scarce results in making it undesirably abundant. The flow of capital into the oil industry must, therefore, be regulated such that not too much nor too little capital is invested in the production of the resource. High investment results in the building up of stocks, a decline in prices, and the devaluation of capital already fixed in production. Little capital investment protects monopoly profits, for capital already invested (and rent-collecting states), but makes less productive fields more profitable leading, eventually, to oversupply, decline in profits and the erosion of monopolies. Thus, the competition among oil companies and resource-owning states for oil resources is fundamentally competition to control investment in its production. This is achieved through negotiating the contradictory process of spatial integration and fragmentation to allow the expansion of capital and its control over oil reserves and production while simultaneously preventing competitors from access to reserves and production.

In summary, to regulate the amount of oil in the market and protect monopoly profits, producers must regulate the capital invested in the production of oil. Some productive oilfields must be kept out of production, inaccessible to capital, if already producing fields are to remain highly profitable. On this analysis, US sanctions against Iran constitute precisely such a mechanism, one which removes a significant part of Iranian oil from the world market by curbing foreign investment in the development of Iran's oil industry in order to maintain the profitability of producers elsewhere, with the added benefit, of course, of weakening the Iranian economy.[3] Iran holds 10 percent of world proven reserves (around 137.5 billion barrels, and potentially more),[4] but it accounts for only 5 percent of world production of crude oil (around four million barrels/day [bbl/d]). Iran produced around six million bbl/d on the eve of the Revolution, and although production plunged to a little more than one million bbl/d in the early 1980s, it has climbed since 1989 to around 4.03 million bbl/d in 2006, reaching 4.14 million bbl/d in 2005 (see Figure 6.1). Iran plans to increase production to around five million bbl/d by 2010, and eight million bbl/d by 2015, which requires significant foreign investment in enhancing oil recovery of existing fields and in exploration for new ones. US sanctions on Iran have so far failed to prevent non-US oil companies from investing in the Iranian hydrocarbon industry, although it has considerably

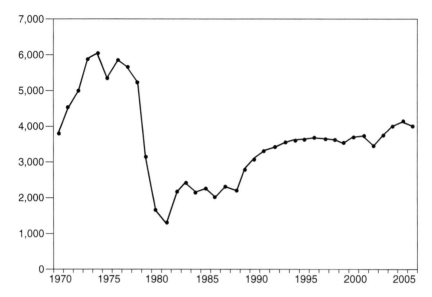

Figure 6.1 Crude oil production in Iran 1970–2006 (million barrels per day) (source: US
     Department of Energy. Energy Information Administration. Office of Energy
     Markets and End Use).

slowed it down, delaying further the integration of Iranian oil into the global
economy. Iranian laws of investment have also placed an obstacle to the full
integration of Iranian oil and gas in global capital. But both have succeeded little
in completely isolating Iran from the global economy, and have contributed to
the production of the contradictory geographical space that mediates the global
competition for oil.

In the following, we examine in two parts the contradiction of geographical
integration and fragmentation in the global competition for Iranian oil. The first
part examines the dual nature of US sanctions, as an expression of the contradiction between the struggle with Iran and struggle for Iran: an attempt to isolate
Iran – to keep foreign capital out of Iran – that is hindered by economic interdependence and competition in the global economy. The second part examines the
production of the geographical contradiction in the attempt by the Iranian
government to attract foreign capital into Iran's oil and gas industry, yet secure
the Iranian oil and gas industry from the control by foreign capital as it is
expressed in legislative and contractual forms that negotiate the tension between
Iran's dependence on foreign capital and desire for economic independence. We
focus especially on the development of the buy-back contract, a type of risk
service agreement that the Iranian government designed to allow yet regulate
foreign investment within the confines of the constitution.

US sanctions: the struggle with Iran, the struggle for Iran

US sanctions targeting Iran's oil industry evolved during the middle 1990s, in a period of intense competition between OPEC (Organization of Petroleum Exporting Countries) and non-OPEC producers which found major oil-producing countries struggling to maintain high prices against slowing demand in glutted oil markets. Members of OPEC struggled among themselves and with non-OPEC oil producers, especially Norway (which climbed to the position of second largest oil producer after Saudi Arabia), Russia, and Mexico, to find ways to cut production in order to salvage depressed market prices. But none wanted to relinquish their market shares to the others – in OPEC, some members struggled to raise their allocated quotas, often exaggerating the size of their reserves, while others ignored their quotas and produced more than their allotted share. With the exception of Mexico, non-OPEC members responded to OPEC's appeal to cut production either by ignoring it or by increasing production, as in the case of Russia. Too much oil on the market, however, threatened the profitability of the oil industry as a whole. To make things worse, oil started flowing out of Iraq, under the control of the United Nations, at a modest rate of 700,000 bbl/d, which, however, accounted for around 1 percent of world oil consumption. The upstream oil frontier in low-cost regions in the Middle East remained closed to major transnational oil companies, making it difficult to replace or increase their reserves and to find outlets for overaccumulated money capital in new production. Oversupplied markets, coupled with declining prices through the second half of the 1990s, lent greater significance to the Middle East, making it at once more attractive to oil companies looking for reserves and seeking to regain high profit margins by tapping into productive low-cost oilfields and more threatening to oil companies producing in high-cost regions such as Russia, North America, and the North Sea. Unless demand increased above the capacity of existing production, or production grew at a slower rate than sluggish demand, producers in the North Sea and the Gulf of Mexico faced potential decline in their profit margins, which would have made further investment unprofitable and taken them out of the market. Opening the upstream sector in the countries of the Middle East, amidst continuing decline in market prices and slowing demand, would have only made matters worse.

Beyond Iran: "threats to US national security"

In March 1995, after several years of negotiations, a Dutch affiliate of the US oil major Conoco won a contract from NIOC to develop two offshore oilfields in the Persian Gulf, Sirri A and Sirri E, discovered in 1972 and 1976, respectively.[5] US laws, since 1979, prohibited imports from Iran and restricted US exports to items related to humanitarian aid, but allowed US companies to do business with Iran through independent affiliates, as long as they sold their products in non-US markets. Throughout 1994, US oil companies had, in fact, bought around 600,000 bbl/d of Iranian oil, at about $4 billion per year, through their subsidiaries to sell in European markets. The $1 billion contract between Conoco Iran and NIOC, brought to the attention of then US President, Bill Clinton, in a letter from the American Israel Public Affairs Committee (AIPAC), did not seem to violate US laws, but was deemed "inconsistent" with US foreign policy of isolating and containing Iran for its alleged support of terrorist groups and disruption of the Middle East peace process. Deals such as Conoco's seemed to directly finance the Iranian regime and, with US companies trading in Iranian oil, which made them Iran's largest trading partner, weakened the State Department's leverage on its allies in Europe and Japan to cut their trade with, and withhold credit to, Iran. Clinton blocked Conoco's deal through Executive Order no. 12957, signed 15 March, preventing US oil companies from investing in Iranian oil. In the meantime, Senator Alfonse D'Amato, enlisted by AIPAC since 1993 to seek comprehensive sanctions against Iran, embarked on designing a bill that would result in the Iran Libya Sanctions Act of 1996.

Energy economists and oil executives in the US promptly concluded that such unilateral measures placed US oil companies at a competitive disadvantage to their European (and, later Asian) counterparts that, as in Iraq and Libya, would be quick to fill the gap left by US companies blocked from investing in what seemed a growing list of countries. There was nothing to prevent non-US companies from investing in Iran (or Libya, Nigeria, and Cuba) and from buying Iranian oil and gas. Indeed, the loss of the Conoco deal turned NIOC almost immediately to Royal Dutch Shell to take the Sirri project, although NIOC ultimately settled on Total. Iran would proceed henceforth to lure one foreign oil company after another by offering lucrative projects in its largely underdeveloped hydrocarbon industry. Only multilateral sanctions appeared to effectively punish Iran by preventing US and non-US oil companies alike from investing in Iran's oil and gas industry without disadvantaging US companies. D'Amato thus started lobbying for legislation that prohibited US companies and their foreign subsidiaries from buying Iranian oil and investing in Iran's oil industry, and which would also prevent non-US companies conducting business with Iran access to US markets and financial services: "a foreign corporation or person will have to choose between trade with the United States or trade with Iran," declared the Senator from New York.[6] The Clinton administration saw in D'Amato's bill an invitation to diplomatic disputes and perhaps litigation, and sought a compromise that would not distance or anger European allies. The Defense and Commerce Departments proposed sanctions that exclusively targeted exports to Iran with potential military use, arguing that unilateral oil sanctions would hurt the US more than Iran. The State Department, however, pressed for a total ban on US oil trade with Iran, including oil purchases and sale of oilfield equipment, in its effort to rally European allies around a comprehensive embargo on Iran. Japan, more vulnerable to US pressure than Germany, Italy, or France, froze a $1.4 billion loan to Iran to build a hydroelectric dam on the River Karun, but the European countries alleviated the financial squeeze by rescheduling, yet again, Iran's $12 billion trade debt.

The State Department also worked on persuading Russia and China not to sell nuclear technology to Iran, with even less successful results. Russia and Iran had signed an agreement in January 1995 to finish building the light-water nuclear reactor at Bushehr, started by the German Siemens Kraftwerke Union in the early 1970s but interrupted by the Revolution of 1979. As is the case today, US and Israeli intelligence considered Iran to be within five years of manufacturing a nuclear weapon, and the US tried to block the deal only to be rebuffed by the Russians on the grounds that the deal did not violate international laws and that it was indeed very similar to a planned sale by the US of a light-water nuclear reactor to North Korea – the US, according to the Russians, was placing non-competitive sanctions on the Russian nuclear industry, one of Russia's remaining competitive industries in the world market. China, equally, rejected an appeal by then Secretary of State, Warren Christopher, to cancel sales of nuclear reactors to Iran, but eventually came round and suspended them in September. Several Chinese and Russian companies, however, would continue to sell to Iran dual-use technologies, which would later bring US sanctions against them – but not against companies making investment in Iran's oil and gas industry.

Clinton signed another executive order (no. 12959) at the beginning of May barring US companies, their overseas branches, and in some cases their foreign subsidiaries, from the purchase of all Iranian exports, blocking all US exports to Iran (excluding material related to humanitarian aid), and prohibiting US investment in Iran. US companies were still allowed to purchase Iranian oil through foreign subsidiaries that operated independently of their US parent companies.[7] The immediate effect of Clinton's order was a surplus of 200,000 bbl/d of Iranian oil that Iran could not sell and had to store in leased tankers and storage facilities abroad, thereby not only depriving Iran of some of its foreign income but also incurring storage expenses. Investment in Iran's oil and gas industry also became more costly as the ban on US exports of oilfield equipment deprived Iran's oil industry, which consisted mostly of US-made equipment, of crucial replacement parts. Yet, the embargo failed to raise oil prices, as the experts predicted and feared, and oil prices continued to collapse until the end of the decade.

Only Israel welcomed Clinton's embargo on Iran. European and East Asian allies refused to join, arguing that the embargo went against the spirit of the fledgling World Trade Organization (WTO). Companies from countries opposed to US sanctions would eventually make substantial investments in Iran's manufacturing and transportation sectors, in addition to larger investments in the hydrocarbon industry, underscoring not only their defiance to US extraterritoriality but also a shift of foreign interest and relations with Iran from trade to direct investment ... a shift that would gradually be accompanied by a geographical shift towards the East, with oil companies from Russia, India, China, and, to a lesser extent, Japan, gaining more foothold in Iran's oil industry. Iran, in the meantime, embarked on actively engaging foreign companies in the development of its energy sector. On the trail of Clinton's embargo, Iran invited 100 companies to Tehran to consider investing in major oil and gas projects. At a time when the oil frontier in the Middle East remained closed to foreign investment in upstream production, the opening of Iran provided a rare crevice into one of the lowest-cost oil regions in the world ... an opportunity that oil companies looking to expand their reserves and prop up their profits were not going to ignore.

By the end of 1995, the Senate Banking Committee, headed by D'Amato, secured the support of Clinton's White House, in addition to unanimous bipartisan support in both Houses of Congress, for a bill placing secondary embargoes on non-US companies making "substantial investments" in Iran, that is investments of $40 million or more, raised from an initially proposed $10 million. The Committee promptly sent a letter to the chairman of Total, which had taken the project relinquished by Conoco, warning that the US viewed any deals financing Iran's energy sector as direct "threats to US national security." It followed it with a similar letter the following spring to JGC (Japan), which was seeking investment in offshore gas projects, threatening that Congress, after passing the bill, might make it retroactive (see Greenberger and Lande 1995; Greenberger 1996). The bill, which made it mandatory that the President punish foreign firms investing in Iran, gave the President, however, the right to delay or waive sanctions if they came into conflict with the national interest or national security – a provision that would prove handy in saving face as European companies went on to defy US sanctions and refused to comply with US threats to disinvest from Iran. The Senate passed the Iran Oil Sanctions Act (IOSA) unanimously, adding, at the last minute, provisions for sanctions against foreign companies making similar investments in Libya, to the opposition of the State Department, which worried that this would open up space for a string of other additions to the bill, i.e. countries such as Cuba, Nigeria, and Russia.[8] Adding Libya to the bill had significant impact on European oil companies, which, due to more lax foreign investment laws in Libya, had greater investments in Libya than in Iran. Unsurprisingly, therefore, European countries responded angrily to US unilateral sanctions and threatened to appeal to the WTO if legislation was passed.

Nonetheless, the House Ways and Means Committee approved the bill in May, requiring the President to impose at least two of a set of six sanctions that included restriction on imports from, and exports and loans from US banks to, the sanctioned entity. A measure sponsored by AIPAC, which participated in debating the bill in Congress, and favored by the International Relations Committee, lowered the $40 million threshold on investment to $20 million on companies from countries that refused to join the sanctions within a year. The House unanimously approved the bill on 19 June and passed it on 23 July 1996. Clinton signed the bill into law on 5 August 1996 as the Iran Libya Sanctions Act (ILSA).

US sanctions against Iran were, in effect, sanctions against non-US firms doing business with both the US and Iran. Firms that had no investment or trade relations with the US were, therefore, less affected by the sanctions than non-US firms (and banks) dependent on US markets for a significant part of their operations. Nevertheless, since parent countries of firms violating ILSA were subject to sanctions, they were expected to pressure their firms against dealing with Iran. As it turned out, few countries were willing to comply with US demands and force their firms to disinvest from Iran. The EU, in fact, went in the opposite direction, threatening to take the US to a tribunal at the WTO and to make it illegal for European firms to comply with ILSA. The EU had filed a complaint with the WTO regarding the Cuban Liberty and Democratic Solidarity Act of 1996, the so-called Helms–Burton Act, which expanded long-standing economic sanctions on Cuba and extended them to foreign companies "trafficking" in property confiscated by the Cuban government from US nationals, including property owned by Cubans who had become US citizens. The dispute was later resolved through negotiations between the EU and the US. However, the EU passed a measure in October allowing Europeans to counter-sue US companies and individuals suing EU companies for trading in confiscated property, and sought legislation in the European Council making the provisions of the Helms–Burton Act unenforceable within EU territory and making it illegal for European companies to comply with it. (Britain, which already had measures against US extraterritoriality, followed suit and made it illegal to comply with the Helms–Burton Act in British territory.) Now, the EU was poised to follow a similar course regarding the "D'Amato law."

The conflict between the US and Iran was soon to turn into a dispute between the US and the EU, not only over their relations with Iran but over the form and structure of the global economy. What distinguished the clash between the US and the EU from other countries defiant to US extraterritoriality, such as Russia and China, and forced both to arrive at contradictory policies regarding Iran, is the degree of economic integration and interdependence between them. Trade and economic relations between the US and the EU were more crucial to each other than the relationship of each to Iran: 40 percent of US overseas investment went to Europe while 60 percent of EU investment was in the US. Annual trade between the US and EU countries amounted to around $250 billion compared with around $20 billion between European countries and Iran. Such economic interdependence was destined to chafe against differences in dealing with Iran, as an expression of fundamentally different globalisms. While the US sought to isolate and contain so-called rogue states to force a change in their political behavior that would allow their entry into a liberal global capitalism centered on the US, the EU opted for "critical engagement," which aimed at changing political behavior by normalizing trade relations and deepening economic integration. Both, however, could not afford to irritate the fledgling and fragile process of economic integration and sought to deepen economic ties among themselves while they bickered over Iran.

US sanctions did manage to slow down European–Iranian trade and European investment in Iran, and, although European oil companies continued to defy US sanctions, they trod this territory carefully. Companies with a large US asset base and market shares, such as BP and Royal Dutch Shell, still preferred to receive (tacit) US approval in their dealings with Iran. Companies with relatively small exposure to US markets, however, such as Total, ENI (Italy), Gazprom (Russia), and Petronas (Malaysia), were less affected by closed access to US markets and could hazard defying US sanctions, albeit with some caution as they remained vulnerable to diminished access to global financial markets (see Table 6.1 for a synopsis of foreign investment in Iran since 1995). Thus, following ILSA, ENI disclosed a $3 billion deal to develop natural gas in Libya that it had signed in June 1996, while the final touches were being put to ILSA in Congress. Petronas similarly announced that its subsidiary Petronas Carigali had acquired a 30 percent stake in the Sirri fields developed by Total (Total justified Petronas's participation as a transfer of shares predating ILSA and not an "additional investment," therefore exempt from it). The first serious test to the potency of US sanctions was brought about by a $2 billion deal in 1997 between Iran and a consortium composed of Total, Gazprom, and Petronas to develop phases 2 and 3 of the giant South Pars gas project in the Persian Gulf. Total had the support of both France, which threatened to appeal to the WTO, and the EU, which threatened to reinstate its complaint against the Helms–Burton Act if the US imposed sanctions on the French firm. Total was not deterred by the threat of US sanctions because it had no significant sales in US consumer markets and its investments in the US accounted for 3 to 4 percent of its annual income. Royal Dutch Shell, Elf Aquitaine, and other oil majors watched with caution as they negotiated deals for later phases of South Pars and other projects in Iran, whose viability depended on the outcome of the confrontation between Total and the Clinton administration.

Despite pressure from Congress on Clinton to impose sanctions on Total and its partners in the South Pars deal, the Clinton administration waived sanctions under section 9.c of ILSA in exchange for a pledge by the EU, at the US–EU summit of May 1998, to cooperate with the US on matters of nonproliferation and counterterrorism.[9] ILSA was, in effect, permanently suspended. Although it remained in force, it was never effectively applied beyond its use by the Clinton and Bush administrations to threaten foreign companies with "investigation" of their deals that violated the law. The fundamental contradiction of ILSA is that the Clinton administration found its provisions for waivers more effective in achieving its principal objectives, ostensibly securing European cooperation to prevent Iran from developing nuclear weapons and supporting terrorism, than the actual application of sanctions – the law itself. Madeleine Albright, whom Clinton had delegated to make decisions on matters relating to ILSA, explained the decision to grant waivers to Total, Gazprom, and Petronas (in a statement following the summit in London) on the grounds that the waiver under section 9.c of ILSA was "important to the national interest" of the US. "We concluded that sanctions would not prevent this project from proceeding," Albright went on, and might lead to retaliation against US firms. ILSA proved "a valuable tool in making clear to others the seriousness of our concerns about Iran's behavior" – not in preventing investment in Iranian oil and gas. Notwithstanding the waiver, France objected to the agreement reached between the US and the EU, arguing that it implicitly acknowledged the extraterritoriality of US laws, even in their suspension, but stopped short of vetoing it. Henceforth, non-US companies would brave the threat of US sanctions to invest in Iran, despite the pressure on profitability from Iranian investment laws (see below).

Opening Iran

Waiver of sanctions against the Total consortium paved the way for major oil companies into Iran's oil and gas industry. Most remarkable, was the deal between Royal Dutch Shell and NIOC in late 1999 to restore the Soroush and Nowruz oilfields, both destroyed during the Iran–Iraq War. Although the project was small in terms of its costs by the standards of the industry ($800 million), its great significance lay in its challenge to US sanctions. Unlike Total, Gazprom, Petronas, and other companies investing in Iran at the time, Shell was quite vulnerable to US sanctions, for it held about 20 percent of its assets in the US and a significant share of US markets – Shell Oil, the company's US subsidiary, generated $2 billion in profits from sales in US markets in 1997. The US Department of State sufficed to launch a "fact-finding investigation" into the deal, but Shell went unpunished. In any case, it had proceeded on the premise, supported by the EU and the British and Dutch governments, that ILSA was inapplicable. Shell Oil, on the other hand, was not part of the contract with NIOC and would not suffer from sanctions against Shell resulting from its contract with Iran.

Shell's investment in redeveloping the two small oilfields (500–550 million barrels) was crucial in establishing investors' confidence in a place under constant threat of economic sanctions (and potential military strikes) and internal limits on profitability. For its part, Iran kept marketing its lucrative fields on the global market, offering oil at well below its market price.[10] Iran, not hiding its desire to lure US oil firms into its oil and gas industry, kept its invitation open with promises of oil and fields reserved for returning US majors and encouragement to defy US sanctions and invest in Iran. US firms in their turn endeavored to reserve a place in Iran's oil and gas industry and did their part in lobbying the administration to remove or, at least, ease sanctions against Iran. Other business interests in Congress, however, were more successful in easing sanctions on Iran, which had solicited a $500 million deal from US farmers for grains and other farm products. The Clinton administration, under pressure from farm state Senators, allowed US exports to Iran through an exceptional lifting of sanctions in April 1999. Another lifting of sanctions, this time on non-oil luxury imports from Iran – carpets, caviare, and pistachios – followed in the spring of 2000. Regardless of the administration's ostensible will to support private Iranian entrepreneurs, craftsmen, farmers, and fishermen, the Iranian regime remained a threat to "the national security, foreign policy and economy of the United States" in the eyes of the President, who duly extended the ban on oil contracts with Iran. The (largely symbolic) opening to Iran by the Clinton administration was rebuffed by the Iranians, who insisted that only an end to the embargo on Iran's oil and gas industry and an end to accusations of Iran's pursuit of weapons of mass destruction and support of terrorism would bring a real rapprochement between the two countries. The US responded, in a somewhat circular manner, that an end to the embargo on oil would only follow an end to Iran's support for terrorism.

Notwithstanding, by the end of the decade there seemed to be an imminent thaw in the relationship between Iran and the US, which made it difficult, and rather embarrassing, for the Clinton administration to keep non-US companies from making deals with Iran. Recovery of Asian economies from the crises of 1998 and economic growth in the US and other Western industrial countries increased world demand for raw material and energy, causing oil prices to start climbing again beginning in summer 1999. Keeping oil out of the market meant an undesirable increase in price. Oil production, moreover, could expand and absorb more investment without jeopardizing prices, as long as demand remained strong. OPEC producers, together with Mexico, removed the limits on production they had struggled to put in place in 1998 without affecting climbing market prices – OPEC managed to raise production four times during 2000. US oil companies renewed their momentum to gain a place in Iran's hydrocarbon industry and, in November 2000, solicited the Iranian oil ministry for potential participation in the development of South Pars in the hope that sanctions against Iran would be removed by the incoming administration.

With the election of George W. Bush in late 2000, and Dick Cheney on his side as Vice President, it was expected that US sanctions against Iranian oil would finally be eliminated. Both Bush and Cheney came from, and had strong connections with, the oil industry. Cheney, as CEO of Halliburton, had lobbied the Clinton administration to lift unilateral sanctions against Iran before moving to the White House. Indeed, Halliburton was one of the most active members of US Engage, a group of around 600 companies formed in 1996 to lobby the administration against unilateral sanctions such as ILSA, and had, until recently, maintained its business in Iran. On closer inspection, however, the Bush–Cheney administration's connections with the oil industry are not with major producers as much as with energy traders (such as Enron), oil service providers (such as Halliburton), and small US independent companies producing in the US, none of which, unlike transnational oil producers, depended on having independent access to upstream production abroad, and all of which suffered from decline in market prices. High market prices not only made production of independents in the US more profitable, and to a certain extent possible, but also more competitive with major transnationals importing cheaper oil from overseas production. Thus, opening access to low-cost oilfields of the Middle East, which would bring cheaper oil with higher profit margins to the market, was not in the interest of the oil interests behind the Bush–Cheney administration. It is, therefore, no surprise that the Bush administration renewed ILSA while it sought to open more space for oil extraction in the US, in Alaska and offshore the continental US, and stepped up the sanctions against Iran, eventually moving them to the United Nations Security Council.

European companies continued to challenge US sanctions under the Bush administration as Congress debated whether to renew ILSA for another five years. The Bush administration wanted to extend ILSA for two years only, as it considered modifying the whole sanctions policy. Cheney no longer lobbied for the removal of unilateral sanctions against Iran. His National Energy Policy of 2001 recommended a "comprehensive review of sanctions" in consideration of their "effectiveness" regarding US "energy security" and minimizing the costs to US interests, but stopped short of recommending a complete end to sanctions. Oil companies, and some in the State Department, continued to lobby Congress to end sanctions altogether, but Congress managed to extend ILSA for another five years, until August 2006. In a concession to the administration, Congress allowed a review of ILSA in two years but eventually renewed it in 2003 and, after lifting the sanctions on Libya in 2004, removed Libya from ILSA (although Libya remained on the list of states that sponsor terrorism). ILSA was amended to the Iran Sanctions Act (ISA) in 2006, which, unlike its predecessor, placed more restrictions on the administration in justifying waivers and went further to place bans on foreign subsidiaries of US companies doing business in Iran, thus ending Halliburton's sojourn there, and to authorize funding to promote democracy in Iran, i.e. regime change.

The Bush administration was as keen on upholding sanctions against Iran as its predecessor and was more rigorous in its campaign to expand them into multilateral sanctions, against the opposition and reluctant endorsement of Germany, France, Britain, Russia, and China. Despite the renewal of ILSA, however, the Bush administration did not impose any sanctions on foreign companies making investments in Iran (and Libya) and failed to curb the expansion of European capital into Iran. As with its predecessor, the Bush administration sufficed to "investigate" companies violating ILSA on a case-by-case basis, only to find that suspending the law of sanctions was more effective in achieving its objectives than applying it. Certainly the Bush administration, also like its predecessor, although it suspended sanctions against European companies, proceeded to sanction companies from Russia, China, and India for trading with Iran, not under ILSA, however, but under other laws relating to proliferation and arms technology. The Bush administration remained skeptical about the effectiveness of unilateral sanctions, especially if they risked trade frictions with Europe and Japan. Thus, US oil companies, awash with cash from recent surges in oil prices but with declining reserves and limited or no access to new exploration and development, watched as their competitors from Europe and Asia made inroads into Iran, Libya, and Iraq.

US and EU Iran policies diverged increasingly as one sought international sanctions and multilateral containment while the other sought increased economic and commercial integration (the EU began trade negotiations with Iran in December 2002), a difference that would lead to the hybrid, and contradictory, "dual approach" strategy regarding Iran's development of nuclear projects. A strategy that combined continued negotiation with Iran under threat of escalating sanctions and potential military intervention. Despite divergence between US and EU policies regarding Iran, growing European influence in Iran and the Middle East was regarded in Washington [DC] in a variety of ways. Conservatives and neoconservatives saw the EU advancing its immediate economic interests over issues of global security, leaving the US alone to deal with threats of terrorism and proliferation. Others, mostly veterans of the Cold War, welcomed EU influence in the Middle East as a moderating influence and counterbalance to increasing Chinese and, especially, Russian economic and political influence, and on a more critical view, as an alternative to failing US policy in the Middle East. Notwithstanding, US transnational (oil) companies held onto the same position regarding increasing penetration of the Middle East by European, Russian, and Chinese capital alike – the increasing presence of European and Asian oil companies made it increasingly difficult for US companies to gain access to (what remained of) Iranian oil. The longer sanctions remained in place, the more eroded the possibility of establishing footholds in Iranian oil and gas production.

The build-up to the war on Iraq throughout 2002 offered some hope for US companies of an opening into the upstream frontier of the Middle East. The campaign against Iraq gave rise to suspicions among France, Russia, and China that their contracts with the Iraqi government to develop Iraqi oil would be lost to US companies, despite assurance to the contrary by the Department of State. Word of an imminent war sent oil prices up. In the event of war, however, oil analysts speculated that short-term supply interruptions might keep prices high for some time, forcing industrial countries to tap into their emergency stockpiles. Yet, a "liberated" Iraq promised to break the hold of Saudi Arabia over the world oil market and to bring changes in the balance of power within OPEC, making oil more readily available and cheaper to obtain (see King *et al.* 2002). In 2002, Iraq produced only 2.8 million bbl/d and exported around 0.5 million bbl/d under the UN oil-for-food program (in addition to small quantities smuggled periodically through the Persian Gulf). Iraq, however, sat atop the second largest oil reserves in the world, which were never developed to their full potential, and is capable of producing up to 6 million bbl/d within a few years, with the requisite investment in exploration and production. Iran would also emerge as a benefactor from the war: without a regional rival and constant threat to its west, Iran would be able to devote more finances to developing its oil and gas industry, placing more oil on the world market to meet growing demand.

None of this happened. The war removed Iraqi oil from the access of US and non-US companies alike, thus removing cheap oil from the market and replacing it with more expensive oil from high-cost regions, thereby increasing world total production while continuing the increase in world prices. Iraq already had contracts with foreign (non-US) companies to explore and develop oil and gas within Iraq, and a simple lifting of sanctions would have been enough to flood Iraq with foreign capital and to flood the world market with cheap oil. Moreover, the war did not relax the tensions on Iran: rather, US–Iran relations deteriorated after the invasion of Iraq, especially after the subsequent discovery of Iran's clandestine nuclear work in late 2003. Iran managed to reach an agreement with Britain, Germany, and France (the "EU-3") to suspend its nuclear projects until the International Atomic Energy Agency verified its civilian nature. Yet, while the EU-3 sought ways throughout 2004 to keep Iran in negotiation over its nuclear energy, in order not to interrupt the ongoing trade negotiations, the US found further cause to step up pressure on Europe, Russia, and China to isolate Iran further and bring it to the UN Security Council, imposing along the way penalties on European banks with branches in the US (most notably UBS and ABN Amro) for conducting business with Iranian companies and banks, and sanctions on Russian and Chinese companies for trading in dual-use technologies with Iran. The five permanent members of the Security Council and Germany, the "big six," four of which have considerable trade with and investment in Iran, remained reluctant about imposing international sanctions on Iran, which translated into imposing sanctions against their own firms.

Iran's resumption of work on its nuclear projects in 2005, however, led the big six to compromise by December 2006 on limited UN sanctions that targeted Iranian entities and persons involved in Iran's nuclear and military institutions, including two of Iran's largest banks. Subsequent UN sanctions on Iran in 2007, coupled with threats of sanctions on European companies (and more sanctions on Russian and Chinese companies), however, failed to keep European and Asian oil companies out of Iran's hydrocarbon industry. The sanctions did, however, manage to slow down its development since they placed limits on the access of Iran and foreign oil companies operating in Iran to global financial markets and US dollars, the currency in which oil is globally traded, making it more expensive and less profitable to conduct business in Iran. European companies and banks, moreover, feared that the US campaign against Iran's nuclear program might lead to a conclusion similar to that of the campaign against Iraq, which raised Iran's ranking as an investment risk. Companies from China, Japan, India, and Malaysia, increasingly filled the cracks left by reluctant European investors as the Bush administration, despite denials by the President himself, refused to rule out the ultimate use of military force against Iran, in case Iran refused to halt its nuclear development. Indeed, as if the threat of more sanctions and potential military strikes (by the US and Israel) were not enough to raise the risk of investing in Iran, the US, in an additional attempt to limit European financial dealings with Iran, "encouraged," in April 2006, the Organization for Economic Cooperation and Development (OECD) countries to raise Iran's rating as a business risk, which increased the cost of loans and guarantees and limited export credits to Iran (see Alden *et al.* 2006; Weisman 2006).

Tightening economic sanctions, however, were partly offset by rising oil prices throughout 2006, which increased Iran's foreign earnings and made it dependent on lesser amounts of foreign capital for the development of its oil and gas projects. Iranian oil companies took up projects previously under negotiation with European oil companies and bigger projects were offered to Chinese oil companies. Iran was now in a position to impose penalties on companies already operating in Iran, some of which under US pressure such as the consortium led by Inpex to develop the Azadegan oilfield, and extract better terms of contracts from deals under negotiation (see below). Yet, the four-year oil boom raised the value of Iran's exports to $51 billion in 2006 from $19 billion in 2002, but not its volume: exports, in fact, declined over the same period from 2.43 million bbl/d to 2.29 bbl/d. Iran's oil production did not increase in any way to meet its projected targets and the US continued to find ways to prevent the influx of much needed investment into Iran to raise the volume of oil production, using a range of legal instruments, other than ILSA. Already existing sanctions were only compounded by conflicts within Iran on how, or even whether, to open the hydrocarbon industry to investment by foreign companies. So-called hardliners have historically struggled to keep foreign companies out and have benefited, ironically, from increasing sanctions as, in the absence of credit and loans from foreign banks to foreign and Iranian private enterprises, they managed to expand their control over the Iranian economy, including the oil and gas industry. Thus, the prospect of opening Iran further was not forthcoming, and pressure of external sanctions and stringent investment laws seemed to curb the expansion of foreign capital into Iran's oil and gas industry. Yet, foreign oil companies keep knocking at the doors of the oil ministry, and Iran, in its turn, has found ways to modify its existing contractual forms to make investment in Iran more attractive, despite the persistence of US sanctions, although its dependence on foreign capital has not led Iran to remove completely laws that regulate the access of foreign companies to reserves.

In short, neither US sanctions nor Iranian law, as we shall see below, have deterred foreign oil companies from investing in Iran, and both have been amenable to bend and change under specific geopolitical and geoeconomic circumstances. What ultimately determines the flow of capital into Iranian oil and gas, or any other place for that matter, is the negotiated relationship between oil companies and (resource-owning) states over the control of the production of oil, ultimately to control the amount of oil in the market and protect monopoly profits. This is achieved through negotiating the contradictory process of spatial integration, to allow the flow of capital into the profitable production of the resource, and fragmentation, to deny competitors access to reserves and prevent overproduction in order to protect monopoly profits. In the following, we examine how this contradiction is embodied and reproduced in Iranian laws regarding foreign investment.

Capital versus the law

While the first part showed how the attempt to isolate Iran had to come across its (internal) opposite, the attempt to integrate Iran, the second shows that the attempt by the Iranian government to protect the Iranian economy from foreign capital and to guarantee economic independence had to run against deep and functional dependence on foreign capital, financial and technological, to resuscitate Iran's hydrocarbon industry – the backbone of the Iranian economy. Iran's attempt at negotiating this contradiction has reproduced and internalized it in a series of legislative and contractual forms that tried to achieve both, i.e. to shield Iranian resources from the control of global capital while trying to integrate resource production in global capital. We look first at the liberalization of Iran's economy in the period following the war with Iraq, which produced a scheme for free trade zones that failed, however, to have the intended effect of opening the whole Iranian economy. Then we examine the development of buy-back agreements as a contractual mechanism to bring foreign capital investment into the oil and gas industry, yet regulate its spatial and temporal extent to ensure continued government control over the resources and the industry.

Window to our liberalization: Iran's free trade zones

At the end of its war with Iraq, and as part of the effort to reconstruct its shattered economy, Iran set up a series of free trade zones, beginning with the Kish Free Zone Organization (1989) and Qeshm Island Free Area (1990), to encourage private investment and bring in foreign investment to boost its non-oil export industries.[11] Kish and Qeshm, both islands in the Persian Gulf, were to be run by a relatively autonomous local government, providing foreign investors with unrestricted movement of capital and repatriation of profits; a 100 percent equity in local joint ventures and ownership of assets (excluding land); a 15-year exemption from corporate and individual taxes; import and export custom duty exemptions; foreign financial and insurance services; and legal guarantees against expropriation or nationalization of investments. Foreigners can visit the islands and, in the case of Kish, make 72-hour trips to mainland Iran, without a visa. The two islands, situated halfway between Europe and East Asia and on the route of around 60 percent of water traffic leaving the Gulf, were expected to attract export-oriented industries and oil refineries to supply regional markets in Central Asia and, by allowing foreign banks to set up branches there, to become a world financial center to rival Dubai, including a commodity exchange in Kish that would trade oil futures by 2005.

What is most significant about Iran's free trade zones, however, is that they were seen as experiments in free-market capitalism that would open a gateway to mainland Iran and pave the way for structural changes in Iran's economy. In a way, Iran's free trade zones represented to the country possible economic liberalization brought about by opening the economy to foreign capital.[12] This was certain to come up against opposition and create division within Iran over the extent, and virtue, of opening the economy to foreign capital, with the (dis)taste of the colonialism of a not-too-distant past still fresh in the national memory. But more to it, the opposition inside Iran had its origin in the conflicting economic interests of the different capitalist classes and their representation in institutions of government, namely parliament and the Council of Guardians. (This opposition would result in the reproduction of the contradiction between integration and isolation in Iran's investment policies.) In (June) 1993, Iran's parliament approved the legal framework allowing foreign direct investment in Kish, Qeshm, and in an onshore free trade zone in the port city of Chah Bahar. Iran followed with an application to join the WTO in 1995, signaling further preparedness to liberalize its economy and join in global free-market capitalism. But, as with the free trade zones, moves that drove the economy towards liberalization and that were supported by Iran's banking interests and the so-called reformers, were opposed by merchants and industrialists who enjoyed the monopoly benefits from existing import and capital controls, and the conservative clerical elite, which, although ostensibly opposed to the liberalization of the economy lest it lead to the liberalization of all of Iranian society and the erosion of Islamic culture, had much to benefit from their monopoly of vital sectors of Iran's economy through their control of the powerful Bonyads in the absence of competition from foreign companies and private companies with access to global financial markets.

Iran's parliament approved further legislation in 1997, permitting foreign companies to open representative and branch offices in Iran and allowing foreign banks to open branches in the free trade zones, beginning in the spring of 1998, with up to a 49 percent share in joint ventures with the government.[13] The latter was amended in 1999 to allow 100 percent foreign-owned banks and insurance companies in free trade zones, and to protect them against nationalization as parliament considered draft proposals for amendments to the Law on Attraction and Protection of Foreign Investment (more on this below).[14] The Council of Guardians opposed the legislation allowing completely foreign-owned banks and insurance companies into the free trade zones, only to be overruled by the Expediency Council.[15] Nonetheless, the passing of this legislation did not automatically translate into a flock of foreign banks and foreign capital. Foreign banks with branches and affiliates in the US had to contend with an administration intent on punishing foreign companies conducting business with Iran. Although the US administration never used ILSA to sanction foreign oil companies – and US companies operating in Iran through their foreign subsidiaries – it had at its disposal a set of legal instruments with which to retaliate against banks conducting business with Iran. Political risks to financial investment in Iran came not from Iranian law or the threat of nationalization, but from the risk of losing access to the US markets and financial system. The free trade zones, intended to attract foreign investment to develop export-oriented industries, brought more imports of cheaper consumer goods and Iranian shoppers from the mainland than either foreign investment or exports of Iranian manufactures or petrochemicals. Between 2002 and 2003 (March), the three free trade zones imported $7 billion worth of imports from other Gulf countries and only $1 billion in foreign investment (almost equivalent, nonetheless, to the $1.3 billion invested between 1993 and 2001). Nor was Iran, through the 1997 legislation, capable of trapping Iranian capital: Dubai, with low-interest loans to investors, was capable of not only diverting foreign capital from Iran, but also Iranian capital, which fled to neighboring financial centers rather than making its way back to investment in local industries. This did not deter Iran from continuing to work on its legal structure to make foreign investment more attractive and to pour government and private money into upgrading the infrastructure of its free trade zones in the Gulf and in the North, in order to make them more competitive in the global network of free trade zones, mainly as platforms for exports to the promising markets of Central Asia.

Capital continues to flow into the Iranian free trade zones, increasingly from the South and the East, mainly India and China. But Iran's free trade zones failed to provide the space needed to attract the requisite foreign investment for the development of competitive non-oil production sectors, precisely because of their continued isolation from the mainland. What the free trade zones failed to achieve was to open the gateway to mainland Iran, let alone expansion of full economic liberalization to the mainland, which was the prospect that made them attractive to foreign investors rather than the mere provision of export platforms to Central Asia or elsewhere. Thus, rather than transcend the contradiction between integration and fragmentation, by integrating with world market and global capital yet isolating the Iranian market and economy from foreign capital, free trade zones came to embody the contradiction of liberal globalization. Instead of diversifying Iran's economy away from oil and providing the catalyst for liberalizing Iranian capitalism, oil is as important to Iran's economic development as ever, and Iran seems keen on protecting the industry from foreign influence, despite its concerted attempts to open it to foreign capital.

Restoring oil and gas production: buy-back contracts

Ironically, despite more stringent laws and regulations concerning investment in the oil and gas industry, foreign companies seem more intent on investing in it than in industries in the free trade zones. In parallel to promoting free trade zones, Iran has worked on attracting foreign capital into the oil and gas industry, which remains the main source of foreign income. Since the beginning of the 1990s, Iran has struggled to restore the productivity of the oil and gas industry to the level it enjoyed before the war with Iraq. Iranian recovery has been plagued by lack of the capital and technology necessary to restore the productivity of oilfields damaged by the war with Iraq, to enhance the productivity of aging oilfields, and, most importantly, to explore for and develop new oilfields. The discovery and development of new oilfields is central to Iran's development, for, in addition to increasing productive capacity, an increase in its proven reserves is necessary for Iran to increase its world market share of oil (hence its foreign income). As a member of OPEC, Iran can only increase its exports by increasing its OPEC quota, and this requires that Iran increase its proven reserves. Iran has, since the end of the war with Iraq, made several discoveries of small oilfields in the range of one to two billion barrels of oil. Two significant discoveries, however, have been made since 1999: the Azadegan oilfield, estimated to comprise 26 billion barrels – Iran's biggest discovery in more than 30 years – followed by the discovery of Dasht-e-Abadan in 2001, estimated to be equivalent in size to Azadegan. Iran's proven reserves have more than doubled since the Revolution of 1979, after which they dipped to around 50 billion barrels at the end of the war with Iraq, increasing to around 90 billion by the end of the 1980s, and, following a series of discoveries in the 1990s, jumped to around 1,256 billion in 2003 and again to their present level of around 137 billion barrels (see Figure 6.2).

In addition to increasing oil reserves and production, the development of upstream gas projects has also assumed increasing importance to Iran's energy policy. Iran sits on the second largest reserves of natural gas, around two-thirds of which are non-associated, that is, natural gas reserves occurring

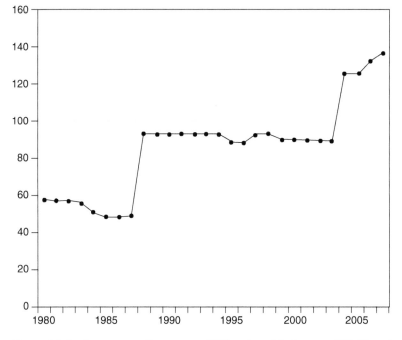

Figure 6.2 Iran's proven oil reserves (billion barrels) (source: US Department of Energy. Energy Information Administration. Office of Energy Markets and End Use).

independently of oil: not as a gas cap and not dissolved in oil. Gas plays a multi-faceted role in Iran's energy development plans: as a domestic energy source that would free more crude oil for export; as a feed for gas-based petrochemical industries; for use in re-injection to enhance the productivity of old oilfields; and as a major export to markets in Asia and Europe. The latter is of primary import-ance with regard to foreign investment in Iran and Iran's position in the gas market. Foreign trade in gas is dependent on finding long-term consumers, and Iran has tried to win new customers by opening the upstream and downstream oil and gas sectors to foreign buyers of gas, entangling trade in liquefied natural gas with contracts for foreign investment in both the oil and gas sectors. Unlike the oil market, which is primarily determined by supply, where oil is produced and stocked before it is sold, hence resulting often in the overaccumulation of inventories and a fall in prices, the market for gas depends on finding contracts for large quantities of gas prior to fixing capital in production, due primarily to the nature of the material, which makes it difficult to store. Customers have to be found before production can proceed at commercial levels, and, unlike oil, in order to secure continued demand, gas contracts tend to be long-term, "locking" the buyer into purchases of agreed-upon amounts of gas over long periods of time. Iran is a latecomer to the gas market and has had, therefore, to compete with already established producers such as Qatar, Oman, and Russia for markets that they have already "locked up," especially markets in the Far East. Iran's strategy, in addition to offering contracts for liquefied natural gas at competitive prices, has also focused on bringing foreign capital into the development of its upstream and downstream gas production. Indeed, almost all trade in gas has involved contracts for investment in upstream production.

(Foreign) investment in upstream production, especially in the more expensive exploration and development, is crucial for the development of Iran's oil and gas industry and for establishing Iran's position in the world market. But it is also of great importance for foreign companies because "greenfield" investment, investment in new production, is more profitable than investment in downstream production or restoration and recovery projects, and, as importantly, expands the company's reserve base and assets. Yet, Iranian law, as we shall see below, precludes both high profitability and expansion of reserves, and has, in addition to tightening US sanctions, delayed, but not completely halted, investment in upstream production. The obstacle of Iranian law is exacerbated further by the potential opening of upstream production to foreign investment in other low-cost regions, such as Kuwait, Qatar, and Saudi Arabia, which would divert capital away from Iran. The competition with other oil- and gas-rich, low-cost regions, and, given high market prices, also relatively higher-cost regions such as Russia, for foreign capital and greater market share prompted Iran to revise and improve the terms of contract to lure foreign companies into the hydrocarbon industry. Instead of resolving the contradictions of investment in Iran – between the attempt to bring foreign capital into the industry and put more oil and gas on the market on one hand, and the attempt to keep Iranian oil and gas shielded from the control of foreign capital on the other – the development of contractual arrangements since the middle 1990s has only managed to internalize and reproduce the contradiction rather than transcend it. In the following, we examine this process in the development of the buy-back contract (Table 6.1 offers a synopsis of buy-back agreements since 1995).

The Iranian constitution is often invoked as an obstacle to foreign investment in Iran's oil and gas industry, but there are no explicit articles in the Iranian constitution that completely prevent the participation of foreign companies in the extraction and production of natural resources and minerals. Instead, the constitution prohibits the formation of monopolies (Article 43.5) and forbids all agreements that result in "foreign control" of resources and the economy (Article 153).[16] The constitution protects against foreign "control," foreign "influence," and lack of "self-sufficiency" and "independence," not only in the economic sphere but in all society.[17] Indeed, the post-Revolutionary constitution left in place most of the laws relating to commerce, protection of foreign investment, contracts, and property rights (see Namazi 2000).[18] What the constitution strictly forbids is the granting of concessions to foreign companies, in all areas of the economy, which gives them exclusive and monopolistic privileges.[19] The constitution, however, and investment laws based on it, leaves ambiguous the question of which sectors of the economy are open to foreign investment. Article 44 divides the national economy into three sectors: state, cooperative, and private, and allocates to the state the administration of "all large-scale and mother industries" including major minerals and foreign trade, in addition to banking and insurance, and to the private sector agricultural, industrial, and commercial activities that "supplement the economic activities of the state." But Article 44 also leaves the scope of the three sectors to "be specified by law." Investment laws, since the Law on the Attraction and Protection of Foreign Investment (Lapfi) of 1955 through to the Foreign Investment Promotion and Protection Act (Fippa) of 2002, allow foreign investment only in sectors open to private Iranian companies, which, only on a literal reading of Article 44, excludes mineral extraction. It remains, therefore, to be determined which industries constitute "mother industries." What makes it even more ambiguous is that the government has not strictly followed this division and has allowed the participation of private Iranian firms in areas not designated as part of the private sector. The question for foreign investors is, therefore, whether they can enjoy legal protection if they participate in areas not designated in the constitution as part of the private sector. In other words, the obstacle to foreign investment in Iran is not the Iranian constitution or Iranian law, much less its absence, but the political and economic risks that emerge from the legal contract between foreign private companies and the Iranian government acting as resource owner, or, to be more precise, administrator and regulator of publicly-owned resources – in addition to the political risk associated with going against US sanctions, as discussed above. The obstacle to foreign investment is fundamentally relational, and is embodied in the limits of questions of profitability, control of reserves, and rent, all of which are implied, but determined, in the law. Rather, the limits to foreign investment and capital accumulation are determined by the relationship between (private) capital and state (capital), foreign oil company and national oil ministry, inseparable from the web of relationships in the larger geopolitical and geoeconomic sphere. This relational view is crucial to understanding the geographical contradiction between integration (expansion of capital into Iran) and fragmentation (protection against foreign capital in Iran) embodied in the process of controlling world oil reserves and production.

Contracts between international oil companies and governments of Third World countries for oil exploration and production have, historically, evolved with the dissolution of colonial and formal imperial relations with host governments. The process has by no means been linear, and has resulted in a variety of contractual forms across space and time, although the general trend has been to give more control to governments over their natural resources. Most governments, in fact, employ several contractual forms, depending on the size of reserves and the cost of their extraction. Concession agreements characterized the international oil industry in its earliest stages. According to concession agreements, oil companies enjoyed complete control over oil operations, including the reserves, production facilities, and the product, in exchange for fixed royalty taxes on profits paid to the host government, which, often falling into the sphere of influence of one imperialist power or another, had control over neither production nor the product. The concession agreement constituted a self-sufficient contract – in other words, it constituted its own legal reference and existed, therefore, outside the domestic law. Concessions covered large areas, often coinciding with the whole territory of the state: the concession granted to Knox D'Arcy by the Persian government in 1901, for example, covered the whole empire, excluding the northern provinces closest to Russia – around 1.3 million square kilometers. Concessions were also long-term, usually for 60–65 years or more (75 years in the case of Kuwait, for example). Riding the waves of national liberation movements and economic nationalism developing in the post-war period, oil-rich governments in Third World countries established petroleum laws that gave governments sovereignty over natural resources (recognized by the UN) and greater degree of participation over production. The control of global oil production by the so-called seven sisters was also challenged in the post-war period by the entry of smaller companies into competition for production contracts in the Third World, often accepting lower profits than the majors that had dominated the industry so far. This allowed governments to renegotiate existing contracts and grant future contracts to foreign companies on the basis of smaller concessions of shorter duration. National oil companies were also established to allow governments greater degree of participation in the production process and to control the product. Some countries fully nationalized their oil industry, even if only formally, while others only partially. Oil companies, under the imminent threat of nationalization spreading throughout the Third World, still refused to cede complete control over production, and, with the help of their home states – the United States in particular – reached a compromise that granted them some control over the management of production operations, resulting, ultimately, in the development of production-sharing agreements (PSAs) followed, more recently, by risk service agreements (RSAs) that transfer more control to governments. The new contractual forms differ from concessions first, in that they preserve the complete sovereignty of the host country over resources, they cover specific, relatively small areas and are granted for shorter periods, rarely more than 25 years.[20] PSAs and RSAs differ from concessions and from each other in terms of ownership of the resource. While concessions grant ownership to the foreign company at the point of production, PSAs guarantee it at the point of export, as a share in the product, while RSAs provide no predetermined ownership of the resource. PSAs divide production shares between government and international oil companies, and allocate to the latter cost recovery shares as compensation for costs of exploration and development. PSAs are gradually and modestly giving way to RSAs (which characterize only about 5 percent of global oil contracts). Ironically, this form of contract, unlike PSAs, opened the upstream sector again to direct investment by foreign companies, but it also transformed the nature of their participation in production. According to RSAs, the government contracts foreign oil companies as providers of technical and commercial, and, in some instances, financial services. In other words, international oil companies increasingly become operators, or contractors, compensated in cash rather than shares in the product for the costs of services rendered to the government, or its national oil company. This is what PSAs were supposed to prevent by granting international oil companies control over management. In some instances, international oil companies operating under RSAs have the option to purchase crude oil on credit, and at a discount in the case of commercial production. RSAs, unlike PSAs, are therefore ideal in places where there are legal limits to foreign access to resources or to the participation of foreign companies in production, but where there is also large reserves that can be produced at low cost combined with the lack of technical or financial means to develop them, as in Iran.

Iran devised the buy-back service contract under its first Five-Year Plan (1990–1995) as a legal mechanism to attract the foreign capital required to expand oil and gas reserves and develop oil and gas production without relinquishing national state control over either. Thus, buy-back contracts are not meant to circumvent the constitution, as they are often portrayed, but are indeed one form of risk service agreement that complies with the constitutional prohibition of concessions to foreign companies. Buy-back agreements limit foreign participation in the exploration for, extraction and production of, oil and gas in space and time. They allow the government to periodically renegotiate the terms of contract to secure higher rents or to terminate contracts if the terms are not met by the contracted foreign oil company, which, accordingly, is reduced to operator. Thus, as discussed above, neither the constitution nor the law is the obstacle to foreign investment in this case, but the implications of the terms of buy-back contracts on the profitability of capital invested in oil and gas, and, as important, on the control of reserves by oil companies and their treatment as company assets. These terms are not specific to Iran and they vary across time and space, as a result and expression of the variation in the relationship between (foreign) capital and the state. Most importantly, they have not stopped oil companies from seeking investment in Iran's oil and gas industry.

Buy-back contracts are essentially short-term risk service agreements between the Iranian Ministry of Petroleum and private companies, according to which the oil company provides exploration, development, or production services over a predetermined period of time in exchange for remuneration of capital and operating costs, interest and bank fees, and profit ranging between 12 and 24 percent – with most ranging between 15 and 18 percent – in amounts of oil or gas. Unplanned increases in costs of production during the operation of the field is the responsibility of the contractor, although NIOC bears the responsibility for fluctuation in oil prices. Buy-back agreements separate exploration and development from production, such that in the case of discovery of reserves determined to be commercially viable, the government, through NIOC, can renegotiate the terms of contract before production can proceed. Thus, according to this two-part form, discovery does not automatically lead to a production agreement. Moreover, if no significant discovery is made, or no new agreement on production is reached, the contract can be terminated with fees paid to the contractor. In general, the exploration part of the contract is limited to two to three years, the operation part to five to eight years, during which the operator secures remuneration fees and after which the operation of the field, including all assets acquired by the contractor during the process, is transferred to NIOC. In return, the contractor receives the right to purchase oil at a discounted price for a certain amount of time. Contractors may, in principle, line up successive contracts to secure longer involvement, or, as in the case of TotalFinaElf in South Pars, participate as service providers for technical assistance fees, even after operation has been transferred to NIOC. The effect is less control over production, and, most importantly, reduced rates of profit.

Buy-back agreements were originally designed to allow the development of existing oilfields, but they were extended in 2003 to include the exploration and development of new fields. From the standpoint of investment, these are two fundamentally different operations. Developing old fields, or fields well into their production life, requires higher technologies than operating new fields, which justifies the participation of oil majors, but yields lower volumes of oil and lower rates of return on investment, making the rate of return of 15–20 percent offered by Iran for enhancing the recovery of aging oilfields acceptable to most companies. Although exploration for new fields and their operation is more expensive and much riskier, it is also potentially more profitable. In the case of discovery, new oilfields produce much higher volumes of oil at relatively low levels of investment, and thus yield high rates of return. In other words, investing in new oilfields compared to fields past their peak (and some of Iran's big oilfields peaked in the 1930s) is similar to investing in more productive fields that yield higher profit margins, thus making the terms of contract offered by the Iranian government, especially the limited rates of return and cap on production, less attractive in the case of exploration and development of new oilfields. Since oil companies do not control production under buy-back contracts, they cannot increase the volume of production to offset the relatively low rate of return. This is exacerbated further by the fact that the contractor is remunerated in quantities of oil after the transfer of operation to NIOC, which may not be able to maintain levels of production. Certainly, the "price risk" is borne by the government, such that if prices increase, the contractor receives less oil; if they drop, the contractor receives more oil. But, if oil prices drop too low, the amount of oil produced may not be sufficient to attain the predetermined rate of return, or even cover costs of production, given the cap on the quantity of oil that can be lifted during the (short) duration of the project. An unplanned increase in costs of production in the meantime, which is borne by the contractor, would slash further the rate of return. Worst of all, the buy-back contract may not move from the exploration to production phase should the Ministry deem it not commercially viable or, alternatively, the role and share of the contractor may be redefined from one phase to another and the contract may even be re-awarded to another contractor.

Iran has continuously modified the terms of buy-back contracts, which are awarded on a case-by-case basis. But modifications have proceeded in both directions. As Congress went on to extend ILSA for another five years in the summer of 2001, NIOC awarded a buy-back agreement to ENI to develop the

Dar Khovin oilfield. In what became known as the "ENI terms," the contract included a "limited risk/reward" component that tied payment to the performance of the contractor and the production capacity of the project.[21] Also to extract better performance from foreign contractors, however, buy-back contracts included penalties on contractors that failed to reach the "production plateau" agreed upon in the contract in due time – this would cost Sheer its contract for the development of Masjid-e-Suleyman, which went to CNPC, while delays in Inpex's work on Azadegan cost it 65 of its 75 percent stake and its operator status. NIOC would also pressure companies negotiating buy-back contracts to conclude negotiations within a limited period of time (six months), after which NIOC would re-tender the projects under negotiation. This would result in Cepsa's loss of Cheshmeh-Kosh, and BP, TotalFinaElf, and Shell's loss of the huge Bangestan oilfield: both were later awarded to Iranian contractors, which by the beginning of the decade were already playing a larger role in the development of Iran's oil and gas. Nonetheless, the development of Iran's oil and gas production still depends on the advanced technical expertise of major transnational oil companies, and this dependence prompted the Ministry of Petroleum to modify the buy-back contract further and provide more incentives for foreign contractors. Reportedly, the most significant amendment concerns the temporal limits of the contract and its two-part form. New contracts link exploration with production, such that, in case of discovery, the foreign contractor is guaranteed priority of participation in development and production without further open bidding. Such is the case of the contract under negotiation between NIOC and Norsk Hydro/LUKoil for the development of Anaran, which Norsk Hydro discovered. In relation to this, NIOC also extends the period of participation in production after the project is transferred to NIOC by granting the contractor the status of "adviser" to NIOC for the field's lifetime, in addition to a reward of a higher rate of return should production exceed expected capacity. The first contract that may be signed under these terms is the one under negotiation between NIOC and Sinopec for the development of Yadavaran.

All the incentives in new buy-back agreements clearly point to a desire on the part of NIOC to encourage deeper involvement by foreign investors, especially in committing higher and more expensive production technologies, to meet Iran's plans for raising production output. To encourage long-term foreign investment further, in 2002 Iran replaced the Law for the Attraction and Protection of Foreign Investment (Lapfi) of 1955 with the Foreign Investment Promotion and Protection Act (Fippa) of 2002, placing under the new law all foreign investment made previously under the old law (Article 24). Despite lingering ambiguities in the new law concerning project ownership and investment in Iranian public companies controlled by the state, the new law was heralded as a significant opening to foreign capital and a great improvement to Iran's investment climate.[22] Fippa offers foreign investors protection of all kinds of investment made under this law (Article 3),[23] and the same "rights, protections, and facilities available to local investments" (Article 8), and, most importantly, protection against nationalization or expropriation and compensation based on the market-determined "real value of the investment" in case of legal expropriation for the public interest (Article 9). Fippa offers further incentive by allowing repatriation and transfer of principal and profits upon completion of projects and deduction of taxes and legal dues (Article 13) in hard currency, not only exports of goods, and, most importantly, of profits from activities conducted in Iran – meaning from limited sales to domestic markets (Article 17).[24] Notwithstanding, the problem with these provisions is that they uphold the constitutional distinction between sectors open to private investment and sectors reserved for the state, which include mineral extraction and foreign trade, keeping it rather ambiguous if foreign investment in oil and gas production is protected by this law. Although the introduction to Article 2 states that foreign investment should be made "for the purpose of development and promotion of producing activities in industry, mining, agriculture and services," Article 2.d leaves it to the Council of Ministers to determine "the fields and extent of investment in each field" in subsequent bylaws.[25] Fippa complies largely with the constitution in terms of demarcation of the private sphere and the prohibition of concessions, but in reproducing and, in some instances, adding to the ambiguities of the constitution, it manages to roll back the limits to foreign investment in a way, however, that reproduces the contradictions of free trade zones and the buy-back contract.

In summary, the contradiction between the attempt by the Iranian government to open the economy to foreign capital and the attempt to withhold sovereignty over resources and to control production is reproduced and internalized in the development of the contractual form and the legal framework determining foreign investment in Iran since the middle 1990s. The contradictory process underscores the following paradox: Iran's economic independence, which rests on the development of its domestic hydrocarbon industry, the expansion of existing and new reserves and increase in oil and gas output, depends ultimately on its opposite – the integration of its oil and gas industry with global capital. The attraction yet regulation of foreign capital produces and depends on the contradiction between geographical integration and isolation.

Conclusion

Transnational oil companies from Europe and Asia have tried to establish footholds in Iran's upstream sector through direct investment against obstacles from their relationships with US sanctions and Iranian law. As other low-cost production regions remain relatively beyond the reach of transnational oil companies, oil companies have flocked to Iran despite stringent limits on profitability from short-term investment and relatively low rates of return, and despite risking punishment by the US that would deprive them of access to lucrative US markets. Although companies that seek investment in Iran come from countries thirsty for the raw material itself, the competition for Iranian oil is irreducible to competition for the resource itself because of increased demand from growing economies. As we saw above, the competition was at its highest during periods of low economic growth and sluggish demand. The competition for oil is

Table 6.1 Foreign investments in Iran under buy-back agreements since 1995

Date	Company	Field	Notes
July 1995	TotalFinaElf 70%; Petronas 30%;	Sirri A and E (Offshore oil)	$760 million. Completed in 2001.
September 1997	TotalFinaElf 40%; Petronas 30%; Gazprom 30%	South Pars, phases 2 and 3 (Offshore gas)	$2.2 billion. Completed 2003.
March 1999	TotalFinaElf 55%; ENI 45%	Doroud (Offshore oil and gas)	$1 billion. Originally awarded to Elf Aquitaine and Agip before they merged with Total and ENI respectively. Completed 2004.
April 1999	TotalFinaElf 47%; ENI 38%; Bow Valley 15%	Balal (Offshore oil)	$240 million. Turned over to NIOC in 2003 after it reached its production level.
November 1999	Royal Dutch Shell 100%	Nowruz-Soroush (Offshore oil)	$800 million. Completed 2005.
July 2000	ENI 60%; Petronas 40%	South Pars, phases 4 and 5 (Offshore gas)	$2.3 billion.
June 2001	ENI 60%; NIOC 40%	Dar Khovin (Onshore oil)	$1 billion. First buy-back with limited risk/reward component (ENI terms) that tied payment to production capacity. Completed 2006.
May 2002	Sheer Energy/CNPC (2004)	Masjid-e-Suleiman (Onshore oil)	$80 million. Originally awarded to Sheer Energy Cyprus under ENI terms. Due to delays in fulfilling the terms of contract, Sheer was replaced in September 2004 by CNPC (China National Petroleum Corporation), which bought Sheer's subsidiary. Completed 2006.
September 2002	LG	South Pars, phases 9 and 10 (Offshore gas)	$1.6 billion.
October 2002	Statoil	South Pars, phases 6, 7, and 8 (Offshore gas)	$2.7 billion.

February 2004	Inpex 10%; Naftiran Intertrade Co. 25%	Azadegan (Onshore oil)	$2 billion. Originally, Inpex led the project (with Japex and Tomen, which withdrew under US pressure) with a 75% stake, but it lost its operator status to Naftiran Intertrade Co. (which has a 25% stake in the project) and its stake was reduced to 10% in October 2006, due to increased costs and delays in financing, largely from US pressure.
October 2004	Sinopec 51%	Yadavaran (Onshore oil)	$2 billion. Still under negotiation by the beginning of 2007; includes a 30-year contract for LNG purchase.
June 2006	Sinopec	Garmsar (Onshore oil)	$20 million.
January 2007	SKS Ventures	Golshan-Ferdows (Onshore gas)	$16 billion. Memorandum of Understanding. Includes midstream and downstream operations.
Under negotiation	Norsk Hydro 75%; LUKoil 25%	Anaran (Onshore oil)	LUKOIL was signed into the project on 14 February, 2003. Under negotiation since summer 2006.
Under negotiation	China National Offshore Oil Co.	North Pars (Offshore gas)	Signed Memorandum of Understanding in spring 2004.

Source: Author from various sources.

essentially competition for its control at the point of production through direct investment in extraction, and this process is mediated by the contradiction between geographical integration and fragmentation, which we examined in its two forms in the case of Iran: the struggle by the US and its "allies" to isolate Iran yet integrate its hydrocarbons in the global economy, as part of a process of global economic integration; the struggle by Iran to assert its position in the global hydrocarbon industry yet guard its hydrocarbon industry against foreign capital in the very process of soliciting foreign investment for its development. Thus, the competition of individual oil companies for Iranian oil and gas is also a collective competition, as extractive industry, with Iran as landlord state controlling the access of capital to resources. Seen from the standpoint of the extraterritoriality and negative territoriality of US sanctions, the struggle of the "international community" with Iran – a struggle to isolate and discipline a "rogue state" – is also a struggle for the integration of Iran in competing hegemonic projects for the global economy. As the competition intensifies, so does the geographical contradiction, becoming ever more decisive in determining the results of the competition.

Notes

1 The expansion of capital, oil scarcity and the contradiction of space

1 See Klare 2001, 2004. Various catastrophic views based on Klare's assumptions are presented by Roberts 2004; Ruppert 2004; Heinberg 2005; and, especially, Kunstler 2005.
2 See Bromley 1991, 1998, 2005; Vitalis 1997, 2002, 2006; Mohamedi and Sadowski 2001; Callinicos 2003; Harvey 2003; Jhaveri 2004; Watts 2006.
3 See Campbell 1998, 2003; Campbell and Laherrère 1998; Deffeyes 2001, 2005.
4 See Adelman and Lynch 1997; Lynch 1998/1999, 2002, 2003; Odell 1998/1999, 2004.
5 Some estimates place world proven reserves at 4.8 trillion barrels (see Mouawad 2007).
6 Standard Oil of New Jersey (Exxon); Standard Oil of New York (Mobil); Standard Oil of California (Chevron); Texaco; Gulf Oil; Royal Dutch Shell; Anglo-Persian Oil Company (BP).
7 Other examples include PetroChina and Sinopec, 90 percent and 55 percent state-owned, respectively; Petrobras (Brazil, 32 percent); ONGC (India, 74 percent). See Vikas and Ellsworth 2007a, 2007b.

2 Contradictions of capitalist accumulation: inter-capitalist competition, the production of raw material and the contradiction of space

1 The "earth itself is an instrument of labor" whose use requires other instruments and a "comparatively high stage of development of labour-power" (Marx 1976: 285). See also Wittfogel 1985; Lefebvre 1939; Schmidt 1971.
2 Benton (1989) emphasizes the importance of extractive industry under similar light. Benton, however, separates the moments of the labor process into discrete points, opposing the *conditions* of labor to the *means* of labor. Accordingly, primary production, or extractive industry, is removed from industrial production and interposed between production and material nature, as a process of "eco-regulation" fundamentally different from the transformative activity in industrial production.
3 Here, also, turnover time is assumed constant, for the rate of profit changes also with the turnover time of capital, which is the sum of production and circulation time. The reduction in turnover time raises the quantity of surplus value produced and realized within a given period of time. Thus, capitals with different turnover times realize various rates of profit as quantities of surplus value in relation to capital advanced within the same period of time, such that the rate of profit is inversely proportional to the length of the turnover period.
4 This is where credit, "fictitious" money, consumption financed by debt, becomes

necessary for completing the process of realizing surplus value (and shortening the turnover time of capital) so that it can be capitalized in production (see Mandel 1995; Harvey 1999).

5 This is the case as far as exchange is not determined by "accidental monopoly" that enables the seller to sell above value, or force other sellers to sell below value. This is where landownership becomes determinant of the realization of surplus profits – by imposing such monopoly (see below).

6 Marx mentions a sixth, the increase in share capital, but does not discuss it further. As Harvey (1999: 178) notes, in the *Grundrisse,* Marx mentions five other factors: devaluation of capital, unproductive waste, transformation of fixed capital into unproductive capital, opening up of labor-intensive sectors that absorb the increase in "surplus" population, and monopolization. Capitalists also resort to "noneconomic" factors, such as evading taxes, inflating prices, exaggerating their assets, and a motley assortment of what can be considered illicit measures. As we are only concerned in this context with the act of squeezing surplus value out of labor, we do not delve further in the analysis of all factors.

7 500,000 workers were laid off in the late 1990s in the oil and gas industry in the US alone due to technological developments across the whole industry (see Mohamedi and Sodowski 2001).

8 For example: "...the same quantity of labour is present in eight bushels of corn in favourable seasons and only in four bushels in unfavourable seasons. The same quantity of labour provides more metal in rich mines than in poor" (Marx 1976: 130).

9 See Smith (1990) on the mediation of the use–value relationship with nature by exchange value.

10 The expansion of capital depends ultimately on the separation of land and resources from their original users, or owners, by what Luxemburg described as the "fiction" of making all (national) land the property of the sovereign, or the state. By "giving" land to the sovereign, land could be ultimately transformed into an alienable commodity that the sovereign could sell or mortgage to foreign banks in return for loans, or rent to foreign capital in the form of concessions for exploration and exploitation. (See Luxemburg's (1951) illuminating discussion of land in India and Egypt under British colonialism.) Mitchell's (2002; see also Scott 1998) dissection of the history of landed property in Egypt goes further than Luxemburg's to show how state lands referred to those managed and controlled by foreign lending banks, whereas the ruling family constituted the biggest private landowner through a system of estates. Revenues from land owned by members of the government went to the estate rather than the government treasury. This required that land be parceled in order to be commodified (for ownership, concessionary exploitation, or taxation).

11 Both transient and permanent improvements to the land are used up as with any other forms of constant capital. The more permanent improvements to the land, however, become the property of the landowner at the end of the lease, as "inseparable accident" of the land. The shorter the lease, the more unused up capital fixed in the land will fall to the landowner, for free: the same land leased again will, therefore, be leased as land of a higher quality, yielding higher rent. For example, land leased for oil and gas exploration yields rent but it yields higher rent if oil is found in it – i.e. if capital as geological knowledge is fixed in it – and even higher rents once oilfields are mapped and developed, even when the same company is involved in all phases. Most oil contracts granted to companies in Iran, for example, did not guarantee automatic oilfield development and production to exploring companies, and were renegotiated in the case of a discovery. This is one major obstacle to the development of production on lands with short lease periods since the capitalist avoids all investments in fixed capital that will not give their full return within the period of the lease and which will be lost to the landowner. This is particularly the case in the history of the oil industry. The reduction in the temporal length and spatial extent that accompanied

the transformation of the contractual form of agreement between foreign oil companies and national government placed more control and higher rents in the hands of the state as contracts became shorter and smaller in their geographical extent (see Chapter 6).

12 "Genuine rent" is rent that is not deducted from profits or wages and it forms a specific category independent from the production price of the commodity. Under "normal" conditions of production, the lease price of land – the surplus that the landowner collects – and rent must coincide (Marx 1981: 890). Marx distinguishes between two forms of rent, each forming the basis of the other: absolute and differential rent. In simple terms, absolute rent originates in the ability of the landowner to offer or withhold land from the circulation of capital, while differential rent arises from differences in the use-value of land, its qualities, location, etc. These are two aspects of rent rather than two types or kinds of rent that exist in pure form. All rent is both absolute and differential, and all landowners collect rent that is analytically divisible into absolute and differential rent. Marx (1981: 885 ff) considers three cases of an "accidental nature" where capital investment on land yields no rent. In the first instance, landed property coincides with capital. In this case, the capitalist and the landowner are the same entity, and the capitalist-landowner can put the land to use as long as capital invested on it can yield the average rate of profit. The barrier which landed property erects to the movement of capital is abolished in this case. But this collusion between capital and landed property, and the hypothetical elimination of the barrier of landed property, disappears as soon as an increased demand for the product requires the capitalist to expand into land that he does not own. In the second case, a particular piece of land that does not yield any rent can be leased for free, but only as part of a greater extent of land leased by the landowner. In such a case, the landowner collects rent for the total land leased to the capitalist rather than for the component parts including the individual piece in question. The barrier to landed property disappears in this instance, insofar as the capitalist can extend production into land that does not produce rent. But this is only possible because the no rent-bearing land to which the capitalist can extend production is leased as an accessory to land which pays rent. Finally, the capitalist may invest additional capital on land already leased when the market price was higher than the production price. The consequent investment is made at a time when the existing market price does not yield rent over and above the price of production. Compared with the above case, total rent is produced not over the spatial totality of land, but over the time period of the lease. Capital invested on the land at one time yields ground rent whereas another part of capital invested at a later time does not, yet the landowner collects rent for the whole period including both capital investments.

3 Imperialism and the geographical contradictions of monopoly capital

1 The relative position of financial capital in relation to industrial capital, developing since the crises of the 1970s, has been recently examined by Duménil and Lévy (2004), Harvey (2005), Bellamy Foster (2006, 2007), F. Magdoff (2006), and Peet (2007). For a revision of the position and development of financial capital in the postwar period, see Panitch and Gindin (2005a). Smith (2005) offers another view and shows, based on developments in US capitalism, a resurgent dominance of military–industrial–energy capital.

2 Although monopoly capital is characterized by the separation of ownership from management of capital, the distinction between ownership in general and management in general is not clear-cut as managers and chief executives are paid in stock and stock options, transferring ownership of social capital increasingly to the administrators. But, rather than "neutral technocracy," the managerial class is already part of the propertied classes – the "most active and influential" – and chief executives

often own significant shares in the companies they run. Baran and Sweezy's (1966) discussion on this topic is on point and still relevant today despite the changes over the last four decades.

3 Examples abound; Mandel (1978) lists 800 protectionist policies enacted by Western capitalist countries in 1974–1975, mostly against each other. Two protectionist measures, however, suffice to signify the dual nature of re-emerging inter-capitalist competition. Section 301 of the Trade Act of 1974, largely directed against Japanese steel and automobile industries, authorized the US to take punitive actions against "unfair traders" and to put pressure on trading partners to accept "voluntary export restraints." (This act is not too dissimilar to the recent threats by the US to repeal normal trade relations with China, see below.) The Multi-Fiber Arrangement of 1973 placed quota restrictions against textile and apparel exports from the developing countries, and protected producers in the advanced capitalist economies collectively until they were able to "adjust" to cheap imports from the developing countries. Thirty years later, the developed countries were still "adjusting." The Multi-Fiber Agreement expired on 1 January 2005, only to be replaced by the Agreement on Textile and Clothing, under the jurisdiction of the WTO, which retained quota restrictions.

4 Most contemporary mainstream and "critical" geopolitical analysis omits the sphere of material production and the processes of capital accumulation from the analysis of the relationship between political power and geographical territory. This is not the place to provide an extended critique of contemporary geopolitical theory. Marxian theorists identified the drawbacks of geopolitical theory almost as soon as it was developed, primarily its omission of the specifically capitalist relations of production, the raison d'être of the capitalist state (see Wittfogel 1985; Bukharin 1936).

5 The so-called Keynesian state provided the model for the "interventionist," developmental state in the post-war period, in its social democratic guise in Western Europe and later in parts of the Third World. In the US, where the state has historically developed as the exemplary "weak" bourgeois state – weak in relation to the (industrial, later financial) bourgeoisie – Keynesianism took a military, rather than a social democratic, turn, providing the basis for the development of a strong military–industrial bourgeoisie. The decline of US economic hegemony beginning in the 1960s and progressing well into the present, contrasted with the ascendance of US militarism, expressing a reversal in the state–bourgeoisie relationship and the quasi-autonomy of an increasingly militarized state from a relatively weakened (industrial) bourgeoisie (see below).

6 Cf. Bukharin (1929: 121): "this entirely erroneous conception formerly found some justification in the fact that the bourgeoisie, following the line of least resistance, tended to widen its territory by the seizure of free lands that offered little resistance. Now, however, the time has come, for a fundamental redivision. Just as trusts competing with one another within the boundaries of a state first grow at the expense of 'third persons,' of outsiders, and only after having destroyed the intermediary groupings, thrust themselves against one another with particular ferocity, so the competitive struggle between state capitalist trusts first expresses itself in a struggle for free lands, for the *jus primi occupantis*, then it stages a redivision of colonies, and finally, when the struggle becomes more intense, even the territory of the home country is drawn into the process of redivision. Here, too, development proceeds along the line of least resistance, and the weakest state capitalist trusts first disappear from the face of the earth."

7 The expansion of money capital in the form of public loans occupies a prominent place in Luxemburg's account of the relationship between capital accumulation and the production of uneven geography. The export of money capital, however, appears always in relation to the export of capital as means of production. Money capital lent to governments in the developing periphery during the imperialist era was primarily paid back in the purchase of industrial means of production. It was invested in infra-

structure (and the armament industry) which, on the one hand, provided a sphere for the investment of overaccumulated capital, and on the other hand created demand for the products of the metropolitan economies at the same time that it enhanced the circulation of commodity capital and the further expansion of capital in the metropolitan economies (see Luxemburg 1951: 426–427). Ultimately, in a prescient analysis that sheds light on the contemporary rise of financial capital and its power over the economic policies of countries plagued with chronic debt, these loans were instrumental in developing and maintaining a relationship of dominance over the developing capitalist economies by allowing the banks in the advanced capitalist economies to exercise their financial control over the domestic economies of the less developed ones, and over their foreign and commercial policies (see ibid. p. 34).

8 See Luxemburg's (1951: 366) discussion of the exchange between German industry and German peasants. In this regard, Harvey's (2003, 2005) reworking of Marx's notion of "primitive accumulation" into "accumulation by dispossession" advances Luxemburg's thesis about the conquest by capital of the non-capitalist environment in the context of the expansion by neoliberal capital of the limits, in society and material nature, to privatization.

9 Bukharin warns that the export of capital should not be considered in abstraction from other economic and political phenomena accompanying it. Capital export in the form of public (state) loans or private investments return to the creditors more than simple interest on capital. It has been often accompanied by conditions which impose on the debtor country the purchase of certain products from capitalists in the creditor country, constrictions on dealing with competing capitals, special trade treaties, etc., but, most importantly, the granting of concessions for specific projects such as the construction of railroads and other public works, and the exploration and exploitation of natural resources. See the example of a 1913 loan to the Persian government by the Russian Discount and Loan Bank of Persia in return for a concession for a railway between Julfa and Tabriz (Bukharin 1929: 98–99).

10 Standard Oil of New Jersey, in 1910, owned 62 companies, and was "connected" with a large number of Dutch, German, French, Swedish, Italian, Russian, etc., enterprises. By the early 1960s, Standard Oil of New Jersey (Exxon) owned 50 percent or more of stock in 275 companies in 52 countries, 77 of which were in the US and 77 in Europe (see Baran and Sweezy 1966: 193 ff). Despite its wide-ranging operations, Exxon, even after merging with Mobil (Standard Oil of New York) in the 1990s, remains a US company, "multinational" in operation but not in management and ownership.

11 Typically, John Gaddis (1997), "the dean of Cold War historians," depicts the Cold War as a struggle between two "informal empires" – a Soviet one, characterized by coercive and military domination and an "American empire" characterized by the voluntary willingness of the US and its post-war allies to manage a sphere of influence under the benevolent hegemony of the US, within which the European satellites retained considerable freedom. Walker (1993) and Agnew (2003) offer more critical and nuanced analyses, but still construe the Cold War primarily as an ideological and binary conflict. The binary division of the Cold War, combined with the preponderance of the US in the West, is also reproduced by Panitch and Gindin (2005a, 2005b) who, although arguing from an analytical and political standpoint diametrically opposite to Gaddis, retain the idea of US super-imperialism, but in this case not so benevolent. Hobsbawm (1994), despite his brief excursion into bringing out inter-capitalist conflicts in the post-war period, concludes that the conflict between the US and the USSR displaced and overshadowed all other conflicts in the post-war period. Halliday (1983) and Harvey (1999, 2001) offer penetrating and complex analyses of the geopolitics of post-war capitalism. Halliday's treatment of inter-capitalist contradiction is largely confined to the "second Cold War," however, while Harvey's (2003) more recent treatment of the Cold War reiterates the binary model.

12　See Hardt and Negri (2000, 2004). For critiques of this notion of empire from different perspectives, see E. M. Wood (2004), Amin (2004), Slater (2004), and Agnew
(2005). Agnew's critique, however, replaces this notion of empire with an equally
problematic notion of "hegemony without a hegemon," while Amin and Slater place
most emphasis on the North–South divide.

13　Harvey (2003; see also Harvey 2001) and Callinicos 2003) have recently examined
the resurgence of inter-capitalist rivalry in the development of global capital. Harvey
is keen on emphasizing the triadic continental structure of the current geopolitical
economy. On the opposite side of the political and analytical spectrum, Brzezinski
(1997) has examined world geopolitics in terms of competition among an intercontinental triad, with an eye, however, on upholding US hegemony.

14　Oil and gas transnational companies are not exempt from the historical geographical
tendency of capital to centralize at the global scale. Yet, in spite of this tendency,
very few transnational oil companies of different "nationalities" have fused together.
The general tendency in the oil industry, since the merger madness of late 1990s, has
been for companies of the same "nationality" to fuse in larger capitals (e.g. Exxon-
Mobil, Chevron Texaco, etc.) and in some instances, as in the case of Russia (see
Chapter 5), to fuse with the national state. The same trend characterizes the arms
industry, which followed similar lines of consolidation in the 1990s in the US,
resulting in huge "national" monopolies such as Lockheed Martin and Northrop
Grumman (see below).

15　The steamboat allowed European "explorers" and merchants to penetrate the inlands
of Africa and Asia, especially the Chinese Empire, sailing up shallow rivers which
were previously inaccessible to older warships. (From control of the sea to control of
the rivers.) Developments in the "art of war" allowed European invaders to suppress
native uprising and resistance, especially in Africa. Ironically, older weapons were
always accessible to colonized revolutionaries through European merchants and
Europeans, therefore, had to "suffer" the effects of their own arms technology in the
hands of colonized people. Nonetheless, European arms were always superior, as
Europeans did not make their newest models always available to their trading partners
in the colonies and the revolutionaries, or governments even, were not able to afford
the new technologies (see Headrick 1981).

16　The "new international division of labor" in more contemporary parlance, however,
refers to the division arising from the migration of industrial production to parts of the
Third World beginning in the 1970s, and the specialization of metropolitan
economies in "white collar" work. See Fröbel, Heinrichs, and Kreye (1980).

17　See also E. M. Wood's (2003) analysis of the British experiment in Ireland. Parry
(1966) made a similar distinction between "effective colonization" and the establishment of "trading stations" as alternative strategies during early European colonialism,
including the British colonization of the American continent which combined both.

18　The same goes for the standard view of an isolationist US, which ignores its interventionist stance in the Americas throughout the nineteenth century and most of the
twentieth and, indeed, its military interventions in the Mediterranean and Southeast
Asia to protect US capitalist interests (see Williams 1972, 1980; Smith 2003, 2005;
Slater 2004). Except in the continental USA, US imperialism differed from, and
found opposition in, the practice of European imperialism by being less dependent on
direct territorial control than on economic imperialism and proxy ruling classes.

19　In 1873–1874 the US imposed 38 percent duties on imports, which increased to 40
percent by 1883, and then to 47 percent in 1887. By 1890 duties on imports had
reached 91 percent for woolen products and 150 percent for fine-grade woolens
(Bukharin 1929).

20　The US government was the largest consumer of zippers, and was responsible for the
development and popularity of the new, uncertain technology with its large demand
for it on the eve of World War I (see Petroski 1991).

21 For various explanations of the economic crises beginning in the 1960s, see Mandel 1970, 1978, 1995; Brenner 1998, 2003; Duménil and Lévy 2004; and Agnew 2005.

22 Average calculated from Baran and Sweezy (1966: 242, 237); see also Varga (1947); figures for labor productivity and assets are from Kolko and Kolko (1972).

23 The tolerance of controls over capital allowed the US Treasury to consider the Soviet Union and the Communist bloc for membership in the Bretton Woods regime, and constant attempts were made to guarantee their participation in the Bretton Woods conference. The US even tried to entice the Soviet Union with a $10 billion loan (Spero 1985). The Soviet Union eventually participated in the Bretton Woods conference, but did not join either the IMF or the IBRD, objecting to the "supervisory power" and the policing function of the IMF. The Soviet Union refused to ratify the agreements reached in the conference, in order not to submit to the "exacting investigations" of gold production, gold and foreign exchange holdings, spending of borrowed funds, and so on – all of which the Soviet Union "customarily kept secret" (see Knorr 1948; Cooper 1975; Scammell 1980; Cohen 1991). From Communist Eastern Europe, only Czechoslovakia, Poland, and Yugoslavia became members of the IMF and IBRD, but Czechoslovakia and Poland withdrew in 1950 and 1954, respectively. Opposite to the economic bloc emerging in the West, and in response to the Marshall Plan, the Council for Mutual Economic Assistance (Comecon) was established in 1949 to reinforce economic cooperation in the Communist bloc.

24 On British and French resistance to US post-war plans for Europe, see Milward 1984.

25 The Korean War also played a major role in boosting the economy of Japan, which, through Special Procurements, received around $3.5 billion, an amount equivalent to Marshall Aid to Germany (Walker 1993: 78 ff).

26 The relationship between the US government and two strategic industries critical for warfare – the arms industry and the oil industry – begins to grow in significance in the late 1940s. It is similar to developments of (European) imperialism in the early twentieth century and again in the 1930s, when the expansion of industry coincided with the perpetual preparation for war and the expansion of the arms industry in times of peace (see Bukharin 1929; Hobsbawm 1987). This triadic association is more visible at the center of the current US administration and is a developing element in relation to developing regional and global competitors, such as Iran and China, whose growing industrial production, increasing demand for oil, and processes of "modernization" of the military are major concerns for the US bourgeoisie.

27 In this light, massive armament during the Reagan years, although still justified in terms of the imaginary struggle against Communism, was a partially successful attempt to reverse the decline in the US economy and to strengthen the imperialist position of the US against other capitalist competitors in Europe and the Third World. Arms production and the military budget of the US were expanded even further, in relative terms, after the collapse of the Soviet Union and throughout the 1990s, well into the present. On armament during the Clinton years in comparison with the Cold War, see Achcar 1998. The manufacturing of a new enemy – "international terrorism" – serves similar purposes today: development of the arms industry subsidized by government spending – transfer of value through taxes into the arms industry – and expanding the market for arms under the pretext of the War on Terror. But as Žižek (2003) recently suggested, the US war on Iraq is the first war between the US and Europe; one may include the new rivals to the East, Russia and China.

28 The US sought to remove all barriers to the expansion of capital into Eastern Europe by implementing an "open-door" policy that would have given US capital an "equal economic opportunity" in the region. In the foreign ministers' council in June 1946, the US pressed for the removal of all trade preferences across Eastern Europe, and for the "enjoyment of all states ... of access on equal terms to the trade and raw materials of the world." Open-door policy in Eastern Europe appeared as a declaration of economic war, an open attempt by US capital to acquire and control local industries and

enhance its position in the global economy, on its way to "world domination." This policy was much more successfully directed at Britain, and France to a certain extent, in the Middle East than it was in Eastern Europe.

29 Stalin drew on a report that Novikov, the Soviet ambassador in Washington, sent to the Kremlin affirming that the US still considered Britain as its "greatest potential competitor," and "despite temporary agreements [between the US and Britain] on very important questions," the Anglo-American relationship is "plagued with great internal contradictions and cannot be lasting" (quoted in Gaddis 1997: 42–43). Yet, Stalin's speech was interpreted in the USA as a declaration of war *on* the capitalist world, particularly the US (Walker 1993). An inquiry sent to the US embassy in Moscow about the motives of Stalin's declaration of war produced what would later become a forming moment of the Cold War, Kennan's "long telegram," which became the basis for an enduring policy of containment. Kennan, (X [Kennan], 1947), already exasperated by the Soviet Union's refusal to join the Bretton Woods institutions, invited the US to assume leadership of "the West" whose only hope against the threat of "oriental" Communism was its capacity to grow, which ultimately rested on its internal political cohesion under the historically-ordained leadership of the US.

30 As Fred Magdoff (2006) argued in his review of Harry Magdoff and Paul Sweezy's analyses of the economic crises of the 1970s, stagnation is the "general economic tendency of mature capitalism." Even during the 1960s, [US] industrial production utilized around 85 percent of its capacity, peaking at 91 percent in 1966: productive capacity averaged 81 percent in the three decades since the late 1970s. Mandel (1995) had developed a similar argument regarding the "asymmetry" between growth and stagnation in mature capitalism, which distinguishes monopoly capital from its previous competitive period – stagnation results automatically from the motion of monopoly capital whereas economic growth requires "artificial stimuli" and "external" interventions in the economy.

31 We are not concerned here with the ideological and behavioral aspects of militarism; see Mann 1987.

32 See Achcar's (1998) extensive and penetrating critique of the Clinton administration's military strategy. Military expenditure measures are also misleading in that they do not account for indirect military-related expenditure. As Cypher (2007: 47) demonstrates, military-related expenditures (MilReEx) in the US exceed the defense budget as presented in the Department of Defense outlays by around 80 percent.

33 See Johnson (2000, 2004); Bacevich (2002).

34 E.g. Joint Combined Exchange Training Programs (JCET), established by Special Operations Command in 1991, and the International Military Education and Training Program (IMET), established by the Department of State in 1990, and the Pentagon's much larger Foreign Military Financing.

35 See Peet 2007, for a similar process in the economic development policy circles, where policy elites circulate between government, Ivy League universities, think tanks, lobbying groups, investment banks, and global governance institutions.

36 The total (reported) sales of the largest 100 arms-producing companies in 2005, excluding companies from China, amounted to around $1,350 billion of which around $315 billion came from the sale of arms. The largest 20 firms accounted for 72 percent of total arms sales (around $227 billion); the largest 12, 62 percent (around $195 billion); the largest six, 45 percent (around $142 billion) (these comprised in 2005 Boeing, Northrop Grumman, Lockheed Martin, BAE Systems, Raytheon, General Dynamics); the largest three, 26 percent (around $82 billion).

   Of the 100 largest companies, 45 are from the US, with the share of 43 of them amounting to around 60.1 percent of total arms sales ($189 billion); the largest six US companies alone account for 40.5 percent ($127 billion); 11 companies from the UK account for 10.8 percent of total arms sales ($34 billion); 11 companies from France, of which eight share 6.8 percent of the total ($21 billion); ten companies from Italy account for 5.8 percent of total arms sales ($18 billion); three European companies share 5 percent of the total ($16 billion); eight German companies share 2.1 percent ($6.5 billion); six Japanese companies, 2 percent ($6.2 billion); and nine Russian companies 1.7 percent ($5.4 billion). Data calculated from Appendix 9A.1 of SIPRI 2007: 374–382.

4 Oil in the development and decline of the Soviet Union

1 Beginning in the middle 1950s, the Soviet Union provided Eastern Europe with 80 percent of its oil imports in exchange for manufactured products that could not be sold on the world market due to their inflated prices. In 1960, the major exports of the Soviet Union comprised machinery, equipment, means of transportation, etc., but by 1985, 60 percent of its imports comprised machinery and industrial articles. Oil and gas came to constitute 53 percent of its exports, divided almost equally between its own "satellites" in the Communist bloc and non-Communist countries, mostly Western European industrial economies (see Bromley 1991; Hobsbawm 1994).
2 See Yergin 1991.
3 During the 1930s, the Soviet Union did establish sufficient conditions in domestic production to reduce foreign imports, but it was still importing heavy machinery, ships, diesel engines, etc., and oil refining technologies from the US, in exchange for raw material and agricultural products, as well as some agricultural machinery, sewing machines, bicycles, etc., through the Amtorg Trading Corporation – a US corporation representing the Soviet Union in US markets (see Ropes 1943, 1944).
4 In 1939, agriculture consumed 60 percent of all oil products (Lydolph and Shabad 1960).
5 The share of coal in total energy consumption was 48.8 percent in 1927–28 compared to 25 percent for oil; 58.9 percent in 1936 compared to 20.5 percent for oil; and 65.9 percent in 1950 against 16.2 percent for oil (Lamet 1952). Lydolph and Shabad (1960) cite 73 percent for coal in 1950. The rigidity of the centrally planned economy contributed to the continued dependence on coal. A structural shift to oil as a source of industrial energy would have involved massive reorganization and bureaucratic procedures in addition to the costs from technological shifts.
6 Baku accounted for about 80 percent of the Soviet Union's crude oil production until World War II. In 1950, it was still the largest oil-producing region, but its production level and relative importance had fallen (Lamet 1952).
7 See Ward 1960. The 15-year oil plan aimed at reducing the share of coal to 30 percent of total fuel consumption (from 70 percent in 1940) and increasing that of oil and gas to 60 percent (Lydolph and Shabad 1960).
8 Soviet oil production for 1950, 1955, and 1960 was 757,000 bbl/d, 1,416,000 bbl/d, 2,900,000 bbl/d, respectively, while its consumption over the same period was 794,000 bbl/d, 1,374,000 bbl/d, 2,525,000 bbl/d (Ward 1960).
9 Between 1987 and 1988, the volume of crude oil exports rose by 5.6 percent, whereas gas exports increased by about 7 percent between 1986 and 1987. In 1988, around 23 percent of total oil production, 11.4 percent of gas production, and 6.6 percent of hard coal output were exported. Oil and gas exports to Western countries in 1989 accounted for 80 percent of the Soviet Union's hard currency earnings (Kuhnert 1991).
10 See Nove 1980. According to Kuhnert (1991), between 1975 and 1988, investment in the energy sector grew from 9.9 percent to 14.6 percent of total investment, and its share of investment in industry grew from 28.2 percent to 42.4 percent, whereas investment in industry grew from 35 percent to 36.4 percent of total investment over the same period: "new construction projects" (*novoe storitel'stvo*) absorbed 60 percent of capital investment in the energy sector.
11 In 1978, 64 percent of the Soviet Union's hard currency earnings came from energy

exports, and this share grew larger by 1980 even though the export of oil declined in absolute terms. The contribution of foreign technology to the industries of the Soviet Union grew enormously between 1970 and 1975. Technological imports accounted for 15 percent of new equipment (Gustafson 1982).

12 The "Carter embargo" was a response by the US to the intervention of the Soviet Union in Afghanistan (see above). Under pressure from US farmers, the Reagan administration lifted the grain embargo, but not the restrictions on trade in high technology to the Soviet Union, in April 1981.

5 Geographical contradictions of state and capital in the development of Russian oil: competition for Russia, competition with Russia

1 PetroAlliance was acquired by Schlumberger in 2003.

2 See figure 2 in Khartukov 2002.

3 LUKoil was one of the few companies that resisted acquisition by the Groups and remained partially state-owned (until ConocoPhillips bought the government's share), with 10 percent of its shares owned by its pension funds. Surgutneftegas was another company to escape the oligarchs by its pension funds acquiring the 40 percent share offered by the government. In contrast, Yukos was the first company to be fully privatized through the loans-for-shares scheme after the government sold its shares to Bank Menatep, founded and controlled by Khodorkovsky. Fifty-one percent of Sidanco was similarly transferred to Oreximbank, run by one of the infamous oligarchs, Victor Potanin, with close ties to another, Anatoly Chubais (Obut *et al.* 1999b).

4 The "nationalization" of Yukos also made a public example of a high-profile company with the effect of disciplining others, rather than repeating the process (see Lavelle 2004). After the crackdown on Yukos, all other companies, foreign and domestic, agreed to pay their tax debts and to increase their tax rates. British shareholders have increasingly harbored worries about the Russian government's demands on TNK-BP for $936 million in back taxes, and, most recently, the Russian Ministry of Natural Resources accused TNK-BP of not developing the Kovykta field fast enough to meet its license requirements. Instead of revoking TNK-BP's license, however, the government reached an agreement with it to yield its controlling stake in the Kovykta project to Gazprom. Quite significantly, Gazprom's agreement with TNK-BP coupled its capture of a controlling stake in Kovykta with expansion abroad through international joint ventures with BP. The Russian authorities have also threatened to revoke production licenses held by Royal Dutch Shell and LUKoil, primarily on the grounds of environmental law violations.

5 Russia ostensibly followed the example of the US which forced, by law, the China National Offshore Oil Corporation to abandon its bid for Unocal under the claim that such an acquisition would jeopardize US national security (Watson 2006).

6 See Konoplyanik (2002). Both Sakhalin consortia contract Russian companies for construction, engineering, and other services. Sakhalin-1 awarded 85 percent of its contracts to local companies in 2003, and Sakhalin-2 contracts 77 percent of labor from Russia in addition to 74 percent of its equipment and material for the duration of the project (Clark 2004; Nicholls 2004). This is not so much the result of the "local commitment" of the consortia, as the *Petroleum Economist* put it, but of limitations imposed by Russian investment laws.

7 At the same time, Access-Renova, which owned Tyumen Oil, increased its stake in Rusiya Petroleum. Currently, TNK-BP owns 63 percent of Rusiya Petroleum, which owns the license and operates Kovykta gasfield in Eastern Siberia.

8 In early 2003, Tyumen Oil (TNK) and Sibneft, through Invest-Oil, an affiliate company acting on behalf of both companies, bought a 75 percent equity stake in Slavneft, one of the two remaining state-owned companies in Russia. China National

Petroleum Corporation was the third bidding company, but the Russian government was keen on preventing foreign companies from winning the bid, especially those in which a foreign government holds a stake of 25 percent or more.

6 Geographical contradictions of Iranian oil: capital versus the law

1   Production costs, including direct lifting costs and production taxes in 2005, were between $4.95/barrel of oil equivalent (boe) in the Middle East, the region with the lowest production taxes, and $8.36/boe in the former Soviet Union and East Europe, the region with the highest production taxes, with the world average at $6.87/boe. Actual lifting costs ranged between $3.17/boe and $6.98/boe in "other Western hemisphere" countries and Canada respectively, with the world average at $5.13/boe.) Historically, except in the US during the early 1980s, direct lifting costs hovered between $4/boe and $6/boe (EIA 2006).

2   Ye *et al.* 2003. The elasticity of short-term demand for crude oil varies between –0.0263 for G-7 countries and –0.0827 for non G-7 countries.

3   I venture, in passing, the following remark regarding Iraqi oil. The invasion of Iraq and its opening to US oil companies did not have as its aim the flooding of the market with Iraqi oil to bring market prices down, as one may infer from comments made by Paul Wolfowitz and others, but precisely the opposite: to control the entry of Iraqi oil into the market, in order not to jeopardize inflated market prices since 2000 and super profits for producers elsewhere, especially in high-cost regions such as North America and the North Sea (see below).

4   *Petroleum Intelligence Weekly* 2006.

5   Conoco's was the first buy-back contract to be granted by the Iranian government to a foreign oil company, with comparatively higher rates of return than the dominant 15 percent of later agreements. The development of Sirri A was granted a 20 percent rate of return; Sirri E, 23 percent (see below).

6   *Wall Street Journal*, 28 March 1995: B4.

7   US oil companies operating in the Caspian Sea were initially exempt from Clinton's embargo because they lacked viable export routes out of the region (except pipelines passing through Iran or Russia). They were allowed to conduct "crude swaps" according to which they made oil from the Caspian available to Iran in the North for an equivalent volume of Iranian oil to be picked up from port cities in the South. This provision, however, came under attack for undermining the effort to build a pipeline between Baku in Azerbaijan and Ceyhan in Turkey to bypass the Russian pipeline network. US companies were subsequently banned from conducting crude swaps.

8   The amendment was proposed by Senator Edward Kennedy, representing the interest of the families of the victims of the Lockerbie bombing in Scotland, who threatened to block IOSA. (Libya has been under US sanctions since 1986 and UN sanctions since 1992.)

9   Section 9.c of ILSA allows the President to waive sanctions on a violating firm if the President can prove that this is in the national interest of the US.

10   In late 1998, Iran offered to presell its oil at $5.80/bbl, half the current market price – largely to pay mounting foreign debt.

11   Kish, a tourist and gambling resort in pre-Revolutionary Iran, was designated as a free economic zone in 1989. The High Ministerial Council for Free Zones issued regulations concerning the Qeshm Island Free Area (QFA) in December 1990.

12   Mehdi Behkish, head of the Iran Chamber of Commerce, described Qeshm as "a window to our liberalisation.... It will be able to show people throughout the country how beneficial the market economy is, the possibilities it can bring" (*The Banker* 1993). Bijan Khajehpour, managing director of Atieh Bahar Consulting, saw the free trade zones "functioning as a back door for reform ideas to see if they could work on

the mainland" (Dawkins and Dinmore 1999). A few years later, Mohammad Ali Najafi, Deputy Chairman of the Kish Free Zone Organization, told Michael Thomas, director of trade for the Middle East Association (London), who took a party of executives of 15 foreign companies on a tour of Iran in 2004: "We are going to set a pattern for mainland Iran. Whatever we do here, we will test, prove and export to the mainland" (Champion 2005).

13 Also in 1997, parliament passed the Law of International Commercial Arbitration, based on the international arbitration model of the United Nations Commission on International Trade Law (UNCITRAL).

14 Parliament also considered amendments to the Tax Code, the Law on Stock Exchange and Securities, and Bankruptcy Law.

15 The Council of Guardians reviews legislation to ensure it conforms with Islamic law. It consists of six clerics appointed by the Supreme Leader and six jurists elected by parliament from among jurists nominated by the judiciary. The Expediency Council is appointed by the Supreme Leader to resolve legislative disputes between the Council of Guardians and parliament.

16 "Any form of agreement resulting in foreign control over the natural resources, economy, army, or culture of the country, as well as other aspects of the national life, is forbidden". (Article 153). All quotations from The Constitution of the Islamic Republic of Iran, Official Gazette of the Islamic Republic of Iran, no. 10,170, 1 BAHMAN 1358 (21 January 1980).

17 The Constitution defines as the duty of Islamic government "the complete elimination of imperialism and the prevention of foreign influence" (Article 3.5); "the attainment of self-sufficiency in scientific, technological, industrial, agricultural, and military domains, and other similar spheres" (Article 3.13). The objective of the Islamic government is to achieve "economic independence of the society" (Article 43) and "prevention of foreign economic domination over the country's economy" (Article 43.8). "The foreign policy of the Islamic Republic of Iran is based upon the rejection of all forms of domination ... the preservation of the independence of the country in all respects and its territorial integrity" (Article 152).

18 The constitution is explicit on the question of private ownership. Article 46: "Everyone is the owner of the fruits of his legitimate business and labor, and no one may deprive another of the opportunity of business and work under the pretext of his right to ownership." Article 47: "Private ownership, legitimately acquired, is to be respected."

19 "The granting of concessions to foreigners for the formation of companies or institutions dealing with commerce, industry, agriculture, services or mineral extraction, is absolutely forbidden" (Article 81). This is reiterated in Article 2 of the Foreign Investment Promotion and Protection Act of 2002 (see below).

20 Concessions still characterize agreements with international oil companies in the US, Canada, and the North Sea – regions where production, and especially exploration costs, are high.

21 ENI also reaped a relatively high rate of return: its fees on the $920 million project were set at $220 million, against capital expenditure of $548 million and bank charges of $142 million (Dinmore 2001).

22 Stock nationalized after the Revolution has not always been paid for, and foreign companies investing in Iran run the risk of litigation by former owners of nationalized stock residing in the US, or Europe, similar to that allowed under the Helms-Burton Act with regards to Cuban property expropriated by the Cuban government.

23 Article 3 defines two types of foreign investment, both of which "enjoy the incentives and protections" provided by the act: direct investment "in fields where the activity of the private sector is permissible" (Article 3.a); investment in "schemes where the return of capital and profits accrued is solely emanated from the economic performance of the project in which the investment is made," including buy-back agreements

(Article 3.b). Article 2 prohibits foreign ownership of any land and certain types of immovable property, and, in keeping with the constitution, Article 2.c prohibits concessions, by which it specifies "special rights" that grant foreign investors a "monopolistic position" (see also Article 2.d below).

24 Article 2.d limits the ratio of goods and services (in value) produced for the domestic market to 25 percent (by sector) and 35 percent (by subsector) of total goods and services.

25 The implementing regulations of Fippa include, under the protection of Fippa, foreign investment made in state-controlled industries, with explicit reference to the "exploration, extraction, and transfer" of oil and gas (see Brexendorff and Ule 2004).

Bibliography

Achcar, G. (1998), "The strategic triad: the United States, Russia and China," *New Left Review* I/228: 91–126.

Adelman, M. A. and Lynch, M. C. (1997), "Fixed view of resource limits creates undue pessimism," *Oil and Gas Journal* 7 April: 56–59.

Agamben, G. (2005), *State of Exception*, trans. K. Attell, Chicago: University of Chicago Press.

Agnew, J. (2003), *Geopolitics: Re-visioning World Politics*, London: Routledge.

—— (2005), *Hegemony: The New Shape of Global Power*, Philadelphia: Temple University Press.

Alden, E., Daniel, C., and Turner, M. (2006), "US looks to financial sector to raise pressure on Iran," *Financial Times*, 8 May: 4.

Amin, S. (2004), *The Liberal Virus: Permanent War and the Americanization of the World*, New York: Monthly Review Press.

Anderson, P. (2007), "Russia's managed democracy," *London Review of Books*, 25 January: 3–12.

Arendt, H. (1951), *The Origins of Totalitarianism*, New York: Harcourt Brace Jovanovich.

Armstrong, P., Glyn A., and Harrison, J. (1991), *Capitalism since 1945*, Oxford: Basil Blackwell.

Arrighi, G. (1994), *The Long Twentieth Century: Money, Power, and the Origins of Our Times*, London: Verso.

Bacevich, A. J. (2002), *American Empire: The Realities and Consequences of U.S. Diplomacy*, Cambridge, MA: Harvard University Press.

Banker, The (1993), "Through the Qeshm window," September 1993: 48.

Baran, P. A. and Sweezy, P. M. (1966), *Monopoly Capital: An Essay on the American Economic and Social Order*, New York: Monthly Review Press.

Barnett, T. P. M. (2004), *The Pentagon's New Map: War and Peace in the Twenty-First Century*, New York: G. P. Putnam's Sons.

Bellamy Foster, J. (2006), "Monopoly-finance capital," *Monthly Review*, 58 (7): 1–14.

—— (2007), "The financialization of capitalism," *Monthly Review*, 58 (11): 1–12.

Benton, T. (1989), "Marxism and natural limits: an ecological critique and reconstruction," *New Left Review*, I/178: 51–86.

Block, F. (1977), *The Origins of International Economic Disorder: A Study of United States International Monetary Policy from World War II to the Present*, Berkeley: University of California Press.

Borawski, J. (1995), "Partnership for peace and beyond," *International Affairs*, 71: 233–246.

Brenner, R. (1998), "Uneven development and the long downturn: the advanced capitalist economies from boom to stagnation, 1950–1998," *New Left Review*, I/229: 1–264.

—— (2003), *The Boom and the Bubble: The US in the World Economy*, London: Verso.

Brexendorff, A. and Ule, C. (2004), "Changes bring new attention to Iranian buy-back contracts," *Oil and Gas Journal*, 1 November: 16–19.

Bromley, S. (1991), *American Hegemony and World Oil: The Industry, the State System and the World Economy*, University Park, PA: Pennsylvania State University Press.

—— (1998), "Oil and the Middle East: the end of US hegemony?" *Middle East Report*, no. 208 (Autumn): 19–22.

—— (2005), "The United States and the control of world oil," *Government and Opposition*, 40 (2): 225–255.

Brzezinski, Z. (1997), *The Grand Chessboard: American Primacy and its Geostrategic Imperatives*, New York: Basic Books.

Bukharin, N. I. (1929), *Imperialism and World Economy*, London: Martin Lawrence.

—— (1936), "Imperialism and communism," *Foreign Affairs*, 14: 563–77.

—— (1972), "Imperialism and the accumulation of capital," trans. R. Wichmann, in K. J. Tarbuck (ed.) *The Accumulation of Capital – An Anti-critique and Imperialism and the Accumulation of Capital*, New York: Monthly Review Press.

Callinicos, A. (2003), *The New Mandarins of American Power: The Bush Administration's Plans for the World*, Cambridge: Polity Press.

Campbell, C. J. (1998), "Running out of gas: this time the wolf is coming," *The National Interest*, no. 51 (Spring): 47–55.

—— (2003), "Industry urged to watch for regular oil production peaks, depletion signals," *Oil and Gas Journal*, 14 July: 38–45.

Campbell, C. J. and Laherrère, J. H. (1998), "The end of cheap oil," *Scientific American*, March: 78–83.

Campbell, R. (1968), "Economic reform in the USSR," *The American Economic Review*, 58: 547–558.

Champion, M. (2005), "Tougher sell: Iran, flush with oil cash, seems to cool to foreign investments," *Wall Street Journal*, 8 February: A1.

Clark, J. (2004), "Sakhalin II partners let pipeline, platform contracts," *Oil and Gas Journal*, 26 April: 22–23.

Cohen, B. J. (1991), "A brief history of international monetary relations," in J. A. Frieden and D. A. Lake (eds) *International Political Economy: Perspectives on Global Power and Wealth*, New York: St. Martin's Press.

Collins, G. (2006), "With oil companies, Russia seeking control plus capital" *Oil and Gas Journal*, 15 May: 18–22.

Cooper, R. N. (1975), "Prolegomena to the choice of an international monetary system," in C. F. Bergsten and L. B. Krause (eds) *World Politics and International Economics*, Washington, DC: The Brookings Institution.

Cornell, S. E. (2004), "The United States and Central Asia: in the steppes to stay?," *Cambridge Review of International Affairs*, 17 (2): 239–254.

Cypher, J. M. (2007), "From military Keynesianism to global–neoliberal militarism," *Monthly Review*, 59 (2): 37–55.

Dawkins, W. and Dinmore, G. (1999), "Impact of Iran protests 'exaggerated,'" *Financial Times*, 22 July: 3.

Deffeyes, K. S. (2001), *Hubbert's Peak: The Impending World Oil Shortage*, Princeton, NJ: Princeton University Press.

—— (2005), *Beyond Oil: The View from Hubbert's Peak*, New York: Hill and Wang.

Dicken, P. (2003), *Global Shift: Reshaping the Global Economic Map in the 21st Century*, New York: Guilford.

Dienes, L. (1971), "Issues in Soviet energy policy and conflicts over fuel costs in regional development," *Soviet Studies*, 23: 26–58.

—— (1972), "Investment priorities in Soviet Russia," *Annals of the Association of American Geographers*, 62: 437–454.

Dinmore, G. (2001), "US faces test on Iran sanctions," *Financial Times*, 2 July: 1.

Duménil, G. and Lévy, D. (1993), *The Economics of the Profit Rate: Competition, Crises, and Historical Tendencies in Capitalism*, Brookfield, VT: Edward Elgar.

—— (2004), *Capital Resurgent: Roots of the Neoliberal Revolution*, Cambridge, MA: Harvard University Press.

Economist, The (2002), "Survey: odd industry out," 20 July: 4.

Energy Information Administration, Office of Energy Markets and End Use (2006), *Performance Profiles of Major Energy Producers, 2005*, Washington, DC: US Department of Energy.

Fröbel, F., Heinrichs, J., and Kreye, O. (1980), *The New International Division of Labor: Structural Unemployment in Industrialized Countries and Industrialization in Developing Countries*, Cambridge, UK: Cambridge University Press.

Gaddis, J. L. (1997), *We Now Know: Rethinking Cold War History*, Oxford: Oxford University Press.

Gillette, P. S. (1973), "American capital in the contest for Soviet oil, 1920–23," *Soviet Studies*, 24: 477–490.

—— (1981), "Armand Hammer, Lenin, and the first American concession in Soviet Russia," *Slavic Review*, 40: 355–365.

Gilpin, R. (2000), *The Challenge of Global Capitalism: The World Economy in the 21st Century*, Princeton, NJ: Princeton University Press.

Glassman, J. (2004), *Thailand at the Margins: Internationalization of the State and the Transformation of Labour*, Oxford: Oxford University Press.

Greenberger, R. (1996), "Threat of sanctions on oil companies that invest in Iran seems to deter deals," *Wall Street Journal*, 8 March: A3.

Greenberger, R. and Lande, L. (1995), "Sanctions on foreign firms investing in Iran's energy sector pass panel," *Wall Street Journal*, 13 December: A16.

Gustafson, T. (1982), "Energy and the Soviet bloc," *International Security*, 6: 65–89.

Halliday, F. (1983), *The Making of the Second Cold War*, London: Verso.

Hardt, M. and Negri, A. (2000), *Empire*, Cambridge, MA: Harvard University Press.

—— (2004), *Multitude: War and Democracy in the Age of Empire*, New York: Penguin.

Harvey, D. (1999), *The Limits to Capital*, London: Verso.

—— (2001), "The geopolitics of capitalism," in *Spaces of Capital: Towards a Critical Geography*, New York: Routledge.

—— (2003), *The New Imperialism*, Oxford: Oxford University Press.

—— (2005), *A Brief History of Neoliberalism*, Oxford: Oxford University Press.

Hassmann, H. (1953), *Oil in the Soviet Union: History, Geography, Problems*, Princeton, NJ: Princeton University Press.

Headrick, D. (1981), *Tools of Empire: Technology and European Imperialism in the Nineteenth Century*, Oxford: Oxford University Press.

Heinberg, R. (2005), *The Party's Over: Oil, War and the Fate of Industrial Societies*, Gabriola Island, BC: New Society Publishers.

Heymann, H. (1948), "Oil in Soviet–Western relations in the interwar years," *American Slavic and East European Review*, 7: 303–316.

Hobsbawm, E. J. (1975), *The Age of Capital, 1848–1875*, New York: Vintage.

—— (1987), *The Age of Empire, 1875–1914*, New York: Vintage.

—— (1994), *The Age of Extremes: A History of the World, 1914–1991*, New York: Vintage.

Jhaveri, N. (2004), "Petroimperialism: US interests and the Iraq war," *Antipode*, 36 (1): 2–11.

Johnson, C. (2000), *Blowback: The Costs and Consequences of American Empire*, New York: Henri Holt.

—— (2004), *The Sorrows of Empire: Militarism, Secrecy, and the End of the Republic*, New York: Henri Holt.

Kennan, G. [X] (1947), "The sources of Soviet conduct," *Foreign Affairs*, 25: 566–582.

Khartukov, E. (2002), "Russia's oil majors: engine for radical change," *Oil and Gas Journal*, 27 May: 20–32.

Khartukov, E. and Starostina, E. (2000), "Russia's oil privatization is more greed than fear," *Oil and Gas Journal*, 3 July: 30–32.

King Jr., N., Fialka, J. J., and Bahree, B. (2002), "Balance of power: in oil fallout from an Iraq war, Iran could gain, Saudis lose," *Wall Street Journal*, 19 September: A1.

Klare, M. T. (2001), *Resource Wars: The New Landscape of Global Conflict*, New York: Metropolitan Books.

—— (2004), *Blood and Oil: The Dangers and Consequences of America's Growing Dependency on Imported Petroleum*, New York: Metropolitan Books.

Knorr, K. (1948), "The Bretton Woods Institutions in Transition," *International Organization*, 2: 19–38.

Kolko J. and Kolko, G. (1972), *The Limits of Power: The World and United States Foreign Policy, 1945–1954*, New York: Harper and Row.

Konoplyanik, A. (2002), "Would Russian oil companies really like to have a PSA regime in Russia?" *Oil and Gas Journal*, 23 December: 20–26.

Kuhnert, C. (1991), "More power for the Soviets: perestroika and energy," *Soviet Studies*, 43: 491–506.

Kunstler, J. H. (2005), *The Long Emergency: Surviving the Converging Catastrophes of the Twenty-First Century*, New York: Atlantic Monthly Press.

Lamet, S. (1952), "Soviet fuel and power," *Soviet Studies*, 4: 1–14.

Lavelle, P. (2004), "What does Putin want?" *Current History*, October: 314–318.

Lefebvre, H. (1939), *Le Matérialisme Dialetique*, Paris: Presses Universitaires de France.

—— (1976–1978), *De L'État, 4 volumes*, Paris: Union Générale d'Edition.

—— (1991), *The Production of Space*, trans. D. Nicholson-Smith, Oxford: Blackwell.

Lenin, V. I. (1975), *Imperialism, the Highest Stage of Capitalism*, Peking: Foreign Language Press.

Luke, T. W. (1985), "Technology and Soviet foreign trade: on the political economy of an underdeveloped superpower," *International Studies Quarterly*, 29: 327–353.

Luxemburg, R. (1951), *The Accumulation of Capital*, trans. A. Schwarzschild, London: Routledge and Kegan Paul.

—— (1972), "The accumulation of capital – an anti-critique," trans. R. Wichmann, in K. J. Tarbuck (ed.) *The Accumulation of Capital – An Anti-critique and Imperialism and the Accumulation of Capital*, New York: Monthly Review Press.

Lydolph, P. E. and Shabad, T. (1960), "The oil and gas industries in the USSR," *Annals of the Association of American Geographers*, 50: 461–486.

Lynch, M. C. (1998/1999), "Farce this time: renewed pessimism about oil supply," *Geopolitics of Energy*, December/January: 9–12.

—— (2002), "Forecasting oil supply: theory and practice," *The Quarterly Review of Economics and Finance*, 42: 373–389.

—— (2003), "Petroleum resources pessimism debunked in Hubbert model and Hubbert modelers' assessment," *Oil and Gas Journal*, 14 July: 38–47.

McMichael, P. (2004), *Development and Social Change: A Global Perspective*, Thousand Oaks, CA: Pine Forge Press.

Magdoff, F. (2006), "The explosion of debt and speculation," *Monthly Review*, 58 (6): 1–23.

Magdoff, H. (1978), *Imperialism: From the Colonial Age to the Present*, New York: Monthly Review Press.

Mandel, E. (1970), *Europe vs America: Contradictions of Imperialism*, New York: New Left Books.

—— (1975), *Late Capitalism*, trans. J. De Bres, London: Verso.

—— (1978), *The Second Slump: A Marxist Analysis of Recession in the Seventies*, trans. J. Rothschild, London: New Left Books.

—— (1986), *The Meaning of the Second World War*, London: Verso.

—— (1995), *Long Waves of Capitalist Development: A Marxist Interpretation*, London: Verso.

Mann, M. (1987), "The roots and contradictions of modern militarism," *New Left Review* I/162, March-April: 35–50.

—— (2003), *Incoherent Empire*, London: Verso.

Marx, K. (1964), *Pre-capitalist Economic Formations*, E. J. Hobsbawm (ed.), trans. J. Cohen, New York: International Publishers.

—— (1975), "Economic and Philosophical Manuscripts," trans. R. Livingstone, in *Early Writings*, New York: Vintage.

—— (1976), *Capital, Vol. 1*, trans. B. Fowkes, New York: Random House.

—— (1978), *Capital, Vol. 2*, trans. D. Fernbach, New York: Random House.

—— (1981), *Capital, Vol. 3*, trans. D. Fernbach, New York: Random House.

Marx, K. and Engels, F. (1948), *Manifesto of the Communist Party*, New York: International Publishers.

Milward, A. (1984), *The Reconstruction of Western Europe, 1945–1951*, Berkeley, CA: University of California Press.

Mitchell, T. (2002), *Rule of Experts: Egypt, Techno-Politics, Modernity*, Berkeley, CA: University of California Press.

Mohamedi, F. and Sadowski, Y. (2001), "The decline (but not fall) of US hegemony in the Middle East," *Middle East Report*, no. 220 (Autumn): 12–22.

Mouawad, J. (2007), "Oil innovations pump new life into old wells," *New York Times*, 5 March: A1.

Naleszkiewicz, W. (1966), "Technical assistance of the American enterprises to the growth of the Soviet Union, 1929–1933," *Russian Review*, 25: 54–76.

Namazi, B. (2000), "The legal aspects of doing business in Iran," *International Financial Law Review*, 19 (2): 23–27.

Nicholls, T. (2004), "Breaking the ice," *Petroleum Economist*, January: 31–32.

North, R. N. (1972), "Soviet northern development: the case of NW Siberia," *Soviet Studies*, 24: 171–199.

Nove, A. (1980), "The Soviet economy: problem and prospects," *New Left Review*, I/119, January/February: 3–19.

Obut, T., Sarkar, A., and Sunder, S. (1999a), "Roots of systemic woes in Russian oil sector traceable to industry evolution," *Oil and Gas Journal*, 25 January: 27–32.

—— (1999b), "Comparing Russian, western major oil firms underscores problems unique to Russian oil," *Oil and Gas Journal*, 1 February: 20–25.

Odell, P. R. (1998/1999), "Oil and gas reserves: retrospect and prospect," *Geopolitics of Energy*, December/January: 13–20.

—— (2004), *Why Carbon Fuels Will Dominate The 21st Century's Global Energy Economy*, Brentwood, UK: Multi-Science Publishing.

Olcott, M. B. (2000), "Regional cooperation in Central Asia and the South Caucasus," in R. E. Ebel and R. Menon (eds) *Energy and Conflict in Central Asia and the Caucasus*, Lanham, MD: Rowman & Littlefield.

Panitch, L. and Gindin, S. (2005a), "Finance and American empire," *The Empire Reloaded: Socialist Register 2005*: 46–81.

—— (2005b), "Superintending global capital," *New Left Review*, 35: 101–123.

Parry, J. H. (1966), *The Establishment of the European Hegemony: 1415–1715. Trade and Exploration in the Age of the Renaissance*, New York: Harper and Row.

Peck, J. (2001), "Neoliberalizing states: thin policies/hard outcomes," *Progress in Human Geography*, 25: 445–455.

—— (2004), "Geography and public policy: constructions of neoliberalism," *Progress in Human Geography*, 28: 392–405

Peck, J. and Tickell, A. (2002), "Neoliberalizing space," *Antipode*, 34: 380–404.

Peet, R. (1991), *Global Capitalism: Theories of Societal Development*, New York: Routledge.

—— (2007), *Geography of Power: Making Global Economic Policy*, London: Zed Books.

Petroleum Intelligence Weekly (2006), "Special Supplement: PIW ranks the world's top oil companies," 18 December: S1–S4.

Petroski, Henri (1992), *The Evolution of Useful Things*, New York: Vintage.

Picciotto, S. (1991), "The internationalisation of the state," *Capital & Class*, 43: 43–63.

Project for the New American Century (2000), *Rebuilding America's Defenses: Strategy, Forces and Resources For a New Century*, Washington, DC: Project for the New American Century.

Roberts, P. (2004), *The End of Oil: On the Edge of a Perilous New World*, Boston: Houghton Mifflin.

Rodgers, A. (1974), "The locational dynamics of Soviet industry," *Annals of the Association of American Geographers*, 64: 226–240.

Ropes, E. C. (1943), "American–Soviet trade relations," *Russian Review*, 3: 89–94.

—— (1944), "The shape of United States–Soviet trade, past and future," *Slavonic and East European Review*, 3: 1–15.

Ruppert, M. C. (2004), *Crossing the Rubicon: The Decline of the American Empire and the End of the Age of Oil*, Gabriola Island, BC: New Society Publishers.

Scammell, W. M. (1980), *The International Economy Since 1945*, New York: St. Martin's Press.

Schmidt, A. (1971), *The Concept of Nature in Marx*, London: New Left Books.

Schumpeter, J. A. (1991), "The sociology of imperialism," trans. H. Norden, in P. M. Sweezy (ed.) *Imperialism and Social Classes*, Philadelphia: Orion.

Scott, J. C. (1998), *Seeing like a State: How Certain Schemes to Improve the Human Condition Have Failed*, New Haven, CT: Yale University Press.

Slater, D. (2004), *Geopolitics and the Post-Colonial: Rethinking North–South Relations*, Oxford: Blackwell.

Smith, N. (1990), *Uneven Development: Nature, Capital and the Production of Space*, Oxford: Blackwell.

—— (2003), *American Empire: Roosevelt's Geographer and the Prelude to Globalization*, Berkeley, CA: University of California Press.

—— (2005), *Endgame of Globalization*, London: Routledge.

Spero, J. E. (1985), *The Politics of International Economic Relations*, New York: St. Martin's Press.

Stockholm International Peace Research Institute (2007), *SIPRI Yearbook 2007: Armaments, Disarmament, and International Security*, Oxford: Oxford University Press.

Sweezy, P. M. (1942), *The Theory of Capitalist Development: Principles of Marxian Political Economy*, New York: Monthly Review Press.

Taylor, P. J. (1993), *Political Geography*, London: Longman.

Tirman, J. (1997), *Spoils of War: The Human Cost of America's Arms Trade*, New York: Free Press.

Varga, E. (1947), "Anglo-American rivalry and partnership: a Marxist view," *Foreign Affairs*, 25: 583–595.

Vikas, S. and Ellsworth, C. (2007a), "Part I: Oil companies adjust as government roles expand," *Oil and Gas Journal*, 26 March: 18–25.

—— (2007b), "Part II: Relationships changing as NOC, IOC roles evolve," *Oil and Gas Journal*, 2 April: 22–26.

Vitalis, R. (1997), "The closing of the Arabian oil frontier and the future of Saudi–American relations," *Middle East Report*, no. 204 (July–September): 15–21, 25.

—— (2002), "Black gold, white crude: an essay on American exceptionalism, hierarchy, and hegemony in the Gulf," *Diplomatic History*, 26: 185–213.

—— (2006), *America's Kingdom: Myth-making on the Saudi Oil Frontier*, Stanford, CA: Stanford University Press.

Walker, M. (1993), *The Cold War: A History*, New York: Henry Holt.

Ward, R. (1960), "Soviet competition in western markets: a commodity case and its implications," *The Journal of Industrial Economics*, 8: 133–150.

Watson, N. J. (2006), "Laws of investment," *Petroleum Economist*, January: 10–12.

Watts, M. J. (2006), "Empire of oil: capitalist dispossession and the scramble for Africa," *Monthly Review*, 58 (4): 1–17.

Weisman, S. R. (2006), "Pressed by US, European banks limit Iran deals," *New York Times*, 22 May: A1.

Williams, W. A. (1972), *The Tragedy of American Diplomacy*, New York: W. W. Norton.

—— (1980), *Empire as a Way of Life: An Essay on the Causes and Character of America's Present Predicament along with a Few Thoughts about an Alternative*, Oxford: Oxford University Press.

Wittfogel, K. (1985), "Geopolitics, geographical materialism and Marxism," trans. G. L. Ulmen, *Antipode*, 17: 21–72.

Wolf, E. R. (1982), *Europe and the People without History*, Berkeley, CA: University of California Press.

Wood, E. M. (2003), *Empire of Capital*, London: Verso.

Wood, R. E. (1986), *From Marshall Plan to Debt Crisis: Foreign Aid and Development Choices in the World Economy*, Berkeley, CA: University of California Press.

Ye, M., Zyren, J., and Shore, J. (2003), "Elasticity of demand for relative petroleum inventory in the short run," *Atlantic Economic Journal*, 31: 87–102.

Yergin, D. (1991), *The Prize: The Epic Quest for Oil, Money and Power*, New York: Simon and Schuster.

Žižek, S. (2003), *Iraq: The Borrowed Kettle*, London: Verso.

Index

Access-Renova 120, 162n7
Achcar, G. 159n27, 160n32
Afghanistan: as buffer zone in great game 64; in Centcom area of responsibility 90; Soviet invasion of 78, 103, 104
Agnew, J. 157n11, 158n12, 159n21
Alpha Group 120
Amin, S. 49, 82, 158n12
Anaran 148, *151*
Anglo-Persian Oil Company (BP) 153n6
Arendt, H. 58, 84, 85
arms: industry/production 66, 67–8, 72–3, 86, 93–4, 157n7, 158n14, 159n26, 159n27 (*see also* Keynesianism: military); market/sales 73, 86, 90, 91–3, 160n36; race 73, 75, 78, 79, 103, 104 (*see also* Cold War)
Azadegan 137, 141, 148, *151*

Bacevich, A. J. 86, 91, 160n3
Bangestan 148
banks: in Iranian constitution 144; in Iranian free trade zones 139–40; and privatization of Russian oil 113, 115, 162n3; and state acquisition of Russian oil 117, 118, 121; and US Iran sanctions 80, 81, 130, 137, 138, 140
Baran, P. A. 51, 52, 156n2, 157n10, 159n22
BP (British Petroleum) 8, 9, *9*, 108, 120, 131, 148, 162n4
Bretton Woods 71, 72, 75, 78, 159n23, 160n29
Britain 75, 79, 97; free trade imperialism 65–7; in great game with Russia 64; in postwar inter-imperialist rivalry 69, 74–5, 160n29; and US Iran sanctions 124, 131, 135, 136
Bromley, S. 102, 153n2, 161n1

Brzezinski, Z. 158n13
Bukharin, N. I. 50, 59, 61, 66, 68, 86, 156n4, 156n6, 157n9, 158n18, 159n26
buy-back contracts 124, 126, 139, 141–9; Conoco 163n5; in Foreign Investment Promotion and Protection Act (Iran) 164n23

capital: centralization 8–9, 37–9, 41, 42, 45, 46–7, 50–4, 55–6, 60, 62, 67, 77, 78, 81, 92, 93, 110–13, 115–21, 158n14 (*see also* monopoly); circulating 14, 31, 32, 35, 37, 39, 43 (*see also* raw material); concentration 6, 10, 13, 31, 35, 37, 44–6, 52, 53, 60, 67, 110; constant 13, 14, 19, 21–2, 23, 30–4, 35–7, 39, 43, 44, 45, 46, 154n11; expansion of 5–7, 8, 10, 19, 39, 41–3, 58–60 (*see also* space); extension into land and resources 5–6, 7, 8, 10, 15–16, 39, 40, 41, 44, 111, 112; extractive 6, 7, 15, 42, 45, 47, 110–11, 112 (*see also* extractive industry); financial 50–1, 62, 83–5, 112–13, 115, 118, 121, 122, 128, 137, 140, 156n7 (*see also* banks); fixed 4, 10, 14, 15, 30, 35, 37, 43, 45, 46, 110, 112, 124, 125, 154n6, 154n11; fusion of extractive and landed 45; fusion of industrial and financial 50, 51; fusion of money and landed 118; fusion with state 41, 47, 54–7, 62–3, 113, 117, 121 (*see also* state: capital); international fusion of 53, 61, 158n14; landed 8, 40, 41, 45, 47, 111, 118 (*see also* landed property); magnitude, in relation to composition 14, 20, 22–3, 25; magnitude, in relation to profit 14, 22, 23, 25, 43 (*see also* rate of profit); migration/mobility/movement of 5–7, 15, 22, 25, 26, 36, 41–2, 44, 45,

Dubai: and Iranian free trade zones 139, 140; and US protectionism 81–2

East Europe: and Marshall Aid 75; postwar 69, 74; Soviet oil exports to 99, 101, 107, 160n1; and triangular trade 72; *see also* Comecon
Elf Aquitaine 9, 107, 132; *see also* TotalFinaElf
Engels, F. 76
ENI 131–2, 147–8, *150*, 164n21
entrepreneurial national oil company 117; *see also* hybrid national oil company
European Union (EU): and inter-imperialist rivalry 62, 80; and US Iran sanctions 131–2, 135
Expediency Council (Iran) 140, 164n15
extractive industry 6, 8, 10, 15, 17–18, 19, 36–7, 38, 41, 44, 45–7, 110, 111, 124, 153n2; *see also* capital: extractive
extraterritoriality 124, 129, 131, 132; *see also* sanctions
ExxonMobil 8, *9*, 116, 120, 158n14

Financial Industrial Groups (Russia) 115
France: in postwar inter-imperialist rivalry 69, 78; and US Iran sanctions 124, 128, 132, 135, 136
free trade zones (Iran) 139–40, 149, 163n12; Kish Free Trade Zone Organization 139, 163n11, 164n12; Qeshm Island Free Area 139, 163n11, 163n12

Gaddis, J. L. 157n11, 160n29
Gazprom 9, *9*, 112, *112*, 116, 117, 119–20, 121, 131, 132, 133, *150*, 162n4
geographical contradiction(s) *see* space
Germany: geopolitics 61; in postwar inter-imperialist rivalry 65–7, 69; and protectionism 66–7; and US invasion of Iraq 81; and US Iran sanctions 80, 124, 128–9, 135, 136–7; in US plans for postwar economic recovery 71
Gulf of Mexico 127
Gulf Oil 8, 153n6

Halliburton 57, 82, 111, 134, 135
Halliday, F. 53, 73, 76, 157n11
Harvey, D. 6, 13, 30, 51, 56, 57, 73–4, 82, 85, 153n2, 154n4, 154n6, 155n1, 157n8, 157n11, 158n13
Hobsbawm, E. J. 64, 65, 67, 70, 77, 95, 157n11, 159n26, 161n1

hybrid national oil company 9, 11, 113, 121–2; *see also* entrepreneurial national oil company

India: and Iranian free trade zones 140; and state capital 58, 62; and US Iran sanctions 124, 129, 135, 137
Inpex 137, 138, *151*
Integra 112
International Monetary Fund (IMF) 62, 71, 83, 102, 108, 159n23
Iran 123–52; constitution *see* Constitution of the Islamic Republic of Iran; free trade zones 139–41 (*see also* free trade zones); gas, in relation to investment in oil 142–3; laws of investment 148–9; oil exports 137; oil production 125; oil production contracts 146–8 (*see also* buy-back contracts); oil reserves 125, 141; and Soviet oil 103; US sanctions 80, 81, 123–38 (*see also* sanctions, United States: Iran sanctions)
Iran Libya Sanctions Act (ILSA) 123, 128, 130–5, 138, 140, 163n9
Iran Oil Sanctions Act (IOSA) 130, 163n8
Iran Sanctions Act (ISA) 135
Iraq: oil exports 127, 136; Soviet oil imports from 103; US invasion of 81, 86, 136, 159n27, 163n3
Italy: and US Iran sanctions 128

Japan: colonial expansion 64, 69, 71, 73, 78, 156n3; and Korean War 159n25; in postwar inter-imperialist rivalry 61; and US Iran sanctions 124, 128, 129, 135, 137
JGC 130
Johnson, C. 90, 91, 93, 160n33
joint ventures: in arms industry 93; in Iran 139, 140; in Russia 111, 118, 120, 162n4; in Soviet Union 76, 103, 107, 108

Kazakhstan 99, 100, 107
Keynesianism: military 72, 92–3, 156n5; protectionism in postwar Europe 69; in US postwar policies 71; *see also* state: Keynesian
Klare, M. T. 1, 153n1
Kovykta 162
Kuwait 143, 145

labor: dead 13, 19, 21, 26, 36; division of 6, 16–18, 45–6; exploitation 6, 13, 14,

CPSIA information can be obtained
at www.ICGtesting.com
Printed in the USA
BVHW041047251118
533564BV00019B/87/P